PEACEFUL INVASIONS

PEACEFUL INVASIONS
Immigration and
Changing America

Leon F. Bouvier

UNIVERSITY
PRESS OF
AMERICA

Lanham • New York • London

JV
6507
.B68
1992

15 9136

may 1993

Co-published by arrangement with the
Center for Immigration Studies
1424 Sixteenth Street, NW Suite 603
Washington, D.C. 20036
(202) 328-7228

Library of Congress Cataloging-in-Publication Data
Bouvier, Leon F.
Peaceful Invasions : Immigration and Changing America
/ Leon F. Bouvier.
p. cm.
"Co-published by arrangement with the Center for
Immigration Studies ... Washington, D.C."—T.p. verso.
Includes bibliographical references and index.
1. United States—Emigration and immigration—
Government policy. 2. United States—Emigration
and immigration—Social aspects. 3. United
States—Population. I. Center for Immigration
Studies (Washington, D.C.) II. Title.
JV6507.B68 1990 325.73—dc20 91-26853 CIP

ISBN 0-8191-8402-0 (cloth : alk. paper)
ISBN 0-8191-8403-9 (pbk. : alk. paper)

The paper used in this publication meets the minimum requirements of
American National Standard for Information Sciences—Permanence
of Paper for Printed Library Materials, ANSI Z39.48–1984.

Acknowledgments

This book has benefitted from the advice and guidance of many individuals. Its origin dates back to 1980 when I served as a demographic advisor to the Select Commission on Immigration and Refugee Policy. It was there that I grasped the multi-disciplinary dimensions of immigration policy; it was there that my views on immigration policy began to germinate. To Rev. Theodore Hesburg, chairman of SCIRP, Larry Fuchs, its staff director, and all my colleagues at that time, many thanks.

My research at SCIRP led to long and fruitful discussions with my friend and colleague, Tom Espenshade. These discussions evolved into academic publications which served as a technical base for further studies about immigration policy.

Later, following the suggestion of my friend, John Tanton, three state-level reports on the impact of immigration were prepared and published by the Population Reference Bureau. The co-authors of these reports, Phil Martin, Ray Marshall, and Vernon Briggs, as well as Tom Merrick and all the PRB staff deserve thanks for their cooperation and patience. *Peaceful Invasions* evolved from these reports on California, Texas, and New York.

For the past two years, I have devoted a considerable part of my time to the completion of *Peaceful Invasions*. It has been a rewarding and challenging experience, and in one sense, troublesome as well. Here I am, a self-proclaimed and proud Liberal advocating reduced levels of immigration! Yet, the research for this book has convinced me, more than ever, that this is the correct position for a Liberal to take.

Peaceful Invasions could not have been completed without support, assistance, encouragement, and guidance from many sources. Through a grant from the Laurel Foundation I was able to gather together an excellent advisory committee. Its members, Tom Archdeacon, Kingsley Davis, Otis Graham, Chris Hale, Tom Merrick, Dudley Poston, and Don Smith, all were very helpful in reading and criticizing more than one version of the monograph.

Many others were of great help. Phil Martin, in particular, counselled me extensively especially for chapters 4 and 5. Chris Hale was of great help in advising me on health matters for chapter 8. To Phil and Chris, thank you both so very much.

CIS Director Dave Simcox and board member Roger Conner lent encouragement as I proceeded with my work. They too were very helpful. Other respected immigration authorities gave of their time to review and make useful comments at various stages in the development of the manuscript. To Michael Teitelbaum and Dick Lamm, in particular, I extend my thanks.

I cannot forget my own academic training which first got me into the demographic profession, of which I am so proud. So, a belated thank you to Sid Goldstein, my graduate studies advisor at Brown University. If it were not for his patience when I was a student and his encouragement over the years, not only would this book not have been written, but I wouldn't have become a demographer!

Elaine Dawson did all the word processing necessary to put my manuscript into its final shape. Her expertise as well as her cooperation were both deeply appreciated. Thank you.

Finally, a very special thank you to my dear spouse, Terri. Not only did she put up with the many inconveniences involved with my disappearing either into my office or to a library, hour after hour, and day after day; she read every word of the book in its many emerging forms, made excellent comments and has been a great source of encouragement throughout the years. Thank you, Terri.

Leon F. Bouvier
Virginia Beach, Virginia
May 15, 1991

Contents

Contents

List of Tables

List of Figures

Preface

Remarkable shifts in the demographic behavior of Americans have occurred over the past two decades. United States fertility reached an historical nadir in 1972 and has been low ever since. Life expectancy has increased. As fertility fell and life expectancy rose, immigration soared; perhaps as many immigrants arrived in the United States during the 1980s as arrived in any previous decade.

Immigration interacts with fertility and mortality to determine the size and composition of the population. Although fertility has remained fairly low for some time, if current levels of immigration are maintained, the United States population will continue to grow, at least for the next century. Because of low fertility, the population of the United States is getting older; because of high immigration, the United States is becoming increasingly diverse.

This book outlines arguments for an immigration policy which will not lead to an ever-growing United States population and which will ease the process of cultural adjustment for newcomers. Such an immigration policy is called "liberal limitationist" because some of the reasons for advocating less immigration to protect United States workers and steer the United States economy toward a high productivity trajectory so that there is more income to share with the poor. Many Americans concerned with the nation's poor have traditionally opposed large-scale immigration for these reasons. Immigration should be limited to prepare America for the twenty-first century, economically, culturally, and environmentally.

Americans have always been ambivalent about immigration. In 1886, the United States dedicated the Statue of Liberty which later came to symbolize America's welcome to European immigrants. A few decades later, rigid quotas were placed on movements from Eastern and Southern Europe. In 1986, the Immigration Reform and Control Act was enacted to reduce the

1

influx of illegal immigrants. Then, in 1990 new legislation was passed that will significantly increase the influx of immigrants.

Supporters of efforts to reduce this new surge in immigration, whether legal or illegal, believe that large numbers of immigrants make it difficult to solve the problems of America's poor and that too many immigrants steer the economy away from the high-tech trajectory necessary to compete internationally. Too many immigrants also make it difficult for cultural adaptation to proceed in an orderly fashion and for population growth to come to an end. Thus, there is no consensus on the immigration policy which should be adopted to deal with the wave of newcomers to the United States in the 1990s and beyond.

WHY RESTRICT IMMIGRATION?

The United States accepted more than 9 million immigrants during the 1980s. In contrast to its major European and Asian trading partners, the United States is the only major nation accepting large numbers of newcomers. Does the United States stand alone as the major immigration country because it knows something about immigrants that Europe and Japan do not? Or has the United States resisted a revision of its immigration policies in a changing world?

The United States has backed into its role as the major destination of immigrants without planning for the current wave of newcomers. Immigrants and immigration have powerful advocates in America; most Americans are immigrants or their descendants, and it is easy to be convinced that further immigration is desirable when today's immigration advocates remind us that there were also restrictionist voices when our forebears arrived.

Today, advocates of more immigration often confuse "pro-immigrant" and "pro-immigration." That is, many advocates believe that more must be done by government for the Latino and Asian immigrants currently arriving on our shores, and that doing more for the immigrants who are already here also means supporting further immigration. A better policy is to be pro-immigrant and assist those already here, but to reduce the number of immigrants needing help by reducing immigration.

This book offers four arguments against the continued influx of large numbers of immigrants. First, the presence of newcomers in large numbers makes it impossible to deal with America's indigenous poor in compassionate and effective ways. The United States has a large, and growing, number of people, especially in the inner cities, with weak ties to the labor market but strong links to welfare programs, crime, and drugs. There are also significant numbers of immigrants in many of these cities. These immigrants gain a foothold in the labor market and then they preserve the status quo because they do not complain about inferior wages or working conditions. As long as eager immigrants are available, private employers are not going to make the difficult and costly adjustments needed to employ the American underclass. Instead, they continue to operate their sweatshops and complain about the unwillingness of Americans with welfare and other options to be enthusiastic seamstresses or hotel maids alongside the immigrants.

The availability of immigrant workers has several effects: Immigrants make it unnecessary to improve "bad jobs," which soon become even less attractive. As these immigrant jobs slip further behind mainstream expectations, welfare and crime become preferred alternatives for unskilled Americans. The availability of immigrants keeps private business from experimenting with effective ways to integrate the underclass into the work force. Employers who depend on immigrants have been much less innovative in finding new workers or new ways to get work done. Instead of permitting such employers to maintain the status quo, a tight labor market in the 1990s may provide a unique opportunity for private businesses to help lift people out of poverty and into the mainstream of American society.

The second reason why immigration to the United States should be reduced is that the availability of such workers steers some of the economy in a losing direction. American products have to compete in international markets. The United States competitive edge can be technological sophistication, quality and reliability, or price. Although large numbers of unskilled immigrants may help American businesses to hold down wages and thus prices in order to remain competitive, a low-wage and low-price strategy cannot succeed in the global economy. Developing countries are becoming more adept at producing goods, such as garments and agricultural products, that are currently made in the United States by immigrant workers. Consequently, even wages which are low by United States standards are not low enough to compete with Chinese seamstresses or Chilean farm workers.

Industries which rely on immigrant workers are often slow to innovate, and when developing countries ship similar products produced at even lower wages to the United States, these American businesses often turn protectionist. The result is familiar. The American industry which "needed" immigrant workers to survive and ensure, for example, that grapes do not cost $2 per pound soon complains that cheaper foreign grapes threaten the survival of the American grape industry and asks for restrictions on imports. This in turn drives up consumer prices.

The third reason for limiting immigration is to ease the adaptation of newcomers into American society and facilitate their acceptance by the resident population. Earlier immigration waves contributed to positive changes in American culture. However, the immigration wave at the turn of the twentieth century (the "third wave") ended after 25 years, partly due to war and depression and also because of the 1920s restrictive legislation. As a result, immigration dropped from over 1 million annually in 1908-09 to under 100,000 in the 1930s.

No such abrupt end to current immigration is in sight. The immigration laws of the 1920s were racist and are an embarrassing blot on the American conscience. Yet, by limiting the admission of newcomers, the new immigrants were encouraged to adapt to American society. Today, with immigration increasing year after year, it is difficult for new Americans to adapt to the United States as did previous immigrants.

The source of immigration has changed dramatically. In the first decade of this century, over 80 percent of all immigrants were European. During the 1990s, over 80 percent may be Latin American or Asian. Both immigration streams increased the ethnic diversity of the United States population, but the earlier wave gave the nation a more diverse European population, while the current wave could give it a more racially diverse population, which combined with low fertility could result in a nation with no ethnic majority.

Current and future immigrants as well as the resident population must adapt to a new social situation. Pressure was exerted on the third wave of immigrants to "Americanize" and to conform to Anglo norms. Instead, a new "melting pot" emerged within the population of European ancestry. What kind of cultural adaptation will be needed to insure that today's different ethnic groups assimilate into twenty-first-century America? With a continuation of current levels of immigration, cultural separatism could easily emerge.

The fourth reason to reduce immigration is to slow down rapid population growth. The United States is the world's fastest growing industrial nation. It adds almost 3 million people to its population annually. If current demographic trends continue, the United States population could reach 333 million by 2020 and 388 million in 2050, or 135 million more people than today. About half of that population growth would be due to immigrants and their descendants who arrive after 1990.

While population growth must eventually come to an end, when and at what point should that occur? There is no scientific way to determine the optimal population for a nation; societies try to adjust to rapid population growth by building schools and houses, and they also try to adjust to no-growth populations by improving housing rather than building anew.

More economic activity means more housing and thus more jobs, but population growth also means more roads, more traffic congestion, and more pollution. The nation's infrastructure is already deteriorating; rapid population growth exacerbates this deterioration by increasing the burden on roads and water systems and creating demands for schools and other types of public investment. Americans are concerned about environmental issues, about air and water quality, and while population growth is not necessarily the major cause of environmental problems, more people are certainly an accomplice. Quality of life can improve more without population growth. Given the built-in momentum for further growth, a population of 320 or 330 million is manageable and attainable if immigration is drastically curtailed. Growth beyond such levels would pose significant problems for the nation's environment and infrastructure.

The underclass, the economic trajectory, cultural adaptation, and population growth are four reasons why the United States should rethink its immigration policy. This book presents a vision of how immigration is re-shaping America and why a continuation of current trends will produce problems that could be avoided.

THE CHALLENGE OF ETHNIC/RACIAL DIVERSITY

Continued low fertility will mean an eventual reduction in the resident population while the immigrant group and its descendants keeps expanding. Significant shifts in the ethnic composition of the nation will result. As long as fertility remains low, such shifts are inevitable.

Immigrants today are mostly young Latinos and Asians who settle in major cities, especially in California, New York, and Texas. If current demographic trends continue, within 25 years Anglos would no longer be the majority population in these states and by 2060 the Anglo population would become a minority in the United States. The United States would then be the only industrial nation with no ethnic majority.

Continued low fertility coupled with the aging of the baby boom generation guarantees a growing elderly population in the future. Again, such a shift is inevitable. The combination of aging as well as a more heterogeneous population could pose serious challenges for the society.

There will be changes in the ethnic composition of the United States in future years. The prospects of such diversity should not be viewed with alarm; rather, Americans should assure everyone equal opportunities to succeed. Twenty-first-century America may well be in the vanguard of similar changes that may occur eventually elsewhere in the world as blurred international borders, rapid communications, and international business link peoples closer. The United States could become the first truly universalistic nation. However, major shifts in racial composition will not occur without difficulties. American culture has shown that it can change, but it should not be asked to change so fast that conflict ensues.

THE FOUR "PEACEFUL INVASIONS"

The United States is a nation of immigrants. Ancestors came at various times from almost all nations on earth. These waves of immigrants — these "peaceful invasions" — have radically changed American society.

The first "peaceful invasion" was the move by thousands of English, Spanish and other Europeans to what eventually became known as the United States. The Native-American population, of distant Asian ancestry, was overwhelmed by these new immigrants. By the early nineteenth-century Europeans — English, Dutch, and Swedish in the east, and Spaniards in the west — dominated the region that by then had been renamed the United States of America. In addition, millions of Africans were brought as slaves into the southern states to make plantation agriculture viable.

A second "peaceful invasion" began around 1840 when the Irish and the Germans entered in large numbers. This wave generated hostilities between the newcomers and the earlier immigrants, as evidenced by discrimination against Catholics and Jews in the nation's larger cities. This immigration changed the country from an Anglo-Saxon Protestant nation to one that included diverse religions.

The third "peaceful invasion" began around 1880 and continued until World War I. Over those 35 years some 20 million Europeans came to America. In addition, Chinese and Japanese immigrants arrived in the western states. Most of the European newcomers were Catholic or Jewish and spoke no English; many were poor and illiterate. The impact of these newcomers was tremendous. Numerous confrontations between residents and newcomers contributed to restrictionist sentiments and laws in the 1920s which limited immigration from eastern and southern Europe and put an end to immigration from Asia. White America was becoming heterogeneous, but Anglo-Saxons remained the majority despite some declines in their fertility.

America is now experiencing yet another "peaceful invasion" — a fourth wave of perhaps one million immigrants annually. The immigrants come mainly from Latin America and Asia. Some come legally, but many slip across United States borders without visas or do not leave the United States as scheduled. With the passage of new legislation in 1990 designed to raise immigration levels, the number of immigrants, legal and illegal, is expected to easily surpass 1 million annually for the foreseeable future.

These four waves of immigrants — these "peaceful invasions" — define what is America. Over the past two centuries, the nation has changed while it adapted itself to newcomers. Each of the first three waves receded after a certain period of time. This contributed to the successful adaptation of each successive wave. It remains to be seen what will occur with the fourth wave, which shows no sign of receding.

THE RIGHT THING TO DO

The large number of immigrants now arriving will influence American society in the twenty-first century. How can the nation maintain its economic health and culture while accepting millions of immigrants?

Legal immigration should be limited to about 450,000 persons per year — a recommendation quite similar to that made by the U.S. Select Commission on Immigration and Refugee Policy in 1981 — the Hesburg Commission. To select these immigrants, more emphasis should be placed on admitting individuals who meet the labor needs of the United States. Under no circumstances should a prospective immigrant's race, ethnic background, or religious preference be a factor in determining if that person should be admitted. Illegal immigration should be reduced to a minimum.

Limiting and restructuring immigration will not solve all of America's problems. Federal and state governments should redouble their efforts to better prepare the disadvantaged youth of the nation for the occupational challenges of the future. Particular emphasis should be paid to minority youth; the 1990s may be the nation's last chance to eliminate the specter of a large and permanent underclass. Industries which have relied on low-wage immigrant labor should be weaned from their dependence on unskilled immigrants even if some industries and jobs disappear.

Resident Americans should accept these new immigrants and demonstrate to them that we are a benevolent community anxious to welcome them into American society. These newest immigrants should, in turn, demonstrate a sincere desire to become twenty-first-century Americans.

America in the twenty-first century can truly reflect the motto, *E Pluribus Unum*. Diversity within a unified society can keep the United States an open society.

PART I

THE DEMOGRAPHIC DIMENSION

Introduction

> ... there is simply nothing so important to a people and its government as how many of them there are, whether their number is growing or declining, how they are distributed as between different ages, sexes, and different social classes and racial and ethnic groups, and again, which way these numbers are moving.
>
> Daniel Patrick Moynihan[1]

Shifts in demographic behavior are the focal point for all discussions in this book. As long as immigration levels remain high, the United States population will continue to grow for a long time despite very low fertility. The nation's population will continue to age; the nation will become more ethnically diverse. Unless there is a clear understanding of how the population changes — in size, age composition, and ethnic makeup — grasping the myriad shifts occurring in all segments of American society can be quite difficult.

Almost twenty years ago, the Presidential Commission on Population Growth and the American Future recommended that in view of environmental, resource, and space constraints, the nation should "welcome and plan for" a stationary population — in other words, zero population growth. Twenty years later, the nation is growing as fast as it was in the 1970s.

Ironically, concern is now being expressed in some quarters about a possible decline in the size of the United States population. A recent Bureau of the Census report suggests that, under certain demographic conditions, the nation's population could peak at 302 million in 2040 and fall to 292 million by 2080.[2] Despite the fact that such a number is 40 million greater than the current population, an article in *U.S. News and World Report* argued that the United States should accept more immigrants to counter this possible decline

11

in population.[3] But such ominous (if indeed a declining population is ominous) warnings may be far fetched. The same Bureau of the Census report included an alternative projection in which the United States population would surpass the half billion mark in less than a century.

Much has been written about how low fertility and the maturing of the baby boom are aging the American society. Little has been written about the other compositional shift taking place in the United States; the dramatic alteration in the ethnic composition of the nation.

Together, growth, aging, and increased heterogeneity will pose serious challenges for all American social institution. On the one hand, if fertility remains at its present low level and immigration is moderate, the population will eventually stop growing. In the process the current majority population will cease being the majority. On the other hand, if fertility and immigration levels increase, the United States population could reach 500 million by the middle of the next century.

These demographically-driven issues are addressed in the following chapters. Part I concludes with a chapter on population growth in countries which send immigrants to the United States. To a considerable extent, immigration levels of the future will depend on population growth in countries such as Mexico and the Philippines.

NOTES

1. Daniel P. Moynihan, "Defenders and Invaders," *Washington Post*, 13 June 1977.

2. U.S. Bureau of the Census, *Projections of the Population of the United States, by Age, Sex, and Race: 1988 to 2080*, by Gregory Spencer. Current Population Reports, Series P-25, No. 1018 (Washington: Government Printing Office, 1989).

3. Ben J. Wattenberg, "The Case for More Immigrants," *U.S. News and World Report*, 27 March 1989, 29.

1
How Did We Get So Big?

At the first census of 1790, some 4 million people were counted. In 1950 the nation's population was 151 million (see Table 1.1). Today, about 254 million people live in the United States.[1] Between 1790 and 1990, population growth in the United States was just under 2 percent per year — no other country has ever maintained such a rate for such a long period. It compares to that in many developing nations today. Since 1950 the annual growth rate has been about 1.3 percent, the fastest for any industrial country in the world.

PAST AND RECENT GROWTH

Populations can grow in only two ways: births must exceed deaths and/or the number coming into the country must exceed the number leaving. While births have always outnumbered deaths in the United States, the phenomenal growth of the past two centuries could not have come solely through such "natural increase." Immigration has played a major role in the growth of the American population. Over 90 percent of today's Americans are the direct or indirect descendants of immigrants who came to the United States since Independence in 1776.[2] As Figure 1.1 shows, changes in the source of immigration have also contributed to significant alterations of the nation's racial and ethnic composition.

Large movements of people from one region to another are often called "waves." A migratory pattern evolves, grows in size and later subsides — a wave. The United States has experienced four major waves of immigration.

The first immigration wave to the new world began early in the seventeenth century with the settlements in Virginia and Massachusetts. It ended around 1830. While most early colonists were from England, a

13

Table 1.1 — Population of the U.S: 1790-1980

Year	Population
1790	3,929,214
1800	5,308,483
1810	7,239,881
1820	9,638,453
1830	12,866,020
1840	17,069,453
1850	23,191,876
1860	31,443,321
1870	38,558,371
1880	50,189,209
1890	62,979,766
1900	76,212,168
1910	92,228,496
1920	106,021,537
1930	123,202,624
1940	132,164,569
1950	151,325,798
1960	179,323,175
1970	203,302,031
1980	226,547,082

Source: *The World Almanac and Book of Facts*, p. 219.

substantial number came from other sources. Of the 1790 population, 81 percent were White. Persons of English background constituted only 61 percent of the White inhabitants. Other European sources included the Scots, Irish, German, Dutch, French, and Swedish. Perhaps no more than 100,000 people arrived between Independence and 1819. Between 1819 and 1850 over 2 million persons immigrated to the United States, primarily from western and northern European countries (see Table 1.2).

The second wave began around 1840 and ended in the 1880s. Soon after 1820, Catholic Ireland replaced Great Britain as the country providing the largest number of immigrants to America. By 1850, Germany was the leading country of origin. Some Canadians, of both English and French ancestry, also arrived in that period. Heavy immigration from Ireland and Germany continued after the Civil War. Between 1860 and 1890 almost 3 million Germans and over 1½ million Irish came to America. By 1890, the Census counted almost 21 million "foreign-stock" individuals (that is, immigrants or the children of at least one immigrant parent) out of a total population of 63 million.

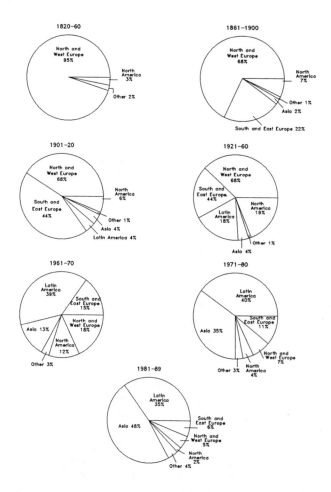

Sources: See Table 1.2.

Figure 1.1 — Legal Immigrants Admitted to the U.S., by Region of Last Residence: 1820-1989

Table 1.2 — Legal Immigration to the U.S.: 1821-1989

Year	Number
1821-30	143,439
1831-40	599,125
1841-50	1,713,251
1851-60	2,598,214
1861-70	2,314,824
1871-80	2,812,191
1881-90	5,246,613
1891-00	3,687,564
1901-10	8,795,386
1911-20	5,735,811
1921-30	4,107,209
1931-40	528,431
1941-50	1,035,039
1951-60	2,515,479
1961-70	3,321,677
1971-80	4,493,314
1981-89	5,801,579

Source: *1988 Statistical Yearbook of the Immigration and Naturalization Service*, Table 1; *Advance Report: Immigration Statistics — Fiscal Year 1989*, Table 1.

By the middle of the nineteenth century, the nation's borders reached the Pacific Ocean and much of northern Mexico became part of the United States after the War of 1847 and the Gadsden Purchase of 1853. With the addition of this land, hundreds of thousands of people of Spanish ancestry became Americans.

February 2, 1848 marks the traditional date given for the arrival of the first immigrants from China. Forty-one thousand of their compatriots joined them over the next decade. By 1870, 123,000 more had settled in America, mostly in California.

The year 1882 is symbolic as a demarcation point between the "Old" and the "New" migrations. It also marks the onset of the "third wave." It was in 1882 that the United States passed the first piece of legislation specifically aimed at restricting immigration by one ethnic group in the Chinese Exclusion Act which excluded Chinese laborers. The 1880s were a turning point insofar as immigrant origins were concerned. While people still came from the traditional sources (that is, Great Britain, Ireland, Germany), many came from "New" sources: Italy, Russia, Poland, Austria-Hungary, Greece, and other southern and eastern European countries. Between 1880 and 1920, over 4½ million Italians entered the United States. Almost 4 million came from

Austria-Hungary as well as from Poland. Well over 3 million came from Russia. Between 1901 and 1910, some 8.8 million people immigrated to the United State — at that time, the highest ever recorded. Although perhaps as many as one-third returned to their respective homelands, this movement from Europe was undoubtedly one of the largest migrant waves in history.

Chinese immigration peaked in the 1870s prior to the passage of legislation which almost put an end to further movements. Japanese immigration began in earnest in the 1870s and reached 1,000 per year in 1891. This movement was abruptly terminated by the so-called "Gentlemen's Agreement" between the United States and the Japanese governments in 1907.

Migration from Mexico began in the late 1800s although many Mexicans already resided in what had once been a part of Mexico. Perhaps as many as 300,000 Mexicans migrated north between 1890 and 1914. With the end of World War I, more Mexicans migrated. It is estimated that close to half a million crossed the border, sometimes illegally, during the 1920s.

The "Quota Laws" of the 1920s led to a drastic reduction in immigration from eastern and southern Europe. The first Quota Act of 1921 limited immigrants from Europe to an annual 3 percent of the number of their countrymen (i.e., foreign-born) enumerated in the 1910 census. The result was a quota of 355,000 — 200,000 for Northern European countries and 155,000 for Southern and Eastern Europe.

The Immigration Act of 1924 lowered the proportion to 2 percent of the foreign-born population — not of 1910 but of 1890 — when the proportion from South and East Europe was quite small. This use of outdated statistics was flagrantly discriminatory. The motives behind the legislation were obvious. The ethnic makeup of the population had to be maintained at all cost. "The total quota for Northern and Western Europe was cut by only 29 percent, whereas that for Southern and Eastern Europe suffered a cut of 87 percent. The quota for Italy, for instance, was reduced from 42,057 to 3,845; Poland's from 30,977 to 5,982."[3]

The National Origins Provision of the 1924 Act further stipulated that the annual quota for each nationality should bear the same ratio to 154,000 as the number of U.S. residents of that descent had to the total population. "Advocates of this plan contended that it would freeze the ethnic composition of the country, apparently on the ethnocentric assumption that a change would be undesirable. About 84 percent of the national quotas went to Northern and Western Europe, 14 percent to Southern and Eastern Europe, and 2 percent to other areas."[4]

In 1952, Congress passed the McCarran-Walter Act over the veto of President Truman. This act not only accepted the racist principle of the 1924 act, but went one step further in incorporating numerous anti-subversive provisions.

Since 1960 over 16 million people have moved to the United States legally.

Additional millions have entered illegally. Currently, well over 650,000 individuals enter the country legally every year. If both legal and illegal entries are counted, immigration during the 1980s probably exceeded 9 million, equalling or surpassing the record set in the first decade of this century. The current movement comes mainly from Latin America and Asia. It is erroneously referred to as the "Fourth Wave," despite the fact that there is no evidence of its imminent decline.

The 1965 immigration legislation explains the numerical rise and ethnic shift that has occurred. The national origins system and discrimination against Asians were abolished. The 1965 law eventually raised the annual quota to 270,000 immigrants, with no more than 20 thousand from any single country. However, spouses, parents and minor children of United States citizens can enter without restrictions.

Also to have important consequences were the changes in the preference system, from the skills emphasized in the 1952 law to family reunification as a rationing criterion. Almost three-quarters of all immigrant slots are reserved for relatives of United States citizens and permanent resident aliens (i.e spouses, children, parents, and siblings).

After 1968, many well-educated Asians took advantage of the professional preference categories to move to the United States or adjust from student or business visas to permanent resident status. After five years of residence they could become citizens and then were eligible to bring in immediate relatives without numerical restrictions, as well as other close relatives under the family reunification provisions of the preference system. Eventually these relatives could in the same way enlarge the family groups in the United States further — a process known as "chain migration." Many Latinos were already residents of the United States in the 1960s, the results of previous immigration. They too followed a similar pattern — through citizenship and the use of the preference system — to bring in more relatives. As a result the "Golden Door" swung wide open to Asians and remained relatively wide open for immigrants from Latin America and these two regions became the major sending areas for post-1965 immigration.[5]

The 1990 legislation increases the number of visas to be issued for occupational purposes. It also sets aside 55,000 slots for diversification of the immigrant stream. Presumably, this would result in more admissions from countries like Ireland and Poland as well as from African countries. The new law also sets a "cap" on total immigration — 700,000 for the years 1992-1994 and 675,000 thereafter. Of that total, 480,000 visas are for family reunification (505,000 in 1992-94), 140,000 for employment-related purposes and 55,000 for ethnic diversity. However, this "cap" is very flexible. Immediate family of U.S. citizens will still be eligible to enter the country without limit, but if that number rises above 220,000, the number of other family-based visas will decrease. However, that latter number cannot fall below 226,000. ". . . if the

GAO's estimates turn out to be correct, the 'floor' of 226,000 visas for relatives other than spouses and children of citizens will push total admissions to 734,000 in 1995 and 754,000 in 1996."[6] As the newest immigrants gain citizenship and some of them apply for the admission of members of their immediate families, the cap's "flexibility" could result in ever increasing numbers of immigrants.

Three types of immigrants can be distinguished: legal, refugee, and illegal. Until 1992 when the new legislation takes effect, the number entering as legal immigrants is based on the 1965 legislation and its subsequent amendments. While a worldwide ceiling of 270,000 is in effect, with no more than 20,000 from any single country, as noted above no restrictions are placed on the number of immediate relatives of United States citizens who can move here. Thus the number of legal immigrants coming from Mexico, for example, was 405,000 in 1989 (including those who received amnesty).

In 1980 Congress passed a new Refugee Act written so as to deal separately with refugees who want to find a new home in this country. According to the 1980 Act, a refugee "is a person who is outside his or her native country of habitual residence and who fears return to the country because of persecution or a well-founded fear of persecution on account of race, religion, nationality, membership in a particular social group or political opinion." The number of refugees accepted in any given year is determined by the president after consultation with the Congress. As many as 150,000 refugees have been accepted in a single year and the authorized total has been well over 130,000.

Illegal, or undocumented, immigrants are persons of foreign origin who have entered the country illegally, bypassing inspection; or who, after legal entry, have violated the terms of their admission, generally by overstaying and/ or accepting unauthorized employment. The number entering the country surreptitiously has climbed since the mid-1970s. While guesses range from 100,000 to 1 million per year, more reasonable estimates lie in the vicinity of 300,000 to 500,000. In 1986, the Congress passed new legislation, the Immigration Reform and Control Act (IRCA), which instituted employer sanctions. Heretofore, while the individual was in this country illegally, it was not illegal for an employer to hire that person. Since 1986, such actions are no longer legal. The same 1986 legislation also provided for an amnesty period during which persons here illegally since at least 1982 could apply to have their status legalized. Some 3 million came forward. As a result of this legislation, clandestine entries fell somewhat for a brief period before climbing again in late 1989. "Since December [1989], the INS' monthly apprehension figures are averaging 50 percent higher than the year before."[7] The 1990 legislation provides for up to 55,000 visas for immediate relatives of aliens legalized under the 1986 law.

Together the change of legislation governing legal entries, the new refugee act, and the increased intensity of illegal movements all have contributed to a remarkable shift in the sources of immigration to the United States. Until the 1960s, most new residents came from European countries. Since 1965 close to 80 percent of all legal newcomers and refugees have come from Asia, Latin America and the Caribbean with only about 15 percent coming from Europe. If illegal immigrants were included, the share coming from Latin America would be even greater.

For Asians, Latin Americans, and Africans, internal diversity is at least as complex as it was for the European immigrants at the turn of the century. In 1989, no less than eight Asian countries sent at least 10,000 migrants to the United States — Philippines, Vietnam, Korea, India, China, Iran, Laos and Taiwan. Thailand and Hong Kong sent just under 10,000. Similarly, from Latin America and the Caribbean, at least 10,000 people came from Mexico, Dominican Republic, Jamaica, El Salvador, and Colombia. The numbers arriving from Africa are smaller, but climbing. In 1989 over 1,000 came from each of the following countries: Egypt, Nigeria, Ethiopia, South Africa, Ghana, and Cape Verde. An additional 492,200 persons already in the United States were "legalized" through the 1986 IRCA legislation (see Table 1.3).

The massive population growth of the past two centuries cannot be accounted solely by immigration. Fertility has also played an important role. At Independence, women were averaging between eight and ten births. By 1850, they were averaging 5.5 births. Fertility continued to fall until after the Great Depression. In 1937 women averaged 2.2 births. Fertility increased slowly during the 1940s and the baby boom began just prior to 1950.

One-third of all Americans are baby boomers, that is, persons born between 1947 and 1964. The decade between 1955 and 1964 produced 43 million births, by far the largest number ever recorded for any ten year period in the nation's history. It was a remarkable era in which couples averaged well over three offspring and the birth rate rose to 25 per 1000 — high for an industrial nation.

Viewing the baby boom as a "catching up" by couples who had been separated because of World War II or by persons who had delayed marriage and/or childbearing in response to the economic insecurities created by the Great Depression partially explains the first few years of the baby boom. Other factors were at work. The proportion of women in their childbearing years was greater than average mainly due to the high fertility of the 1920s. The proportion of women who remained single fell significantly. Childlessness declined to a new low. The three or four child family became the norm as people moved to the suburbs and had more space to raise children. The prosperous postwar economic situation encouraged parents to have an extra child. The average age at marriage decreased and people began having their

Table 1.3 — Immigrants Admitted by Country of Birth (1989)

Mexico	58,443	(405,172)
Philippines	49,535	(57,034)
Vietnam	37,571	(37,739)
Korea	32,204	(34,222)
India	28,498	(31,175)
China	27,394	(32,272)
Dominican Republic	25,553	(26,723)
Jamaica	21,899	(24,523)
Iran	17,128	(21,243)
El Salvador	13,451	(57,878)
United Kingdom	12,841	(14,090)
Laos	12,467	(12,524)
Taiwan	12,457	(13,974)
USSR	11,001	(11,128)
Colombia	10,504	(15,214)

Numbers in parenthesis include those admitted through IRCA legalization.

Source: *Advance Report*, "Immigration Statistics: FY 1989," INS.

children sooner after marriage and closer together. All these factors contributed to the baby boom.

An increase in fertility after World War II was expected. What was not expected was the duration of this increase. The decline in fertility that followed the baby boom was also expected. It had to end sometime. What was not expected was the incredibly low fertility rates that followed which led to the coining of terms like "baby bust" and "birth dearth." By 1972 women were averaging but 1.8 births and by 1975 the birth rate had fallen to 14.8, the lowest in history. Between 1970 and 1979 some 33 million births occurred in the United States, in marked contrast to the 43 million of the 1955-1964 decade. Remarkably, the average of 1.8 births per woman remained fairly constant for about fifteen years. New increases were noted in 1988 when the fertility rate approached 1.9. By 1990, American women were averaging just over 2 births and it appeared that the baby bust had about run its course.

The unsettled economic conditions that began late in the 1960s led people to postpone marriage and/or childbearing. People felt that they could not afford to have as many children as their parents had. Because of the size of the baby boom generation the competition for employment was intense among persons in their twenties and this may have heightened feelings of economic insecurity. In addition, more effective contraceptives, such as the Pill, became available.   Sterilization of males as well as females became generally acceptable, and abortion laws were liberalized.   The women's liberation movement also contributed to fertility decline.   Not only did more women secure employment, but more women went to college.   More women work outside the home than ever before.

These many factors have led to changes in the marriage and childbearing cycle.   People are getting married later in life and births are postponed sometimes until women are in their mid-thirties. About one-third of all births are to women over 30.   Often a one-child family results from such postponements.   Whatever the causes, fertility reached an all-time low in the 1970s and 1980s and only very recently experienced an increase.

Data on mortality for the early decades of the nation's history are sparse. At the onset of the nineteenth century, life expectancy was about 35 years. The death rate dropped steadily throughout the nineteenth century and by 1900 newly born Americans could expect to live 47 years.   By 1950 life expectancy had attained a record high, for then, of 68 years.

Progress in extending life continues.   Life expectancy rose from 68 years in 1950 to 75 years today.   The infant mortality rate recently fell to 10 per 1000 births for the first time, and has since dropped slightly to 9.1.   In 1950 the infant mortality rate was close to 30.   Progress in reducing mortality over the past forty years has been little short of remarkable.   Yet, there is much more to be done.   American minorities have not shared as much as they should in this progress and despite the success of the past few decades, the United States remains almost last among the industrialized nations in mortality.   Those countries with universal health care programs invariably do much better.   Sweden, for example, has a life expectancy of 78 years and an infant mortality rate of 5.8.   It is difficult for Americans to face the fact that a newborn American baby is almost twice as likely to die before reaching its first birthday as is a Swedish baby.

The combination of massive immigration, high, though falling, fertility and increasing life expectancy explain the phenomenal growth that took place in the 200 year period between 1790 and 1990.   All phases of demographic behavior were conducive to rapid population growth.

Because of the comparatively small number of immigrants compared to the total population, some reporters minimize the impact of immigration on population growth.   For example, Robert Christopher concludes that:

> Even if one were to accept the largest halfway supportable estimates for the annual influx of illegal immigrants, immigration into the United States in the latter half of the 1980s was running at a yearly rate equal to only one-third of one percent of the national population — or to put it another way, at considerably less than one-third the rate that prevailed in the first decade of the twentieth century.[8]

These statistics are correct, but they miss the point. A more relevant question is: "What proportion of population growth is due to immigration?" This necessitates looking at fertility and mortality as well as immigration levels. Over the past decade, over one-third of all growth came from immigration, and this share will increase in future years.

AGING OF THE POPULATION

In 1900 the median age of all Americans was but 23. Half the population was younger than 23 and half was older. By 1950, it was 30, then it fell slightly to 28 in 1970. Since 1970, the median age has once again risen and it is now about 32, the highest ever recorded.

In 1900, children under 15 comprised over 33 percent of the population. Today, children are about 23 percent of the total population. On the other hand, the proportion 65 and over has grown continuously; from 4 percent of the population in 1900 to about 12 percent of the population today. In 1900 just over 3 million Americans were 65 or over; by 1950 that number had surpassed 12.2 million; now over 30 million people are in that age group. There are now about 58 million children are under 15; that number has remained virtually the same over the past twenty years! There can be little doubt about it — the nation is aging.

THE DIVERSIFICATION OF THE NATION

In 1950 the four million Latinos, or Hispanics, enumerated in the census represented 2.7 percent of the nation's population. By 1980 that share was up to 6.4 percent and 14.6 million Latinos lived in the United States. The 1990 Latino population is about 23 million and their share of the total is 9 percent.

The number of Asians and Others has also grown rapidly in recent years. In 1950 they numbered just under 600,000. By 1980 close to 3.5 million Asians and Others were counted in the census. Since then their numbers have more than doubled to 9.2 million. Proportionately, that population has risen from 0.4 percent in 1950 to 1.5 percent in 1980 and about 3.7 percent today.

The Black share of the population has gained a little since 1950 when it was 10 percent of the total population. By 1980 it had grown to 11 percent and is now about 12 percent. Immigration from Caribbean and African countries has expanded in recent years but the slightly higher than average fertility of Blacks has been the main contributor to this moderate gain.

The share of the majority population of European ancestry, the Anglos, or Non-Hispanic Whites, has fallen over the past forty years. At mid-century, they comprised almost 87 percent of the nation's inhabitants. By 1980 that was 81 percent and today just over three-quarters of all Americans are Anglos, or persons of European ancestry. For all practical purposes Europeans have ceased migrating to the United States, although this may change because of the immigration legislation passed in 1990. Furthermore, Anglos have the lowest fertility of the four groups being discussed.

The immigrants of the past few decades are not distributed uniformly across the nation. About one-third of all the people who move to the United States settle in California. Following well behind California are Texas, New York, Florida and Illinois. Over 70 percent of newcomers now live in one of these five states which are home to over one-third of all Americans. In California, Anglos now comprise only 57 percent of the state's population, while Latinos represent almost 26 percent, Blacks 7 percent, Asians and Others 10 percent. The majority population only comprise 60 percent of all Texans compared to 26 percent for Latinos, 12 percent for Blacks, and 2 percent for all others. The New York state picture is similar. While 68 percent of the state's people are Anglos, 16 percent are Blacks, 12 percent Latino, and 4 percent Asians and Others.

THE ETHNIC GROUPS

Throughout this book the American population is categorized by broad ethnic groups, some of which are also racial groups. The history of the American people cannot be understood without reference to the various ethnic groups that have contributed to its development. Similarly, the future of the American people cannot be understood without such references. Minorities themselves are adamant about being recognized as separate entities. Witness the pressure exerted in 1980 by Latino organizations to have the Census Bureau include a question of all respondents to determine if they were Latino.[9] Witness too the extraordinary efforts on the part of the Bureau of the Census to enumerate minorities in the 1990 census. Given the continuing strong relationship between ethnicity and economic class, any description of changing America, particularly as it relates to immigration, should include a discussion of the ethnic groups that comprise the nation's people.

If this book were written 50 or 100 years ago, it might have been appropriate to divide the population of European ancestry into its principal ethnic subgroups: Irish, Italian, Polish etc. Today such detailed categorization is no longer relevant. The American population of European ancestry is rapidly becoming a new un-hyphenated group. Now the concern is with those ethnic groups that remain identifiable either physically, culturally, or economically. The Office of Management and Budget (OMB) also offers guidelines in setting up broad ethnic categories: Anglo, Black, Latino, Asian.

Because the number of Native-Americans and Pacific Islanders is too small to develop statistical analyses, in this book they are included in the category, Asian and Other, where they constitute a minute proportion of that subgroup.

How are each of these groups defined? Anthropological and biological sources are of little value and broad and rough social and governmental definitions must be used, definitions that sometimes strain credulity! Anglos include all the people descended from European sources as well as other White sources like the Middle East. Blacks are all the people descended from sub-Saharan African sources, whether directly or indirectly. This group includes people of West Indian descent, newcomers from sub-Saharan African countries and the descendants of those taken into slavery to the United States three centuries ago. Latinos include everyone descended from a Latin American source and the Spanish-speaking Caribbean islands. Asians include all the people descended from any Asian country except those in the Middle East.

These arbitrary definitions pose many anomalies. For example, what about a person of Japanese background coming from Sao Paolo, Brazil? Is that person Asian or Latino? What about the pure Indian from Guatemala? Is that person Latino? In the case of the former, most Americans would probably say that person is Asian; as for the latter, most Americans would define that person as Latino.

The people in these four categories are far from homogeneous. The aforementioned Indian from Guatemala, the Cuban of earlier Spanish descent, the mestizo from Mexico, the Brazilian of Portuguese ancestry, the third-generation Puerto Rican resident of New York City — all are Latinos in the eyes of the federal government.

The Asian category is even more diversified. Indians, Japanese, Filipinos, and Indonesians differ racially from each other. Yet, they all come from Asia and, as with the government guidelines, they are lumped together. If more were known about the true ancestral lines of African-Americans, they too would be quite heterogeneous. Blacks from Haiti and Barbados undoubtedly differ on many cultural indicators between themselves and from recent African arrivals and from the descendants of African slaves who came directly to the United States some three centuries ago.

The Anglo group is also diverse. It includes descendants of those who came from Great Britain on the Mayflower as well as new residents from Poland and Portugal. The author of this book is a second-generation American of French-Canadian parentage. Yet, by current linguistic standards, he too is an Anglo!

How should these groups be labelled — ethnic or racial? For the most part the term "ethnic" will be used. Admittedly "ethnic" encompasses some distinctions that are often considered racial. This convention is followed in part for simplicity, but also because some of the most common current categories have at best ambiguous racial bases. For example, South Asians are generally classified as non-white, but many are, in fact, Caucasian. People of mixed black/white origin are usually classified as Black without regard to whether the greater proportion of their ancestry is White or Black. Latinos are often classified as White even though many of them are racially mixed.

Sociologist Nathan Glazer discusses the ambiguity involved in these terms:

> The term 'ethnic' refers to a social group that consciously shares some aspects of a common culture and is defined primarily by descent. It is part of a family of terms of similar or related meaning, such as 'minority group,' 'race,' and 'nation,' and it is not often easy to make sharp distinctions between these terms. 'Race' of course refers to a group that is defined by common descent and has some typical physical characteristics. Where one decides that a 'race' ends and an 'ethnic group' begins is not easy.[10]

Given such uncertainty, the term "ethnicity" will generally be used, but whenever appropriate "race" will serve as the descriptive term. Far too many people avoid this term. No negative connotation should be implied from its use. Members of various races are justifiably proud of their racial identity.

Ethnic categories have been selected because they are relevant to understanding American society. Unfortunately, these ethnic groupings far too often serve as surrogates for economic groups. As Irving Howe expressed it more then ten years ago:

> The central problems of our society have to do, not with ethnic groupings, but with economic policy, social roles, class relations. They have to do with inequities of wealth, with the shameful neglect of a growing class of sub-proletarians, with the readiness of policy-makers to tolerate high levels of unemployment. They have to do with the 'crisis of cities' a polite phrase masking a terrible reality — the willingness of this country to dump millions of black (and white) poor into the decaying shells of once thriving cities. Toward problems of this kind and magnitude, what answers can ethnicity offer? Very weak ones, I fear.[11]

As the nation looks to the twenty-first century, it must address numerous issues. Many are the result of past and current demographic behavior. The population is growing; the nation is aging; the nation is becoming more heterogeneous. As long as there are ethnic-related economic differences the issues surrounding increased diversity will continue to mount in significance.

NOTES

1. "Census reports it missed up to 6.3 million people," *The Virginian-Pilot*, 19 April 1991, 3. This estimate of the population of the United States as of July 1, 1990 is

somewhat higher than the official census count of 249,632,692. At every census, a certain proportion of the population is not enumerated. The Census Bureau estimates that it may have missed as many as 6.3 million persons in the 1990 census. The Bureau further estimates that it may have missed 2 million Blacks and 1.8 million Latinos.

2. Campbell Gibson, "The Contributions of Immigrants to the U.S. Population Growth: 1790-1970," *International Migration Review* 9 (Summer 1975): 157-176.

3. William S. Barnard, *American Immigration Policy* (New York: Harper and Row, 1950), 27.

4. Ralph Thomlinson, *Population Dynamics* (New York: Random House, 1965), 253.

5. Leon F. Bouvier and Robert Gardner, "Immigration to the U.S.: The Unfinished Story," *Population Bulletin* 41, no. 4 (1986): 13-14.

6. Dick Kirschten, "Legislating by One Senator's Rules," *National Journal* 27 October 1990, 2603.

7. Richard Behar, "The Price of Freedom," *Time*, 14 May 1990, 71.

8. Robert C. Christopher, *Crashing the Gates: The De-Wasping of America's Power Elite* (New York: Simon and Schuster, 1989), 278.

9. Harvey M. Choldin, "Statistics and Politics: The 'Hispanic' Issue in the 1990 Census," *Demography* 23, no. 3 (1986): 403-418.

10. Nathan Glazer, *Ethnic Dilemma* (New York: Hawthorne Press, 1983), 234.

11. Irving Howe, "The Limits of Ethnicity," *New Republic*, 25 June 1977, 19.

2
How Big Will We Get?

Between 1950 and 1990, the population of the United States increased by 100 million; 134 million more may be added by the middle of the next century. A population of 388 million Americans is projected for 2050, at which time still more growth would be forthcoming. Barring totally unforeseen developments, the United States should remain the world's most rapidly growing industrial nation.

The new breed of "demo-doomsayers" concerned about imminent population decline need have no fear. If current patterns of immigration, fertility, and mortality are maintained, growth will continue at least throughout the twenty-first century.

PROJECTIONS VS. PREDICTIONS

The selection of the word projections and not predictions nor even forecasts is deliberate. Predictions of things to come are best left to seers and psychics. Forecasts are best left to meteorologists. A population projection is simply the number of people who will comprise the population of an area at some future point in time according to clearly stated demographic assumptions.

A population projection is intended to answer the question: "What if . . .?" It need not even be realistic. In fact, population projections are sometimes used to demonstrate the utter impossibility of maintaining certain rates of growth. For example, in 1974 demographer Ansley Coale calculated that if the then current rate of world population growth continued indefinitely, in less than 700 years there would be one person for every square foot on the earth's surface.[1] Clearly this was not intended as a prediction! Rather it illustrated rather vividly that the planet cannot maintain such a rate of growth indefinitely. At the other extreme, with its low fertility the United States risks running out of people. A projection of the United States population assuming continued fertility and mortality at 1985 levels, and no immigration, shows that the nation would indeed run out of people — in six thousand years! Again, this is definitely not a prediction but merely an illustration of something that undoubtedly will not occur.

Such examples are extreme, yet they demonstrate what demographer Peter Morrison meant when he wrote: ". . . the purpose of projecting population is not exclusively, or even primarily, to make accurate predictions. Rather, it is to identify and chart the likely effects of influences and contingencies that will determine future population size."[2]

Most projections try to be realistic. The assumptions generally reflect what appears reasonable at a given point in time. Populations rise or fall because of shifts in fertility, mortality, and/or migration. Assumptions are made about future levels of such demographic behavior. The person making the projections must be clear about the intent of the effort. Are the projections realistic or are they intended simply to show the absurdity of some assumptions? Far too many projections are reified. Looking for quick and easy answers, those not well versed in demographic research too often ignore the assumptions and only emphasize the projections.[3]

Given this tendency, those making projections should be clear about their assumptions and their stated goals. The assumptions used in this book reflect reasonable demographic behavior. Nevertheless, they are just that — projections that indicate what the population of the nation would be in a specific year according to stated assumptions. In no way should they be seen as predictions nor should they be considered to be the final word. It is common practice to constantly revise projections based on the most up-to-date evidence. As historian Paul Kennedy has written: "Many a final chapter in works dealing with contemporary affairs has to be changed, only a few years later, in the wisdom of hindsight. It would be surprising if this present chapter survived unscathed."[4]

Aside from concern with the improper understanding of projections, another issue deals with the length of the time interval for which they are made. The longer the period, the less reliable the projection. Anyone who speculates on what the future holds is well-advised to concentrate on dates as far removed from the present as possible, since the longer the prognostication interval, the fewer the number of critics who will remember and point out errant predictions![5]

Short-term projections are usually grounded in a detailed analysis of current trends. These projections amount to forecasts of a sort, but chiefly of forecasts of the near-term future, so long as the underlying trends do not change substantially. Of course, these trends can affect that future and thus falsify themselves, by alerting policy makers to the need for policies to thwart an undesirable future. Long-term trends could be called "scenario builders." These describe a future that could be a plausible outcome of current trends, but not the only possible outcome. Their value lies in alerting policy makers to what might happen, but the other side of the same coin is the high degree of uncertainty attached to the outcomes they foresee. They are especially vulnerable because of the requirement that they make assumptions that hold over a long period of time: for if there is one universal in projections, it is the constancy of change — underlying trends will change, usually in unforeseen ways.[6]

Fluctuations have occurred and will continue to occur in the future. The projections in this book go to the year 2050, but confidence in the first thirty years is far greater than in the last thirty years!

DEMOGRAPHIC ASSUMPTIONS

These projections answer one question: "What if trends in current demographic behavior remain unchanged in future years?"

Immigration poses a particularly difficult challenge when developing population projections. Not only are variations dependent on the economic conditions at both ends of the potential move, but the receiving country, in this case the United States, can also change its immigration laws as it has done in the past and continues to do so, witness the 1990 legislation. Yet, immigration is the most important variable in these projections.

Future legal immigration is assumed to increase somewhat from its previous level, given the 1990 legislation. But determining that level is not easy. Two other movements must also be considered: illegal immigration and emigration. Estimating with any assurance how many people enter the country illegally is not possible. Nor is the number of people who leave the United States in any given year known. The INS long ago did away with collecting such data. Even less information is available on how many illegal immigrants are sojourners, returning to their native land whenever the economy warrants it.

Given all these holes in the statistical sources, some educated guesses about the level of net immigration to the United States must be made. Demographers Long and McMillen, analyzing Census statistics and critiquing the Census Bureau's projections, estimate that "actual levels of [illegal immigration] may have been such that total net immigration is closer to 750,000."[7] Another study has calculated that legal immigration alone may reach 900,000 by 1995.[8] These two estimates were based on the pre-1990 immigration law. The GAO estimates an increase of about 200,000 in annual legal immigration after passage of the 1990 legislation.[9] Net immigration (including illegal immigrants and refugees and deducting out-migrants) is thus assumed to be in the vicinity of 950,000 per year, divided as follows: 360,000 each from Asian and Latin American/Caribbean sources; 180,000 from European and Canadian sources; 50,000 from African sources. The European share is considerably greater than it was in the 1980s. European immigration will probably increase after 1992 when the 1990 legislation goes into effect.

Presently, American women average 2.0 births. However this varies by ethnic groups. It is lower for Anglos (1.8), a little higher for Asians (2.2) and Blacks (2.3) and still higher for Latinos (3.0). The rates for Latinos and Asians are estimated, as nation-wide information on these groups is as yet unavailable. The fertility of Anglos, while having gone up slightly since 1988, remains at about 1.8. However, based on data from California, the fertility for all other groups has increased considerably. Furthermore, as these minorities' share of the nation's population grow, that too will contribute to increases in overall fertility.[10] It is assumed that the fertility of all minority groups will gradually converge to 2.0 births by 2050 and that of Anglos will remain at 1.8. This will result in an overall fertility rate in 2050 of about 1.9. Although many European countries have lower fertility, further declines in the United States are not anticipated, particularly in light of the shifting shares of the population that will see large increases among groups that exhibit higher fertility.

Some may question the assumption that minority fertility levels will fall. As education levels increase and second- and third-generation acculturation develops, fertility usually falls. Improvements in education have been noted among all minorities in recent years and there is no apparent reason for this not to occur in the future. As immigrants and their descendants become more proficient in English, a good indicator of acculturation as well as increased education, fertility falls. Looking at Mexican-origin women aged 20-44, Swicegood, et al, found: "Women who speak only English have two children on average as compared to more than 3⅓ children for women speaking no English at all."[11] However, the decline in fertility will be retarded by the fact that within these immigrant groups, shifting population shares will also take place. Among Asians, the share of higher fertility Filipinos and Southeast Asians will grow at the expense of low fertility Chinese and Japanese. Among Latinos, newer immigrants from higher fertility sources will be increasingly numerous.

Current levels of life expectancy for all groups are assumed to converge to 76 years for males and 80 years for females by 2050. While the life expectancy of Blacks as well as Latinos is now lower than that for other Americans, in the long run such differentials should hopefully be eliminated. As with fertility and immigration, these mortality assumptions are quite conservative. Some experts are convinced that "living to a hundred" is in the foreseeable future.

Few will agree with all these assumptions. The scenario simply illustrates what would happen under certain stated conditions and nothing else.

THE PROJECTIONS

According to the assumptions, the population would rise to 279 million by the year 2000, 333 million in 2020 and 388 million by the middle of the next century. In just 60 years the nation would have added 134 million more people and would still be growing.

These additional 134 million people will not be distributed randomly across the nation. California, which currently accepts more immigrants than any other *nation*, can expect to reach a population of 50 million residents before 2020, Texas 30 million, and Florida almost as many. Today, California's population is about 31 million; Texas 17 million; Florida 13 million.

Some people argue vehemently not only for more immigrants (for the good of the economy) but for larger families (for the survival of the nation). Because of the attention given to these suggestions, a "High" scenario has been prepared to illustrate the impacts of such changes in demographic behavior.

In this scenario, the fertility of all ethnic groups converges at 2.3 births per woman by 2050. Much has been written in recent years about the nation's low fertility and the fear of eventual population decline. Authors who have lamented this low fertility have become the latest "demo-doomsayers." Journalist Ben Wattenberg, for example, has urged American women to have more children.[12]

For this scenario, net immigration is increased from 950,000 to 1.5 million per year. This may seem ridiculously high to some; it is not that far-fetched. Some writers have argued forcefully for the need to elevate immigration levels to solve possible future labor shortages. Economist Julian Simon has suggested that "each year about 1 million immigrants be admitted legally for the next three years. This quota could be reviewed every three years and boosted — say by another million per year — if no major problems arise."[13] The *Wall Street Journal* argues vehemently for totally open borders.[14] Discussions about a United States-Canada-Mexico Free Trade Agreement occasionally center on the possibility of open borders among the three nations. "If free movement of goods becomes a fact, can free (legal) movement of people be far behind?"[15] Potential political and economic problems in countries like Mexico and the Philippines, could result in additional millions of "economic" refugees and illegal immigrants.

The 1990 legislation passed by Congress could eventually yield legal immigration of well over one million per year and would allow entire groups of people to qualify as "refugees." President Bush has expanded the meaning of "refugee" to include any Chinese women forced to practice certain forms of birth control against their will.

Such high levels of immigration would have a strong effect on fertility as the share of the total population made up of new immigrants and their offspring increased. Thus, the High scenario projections should be taken seriously. Indeed, a recent study criticizes Census Bureau projections: "their middle and high projections are too conservative because they discount the possibility of higher fertility levels and future baby boom/bust cycles, underestimate the likely rate of progress that may be made in reducing mortality rates, and underestimate the possible size of future immigration."[16]

Under this book's high scenario, the nation's population would surpass 300 million by 2005, and by mid-next century the nation would have more than 463 million inhabitants — 210 million more than at present. In 2050 it would still be growing by almost 1 percent per year. The half-billion mark would be reached before 2060!

While some Americans express concern about possible population decline, others are worried about continued growth and some advocate eventual negative growth. Former Deputy Assistant Secretary of State for Environment and Population Lindsay Grant writes: "At some stage, one must ask the question: 'How many of us do we want?' There is no precise mathematical formula that can give us the answer, but in retrospect 150 million doesn't look too bad."[17] A "Low" scenario has been prepared to illustrate its impact on American society.

In this scenario, mortality remains as in the basic projection series, but fertility levels are projected to converge at 1.8 for all groups by 2050. Legal immigration approximates 450,000 and illegal immigration is reduced to a minimum. Thus, net immigration is about 350,000 assuming emigration of 100,000. This is not an unreasonable or farfetched scenario and resembles the recommendations made by the Select Commission on Immigration and Refugee Policy in 1981 chaired by Rev. Theodore Hesburg. The population in 2000 would reach 271 million; in 2020, 302 million; in 2050 it would reach 316 million with no further growth anticipated. While such a scenario is not unreasonable or farfetched, it is the least realistic of all. It would require drastic turnarounds in the prevalent political atmosphere and would necessitate a tremendous commitment to the policing of the nation's borders (See Table 2.1 and Figure 2.1).

ETHNIC AND AGE COMPOSITION CONSEQUENCES OF POPULATION CHANGE

The growth in the nation's population will have important consequences for the composition of that population. With resident fertility remaining low

Table 2.1 — Projected Population of the U.S. by Scenario, 1990-2050 (in 000s)

		Scenario	
	"High"	"Basic"	"Low"
1990	254,000	254,000	254,000
2000	284,755	279,146	271,071
2010	318,238	305,337	286,929
2020	354,662	333,453	301,768
2030	389,854	356,816	310,537
2040	424,789	374,484	314,048
2050	463,779	388,460	316,350

and with immigration remaining fairly high, it would be surprising if the ethnic and age composition of the nation were not affected.

The shifting ethnic composition will continue *a fortiori* in the twenty-first century. Should current demographic trends continue, as in the Basic Scenario, Anglos would comprise but 65 percent of the 2020 United States population — a far cry from the 87 percent of 1950. By 2050, just a little over half of all Americans would be of European background. The proportion of Blacks would grow slowly to 13 percent in 2020 with no significant increase thereafter. Newer immigrants from Latin America and Asia would comprise ever growing shares of the future population. By 2010 Latinos would have passed Blacks and be the largest minority group. By mid-century about 22 percent of the population would be of Latino origin. Asians would also see their share climb rapidly. By 2020 it would surpass 7 percent and would reach 11 percent thirty years later.

Numbers portray a more vivid view of the changing ethnic picture. The Anglo population would peak at 218 million in 2030 and then would fall to 208 million in 2050. The Black population would grow from 31 to 53 million. Growth among Latinos and Asians would be substantial. Latinos now number 22 million. They would grow to 50 million in just 30 years and to 84 million by 2050. The Asian population would increase from 8 to 24 million in 2020 and to 44 million by mid-century.

Given that immigrants are most likely to continue to settle in a few states, the ethnic shifts in such states would be particularly striking. California may

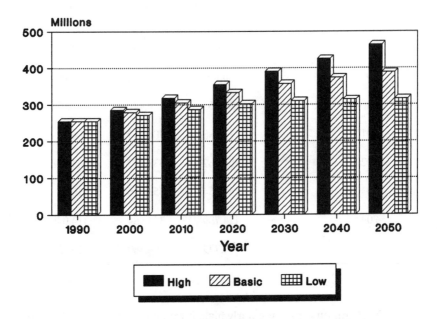

Figure 2.1 — Projected Population of the U.S. by Scenario (in 000s)

become a "minority-majority" state as early as 2000. That is to say, there would be no ethnic majority; all groups would be minorities. By 2025, Latinos would surpass Anglos as the largest minority. Texas may attain a similar "minority-majority" status by 2015 while Latinos would probably catch up to Anglos by 2050. A similar picture could emerge in New York state. By 2020 Anglos would only makeup 44 percent of all New Yorkers. By 2050, Blacks as well as Latinos could outnumber those of European ancestry. To be sure, state-level projections rest on shaky ground. Internal migration must be considered and that is subject to many twists and turns over time. Nevertheless, the trends should be in the direction noted.

If fertility remains low and if the new immigrants and other minorities gradually lower their fertility to 2.0, if life expectancy improves for all Americans, if net immigration averages 950,000 per year with about three-quarters coming from Asia and Latin America and the Caribbean, these numbers and proportions will describe the United States of the twenty-first century. (See Table 2.2 and Figure 2.2.)

As Table 2.3 indicates, the aging of America will continue into the next century. The nation's median age would rise from 32 in 1990 to 38 in 2020. By 2050 roughly half of its population would be under age 40 — in marked contrast to the situation just fifty years ago when half the population was

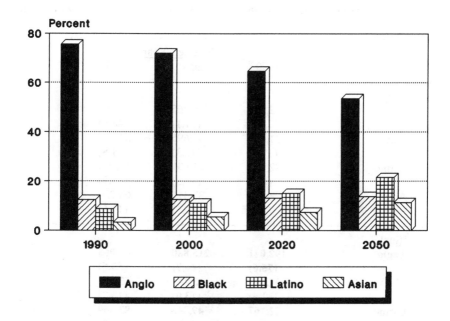

Figure 2.2 — Projected U.S. Population: 1990-2050, by Ethnicity (Basic Scenario)

under age 25. The share of persons over 65 would rise to 15 percent in 2020 and almost 20 percent in 2050. In contrast, that of children under 15 would fall to 19 percent in 2020 and 18 percent in 2050. For the first time in the nation's history there would be more people over 65 than below 15.

There are now about 30 million elderly, that is, over 65. By 2020 that number would increase to 51 million. The baby boom's impact will come later and in 2050, the nation could have as many as 76 million people aged 65 or more. That projected number is quite reliable since all those people were born prior to 1985. The only question may well be — how much greater than 76 million could it become? Some gerontologists are convinced that such projections are far too low. According to a recent study, the United States population over 65 may soar to 87 million by 2040 — 20 million higher than the government's estimate and three times the current level.[18] Thus, the impact of any major increase in life expectancy could be substantial.

Gains among children under 15 will be far less spectacular. That population which now numbers 58 million would reach 66 million in 2020 and 71 million in 2050. Such are the effects of long term low fertility.

All ethnic groups will continue to age. By 2050 the median age for both Blacks and Asians will be almost as high as that for Anglos — 38 and 36

Table 2.2 — Projected Population of the U.S. by Ethnicity by Scenario, 1990-2050 (in 000s)

		Selected Years	
	1990	2020	2050
"High"			
Anglo	192,041	216,765	226,759
	(75.6)	(61.1)	(48.9)
Black	31,413	43,695	54,880
	(12.4)	(12.3)	(11.8)
Latino	22,167	61,891	118,903
	(8.7)	(17.5)	(25.7)
Asian	8,401	32,311	63,236
	(3.3)	(9.1)	(13.6)
"Basic"			
Anglo	**192,041**	**215,880**	**208,065**
	(75.6)	**(64.7)**	**(53.6)**
Black	**31,413**	**43,341**	**53,143**
	(12.4)	**(13.0)**	**(13.7)**
Latino	**22,167**	**49,842**	**83,669**
	(8.7)	**(15.0)**	**(21.5)**
Asian	**8,401**	**24,389**	**43,584**
	(3.3)	**(7.3)**	**(11.2)**
"Low"			
Anglo	192,041	204,073	186,082
	(75.6)	(67.6)	(58.8)
Black	31,413	40,640	44,928
	(12.4)	(13.5)	(14.2)
Latino	22,167	42,189	64,534
	(8.7)	(14.0)	(20.4)
Asian	8,401	14,865	20,805
	(3.3)	(4.9)	(6.6)

respectively. The Latino median age in 2050 will only be 33. Higher fertility and high levels of immigration by young adults account for this retardation in aging. Immigration, in general, will arrest the aging process of the overall society, but it will not come remotely close to ending it.

Differential aging among ethnic groups could pose interesting challenges for the future society. Because minorities are younger than the majority, the

Table 2.3 — Projected Population of the U.S. by Age, by Scenario, 1990-2050 (in 000s)

| | | Selected Years | |
	1990	2020	2050
"High"			
0-14	57,823	74,934	100,153
	(22.7)	(21.1)	(21.6)
15-64	165,675	230,181	287,723
	(65.2)	(64.9)	(62.0)
65 +	30,524	49,507	75,903
	(12.1)	(14.0)	(16.4)
"Basic"			
0-14	**57,823**	**65,676**	**70,751**
	(22.7)	**(19.7)**	**(18.2)**
15-64	**165,675**	**216,376**	**241,998**
	(65.2)	**(64.9)**	**(62.3)**
65 +	**30,524**	**51,401**	**75,711**
	(12.1)	**(15.4)**	**(19.5)**
"Low"			
0-14	57,823	57,305	55,684
	(22.7)	(19.0)	(17.6)
15-64	165,675	196,089	195,935
	(65.3)	(65.0)	(61.9)
65 +	30,524	48,374	64,731
	(12.1)	(16.0)	(20.5)

shifts in ethnic composition will occur earlier in the younger age groups. Among children under 15, the majority group comprises but 69 percent of the total, considerably less than its 76 percent of the overall population. By 2020 the share under 15 could fall to 54 percent and down to 47 percent by 2050. On the other hand the Latino share would rise from 12 to 23 and eventually 30 percent by 2050. At the other extreme of the life cycle, Anglos now comprise over 95 percent of the elderly population. Their share will remain relatively high. Eight of ten elderly will be Anglos in 2020. Even at mid-century, they will comprise two-thirds of the nation's elderly.

DEMOGRAPHIC BEHAVIOR REVISITED

This perhaps dull repetition of numbers after numbers takes on some life when it is realized that these shifts now taking place are simply the result of dramatic changes in demographic behavior. The very nature of American society has been changing, and as the projections suggest, will continue to change for the foreseeable future.

In 1950 the nation had just passed the 150 million mark. Over the next century another 234 million people could be added. What was a still a relatively sparsely-settled region could be on the verge of true overcrowding. In 1950, the median age was 30, 27 percent of the population was under 15 and 8.1 percent was 65 or over. By 2050 the median age could be 40, 18 percent would be under 15 but 20 percent could be 65 or more. What was a still young nation, by developed society standards, could be a mature and even aging nation. In 1950, 87 percent of all Americans were of European ancestry and another 10 percent were Blacks. All other groups combined (that is, Latinos, Asians, Native-Americans, Pacific Islanders) together made up but 3 percent of the population. One hundred years later, Anglos could represent but 54 percent of the population and Blacks 14 percent. Latinos could comprise a hefty 22 percent and Asians and Others the balance of 11 percent. What was an overwhelmingly European-background people could become one of the most ethnically diverse of the world's industrialized nations.

There is nothing wrong with an aging society. There is nothing wrong with increased ethnic diversity. Yet, these shifts in the composition of the United States population will present formidable challenges in the future.

The nation is already anxious about its future social security responsibilities, despite the 1983 legislative adjustments. The nation is concerned about a possible shortage of young adults to cope with the economic and military demands of the future. A society cannot witness such massive changes in age composition without making serious adjustments. These are major but solvable problems.

If the United States truly were a color-blind society, changes in ethnic composition would be of little consequence. Unfortunately that is not the case. Minorities and most of the newest immigrants are disproportionately represented in the nation's lower class. With continued immigration and somewhat higher fertility rates, the lower class group will continue to grow. The majority population is overwhelmingly middle and upper class. With little immigration and low fertility, its numbers will fall. The problem is not one of shifting ethnic composition, but rather one of a expanding lower class and a declining middle and upper class. Normally, this would suggest some upward mobility on the part of the children of the lower classes. However, in large part because of historical patterns of discrimination against minorities, an unfortunate relationship between class and ethnicity exists in the United States and continued high levels of immigration reinforce this relationship. Unless something is done soon to end this relationship between class and ethnicity, conditions could worsen.

Finally, the nation will have to cope with continued rapid population growth, and much of that growth will come from immigration. These are the issues that are emerging from the demographic shifts taking place in the United States.

NOTES

1. Ansley Coale, "The History of the Human Population," *Scientific American* 231 (1974): 51.

2. Peter Morrison, *Forecasting Population of Small Areas: An Overview* (Santa Monica: Rand Corporation, 1977), 12.

3. Carl Haub, "Understanding Population Projections," *Population Bulletin* 42, no. 4 (1987).

4. Paul Kennedy, *The Rise and Fall of Great Powers* (New York: Random House, 1987), 438.

5. W. Parker Frisbie, *Trends in Ethnic Relations: Hispanics and Anglos* (Austin: Texas Research Center Papers, 1986), Series 8, 1.

6. Richard D. Alba, paper presented at conference on "People and Jobs: Adjustment Policies for 1990 and Beyond" (Albany: Rockefeller Institute of Government, 1989), 1-2.

7. John F. Long and D.B. McMillen, "A Survey of Census Bureau Publication Projection Methods," in *Forecasting in the Social and Natural Sciences*, ed. K.C. Land and S.H. Schneider (Dordrecht, Netherlands: Reidel, 1987), 156.

8. "Five Year Estimates of Immigration under Current Legislative Options, 1990-1995," *Scope* (Washington: Center for Immigration Studies, December 1989), 1.

9. Kirschten, "Legislating," 2603.

10. Leon F. Bouvier, "Shifting Shares of the Population and U.S. Fertility," *Population and Environment* (forthcoming, 1991).

11. Gray Swicegood, F.D. Bean, E.H. Stephen, and W. Opitz, "Language Usage and Fertility in the Mexican-Origin Population of the U.S.," *Demography* 25, no. 1 (1986): 17-34.

12. Ben J. Wattenberg, *The Birth Dearth*, 2nd ed. (New York: Pharos Books, 1989).

13. Julian Simon, "Getting the Immigrants We Need," *Washington Post*, 3 August 1988.

14. "America the Vital," *Wall Street Journal*, 16 March 1990, A-12.

15. "Mexico beckons, protectionists quiver," *The Economist*, 20 April 1991, 24.

16. Dennis A. Ahlburg and J.W. Vaupel, "Alternative Projections of the U.S. Population," *Demography* 27, no. 4 (1990): 648.

17. Lindsay Grant, "Too Many Old People or Too Many Americans?" *The NPG Forum* (July 1988): 1.

18. Howard Fields, "New Study Claims Census Figures Low," *AARP News Bulletin* 30, no. 1 (1989): 3.

3
The International Situation

The enormous potential for future immigration to the United States is directly related to the demographic situation in the Third World. Rapid population growth in developing countries will play an important role in determining how many people will want to enter the United States in future years.

By 2010 at least 700 million more people will be in the labor force of Third World countries than there are today. That *increase* equals the total labor force of all the industrial countries today! To be sure, restrictive immigration legislation can be passed, but as the late Prime Minister Houari Boumedienne of Algeria once predicted: "No quantity of atomic bombs could stem the tide of billions . . . who will some day leave the poor Southern part of the world to erupt into the relatively accessible spaces of the rich Northern Hemisphere looking for survival."[1]

THE DEMOGRAPHIC SITUATION IN DEVELOPING COUNTRIES

Of the world's 5.3 billion inhabitants over 4.1 billion (three-quarters) live in the developing regions. By the middle of the twenty-first century nine out of ten of the planet's people will be Third World residents, barring some massive movement of the type predicted by Boumedienne. The demographic reasons for this rapid shift in population distribution are simple: high fertility versus very low fertility. Women in developing countries, as a whole, (excluding China) average almost 5 births while women in the more developed countries average less than 2 births. Although life expectancy is higher in the latter regions (73 versus 58 years), the difference is far from sufficient to compensate for the difference in fertility.

43

Given this high fertility, developing countries have young populations with a tremendous momentum for growth. Even though fertility levels are falling in some places, many developing countries could double their populations over the next 30 to 50 years. Nigeria is expected to grow from 115 million to 274 million between 1990 and 2020. Iran could increase from 54 to 130 million. Egypt could grow to 103 million from 55 million today. And so the story goes in developing country after developing country.

It is not surprising, therefore, that year after year millions of Third World people migrate to the industrialized countries. Yet, few move simply because they feel there are too many people. They move for economic reasons; they can't find jobs. They move for family reasons; they can't find secure housing. They move for educational reasons; there are not enough schools and teachers to instruct their children. But in the background lies rapid population growth, as the *sine qua non* of the equation. In many countries half of the adult population is either unemployed or underemployed; there are too many people. In many countries housing starts (if any) lag far behind demands; there are too many people. In many countries, despite the best intentions, it is economically impossible to build a sufficient number of schools and to adequately prepare enough teachers; there are too many people.

These "push" factors are at least indirectly caused by overpopulation. The decision to move — a difficult decision for individuals and families to make — is further enhanced by the "pull" factors at the intended place of destination. The perceived promise of jobs, of a place to live, of schools for children eases the pain of leaving one's society and culture. Were it not for the strong "push" factors, the attractions in the foreign land would most likely be insufficient to draw migrants. People prefer to remain in their homeland rather than make the sometimes dangerous journey to a strange and possibly hostile nation. Overpopulation is thus a major contributor, albeit indirect, to this mass emigration.

THE NEW POPULATION EXPLOSION

Fertility levels have dropped substantially in many developing countries. South Korea, Mexico, and the Dominican Republic are prime examples of the success of national family planning programs. Yet rapid population growth remains unabated. More people will be added to the world's population in the nineties than in any previous decade in history — almost one billion.

Human populations grow exponentially. Far too often, persons concerned solely with economic growth ignore the power of exponential population growth. The noted economist Kenneth Boulding once commented: "Anyone who believes exponential growth can go on forever in a finite world is either a madman or an economist." At an annual growth of 1 percent, a population doubles in just under 70 years. The Philippines current growth rate of 2.8 percent, if maintained, would result in a doubling of that nation's population in just under 28 years. Furthermore, the *number* being added itself doubles. In the Philippines the population would double from 60 to 120 million in the first "doubling period," and from 120 to 240 million in the second "doubling period."

There is also a built-in momentum for growth in any young population. The main source of population momentum is fertility. The number of births in any given year depends not only on the number of children women have but on the number of women of childbearing age. Many women averaging two births may yield more births than fewer women having many children.

Declining mortality can also contribute to the momentum. Whenever mortality begins to fall in developing countries, the proportion of youth rises primarily because fewer infants and young children die. Children who would have died when mortality was higher are more likely to survive to adulthood.

Changing mortality rates explain the remarkable population "explosion" that occurred in several developing countries in the 1950s and 1960s. Fertility rates, while high, did not go up; indeed, they began to fall in many places. The significant decline in mortality, mainly among infants and children, resulted in a baby boom similar to that experienced in the United States in the same period. However, the cause was quite different. In the United States the rise in fertility accounted for the baby boom; in developing countries the fall in infant and childhood mortality had the same effect.

The baby boom "echo" in the United States produced an increase in births in the 1980s as compared to the 1970s. In many developing countries a similar echo is now taking place as the millions of babies who survived in the 1960s and 1970s are now young adults. This is contributing to a second population explosion. The number of young adults is disproportionately large in most developing countries because of previous high fertility and declining child mortality. That generation not only produces more babies. That generation looks for employment. That generation is restless and easily moved to violence in the absence of any improvement in quality of life. That generation is increasingly aware of the "good life" elsewhere. That generation is most likely to cross international borders looking for a share in that "good life."

In sum, even if fertility falls, a rapid decline in mortality can more than compensate. A "death dearth" has the same impact as a baby boom. The tragedy lies in the insufficient assistance given to the developing countries to reduce fertility rates when the first evidence of success in lowering mortality was noted. The so-called "doomsayers" of the 1960s, concerned about overpopulation, were correct. Even though fertility began to fall in many developing countries in the 1970s, the momentum for growth was already in place. As a result, a second population explosion brought about by the failure to lower fertility rates when mortality began to fall some three decades ago is now just emerging.

SOURCES OF IMMIGRATION TO THE UNITED STATES

As Table 3.1 shows, during the 1980s ten countries provided more than half of the seven million legal immigrants to the United States: Mexico, Philippines, Vietnam, Korea, China, India, Dominican Republic, Jamaica, El Salvador, and Cuba. With the exceptions of Koreans and Cubans, all come from countries experiencing the second population explosion. Many of these immigrants are between age 20 and 35.

Table 3.1 — Immigrants Admitted from Top Ten Countries of Birth, 1981-89

Mexico	974,682
Philippines	458,080
Vietnam	329,606
Korea	304,008
China	278,342
India	226,560
Dominican Republic	209,742
Jamaica	187,311
El Salvador	134,188
Cuba	131,911

Source: *1988 Statistical Yearbook of the Immigration and Naturalization Service*; *Advance Report — Immigration Statistics: Fiscal Year 1989.*

There is a massive movement of young adults coming from countries where rates of population growth are high and where job opportunities are slim. Many come as legal immigrants, some come as refugees, and a surprisingly large number enter the country illegally or overstay their visas and become illegal residents. How many will peregrinate in the 1990s and in the early part of the next century? If a recent poll of residents of Mexico taken by the *Los Angeles Times* is any indicator, that number could be large. More than 4.7 million Mexican citizens believe they are very likely to move north in the next year; 1.3 million would go to California.[2] Much of this is "wishful thinking" on the part of the respondents. Yet, it serves as an indicator of the strong desire on the part of millions of people to emigrate to the United States.

MEXICO AS A TYPICAL SENDING COUNTRY

The demographic shifts that have occurred in the leading sending countries will provide an almost inexhaustible source of potential immigrants for the foreseeable future. The focus here is on Mexico but similar situations exist elsewhere.

A visitor to Mexico in 1950 would have found a languid and uncrowded country of 27 million. If our visitor returned today, she would find a teeming nation of almost 85 million. The returning visitor would be struck by the number of young people. While the visitor was aging, the Mexican population was becoming more youthful. She would find nearly half the population less than 15 years old and over 60 percent under 25.[3]

Surging growth and growing youthfulness have fed Mexico's soaring emigration in recent decades. Given the projected rise in population the prospects are for even greater emigration pressures in the future.

Between 1950 and 1990 Mexico's population more than tripled. The significant decline in mortality mainly among infants and children — the "death dearth" — was the prime contributing factor. Fertility did not rise, but fell slightly. Fifty years ago, the working class Mexican mother of six could expect that perhaps two of her offspring would die prior to reaching adulthood. Today, it is far more likely that all her children will live.

Changing fertility and mortality sparked a "youth explosion." The proportion of people under 15 spurted from 40 percent in 1940 to almost 50 percent by the late 1970s. With such a young population, a momentum for further growth is "built-in." As this large generation moves into and through its reproductive years, it carries considerable potential for even further growth regardless of future birth rates.

Dramatic increases in the number and proportion of children and young adults are the first shock waves of a population explosion that began some two decades earlier. Their impact will be felt for years to come. Even with sharply reduced fertility, the *number* of Mexican births will rise simply because the *number* of women of reproductive age will be larger.

Continued growth can be expected even though fertility has been falling and, according to the United Nations,[4] is projected to continue falling to 2.2 births per woman by 2025. Mexico's population will approach 110 million within a decade and might surpass 154 million by 2025. The seeming paradox of falling fertility with rising population illustrates the powerful momentum for growth in any young society. (Figure 3.1 demonstrates the rise of Latin America's population despite falling fertility.)

The effects of the population explosion of the 1960s and 1970s are only now being seen in the massive proportions of young adults and children, a trend that raises disturbing questions about its long-term consequences. The large number of children born before fertility declined in the 1970s are now

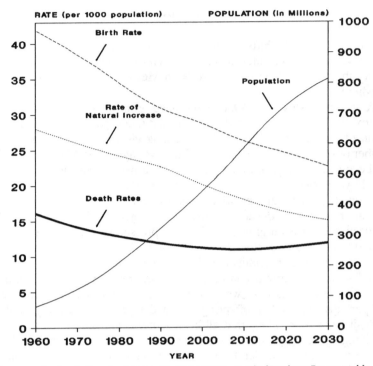

Source: Cantro Latino Americano de Demografia. *Latin American Demographic Situation as Assessed in 1980.* Series A, No. 168 (Santiago, Chile: 1981).

Figure 3.1 — Latin American Birth, Death and Natural Increase Rates and Total Population: 1960-2025

in the critical youth group — a group that will grow alarmingly for the next 20 years. Some 3 million persons between 15 and 24 will be added to the Mexican population before 2000 and another 2 million will be added in the following decade. What impact will such growth have on the social and economic order of the nation in the twenty-first century? Can Mexico support a population of 110 million, much less a population of 154 million? Can the nation's political and social systems bear up under the weight of such numbers? Will emigration take on increased importance?

Mexico's labor force in 1985, according to the International Labor Organization (ILO) was 26 million. The labor force expanded by 3.2 percent annually during the 1980s and ILO projects a 2.9 percent annual growth rate in the 1990s. As Mexico moves into the nineties the number of new entrants into the workforce each year will grow to more than 900,000, and surpass 1 million by the end of the century. The nation's labor force will have risen from 14 million in 1970 to 40 million in 2000, an increase of 180 percent! After the turn of the century, the labor force will continue to grow by more than one million a year until 2010 when the changing age distribution resulting from lower fertility will lower the pace of growth.[5]

The ten million young Mexicans reaching working age by 2000 are prospective claimants on Mexican society for jobs that are reasonably stable and satisfy basic needs. If their claims are unmet, they may follow several routes: apathy and withdrawal, joining millions of other unemployed Mexicans already in the country's shadowy subsistence economy, crime, vice or political extremism in pursuit of revolutionary changes, and seasonal or permanent migration to the United States.

The heavy migration from Mexico since the 1970s may be only the leading edge of a far larger wave of migrants who will sojourn or settle in the United States over the next few decades. Many of the demographic, social, and economic factors driving this wave are already at work. Major lures are the presence in the United States of large Mexican communities, village and ethnic networks to provide jobs and support to the migrants, and certain American industries that have accepted dependence on Mexican workers.

To some degree, Mexican migration has acquired a dynamic of its own. Yet long term migration pressures will depend greatly on the health of the Mexican economy, as well as the quality of Mexico's political life and its success in improving the distribution of income.

What are the prospects that Mexico can spur creation of new jobs for at least 10 million new workers over the next decade? Even under the most sanguine growth projections, Mexico will be unlikely to create the more than 900,000 jobs it needs annually. Applying the optimistic job creation multiplier of .6 for each percentage point of growth — and with equal optimism applying the multiplier to current employment in the traditional as well as more modern sectors of the economy — a healthy and sustained annual growth of output of 5 percent would yield yearly employment growth of 3 percent — 700 to 800,000 jobs a year. Mexico would still reach the year 2000 with 7.7 million unemployed, 19 percent of its labor force, and 9 million still underemployed.

In the absence of major and unforeseen social and economic changes, conditions in Mexico point to heavy incentives for migration northward: a dizzying growth in the younger population most prone to migration; the availability of jobs to only half to three-quarters of those entering the labor force, and the declining economic appeal of available jobs compared to possible alternatives in the United States as the peso's value continues to fall.[6] "An appreciation of the social nature of immigration . . . suggests that Mexican migration to the United States will persist and that it will be more difficult and costly to control than many Americans believe."[7]

The situation in Mexico appears grim. Yet the same trends are underway for a host of other countries which are traditional sources of migration to the

United States: Philippines, Jamaica, El Salvador, Dominican Republic, and so on. Strong pressure for emigration is gradually building up in these developing countries. Other such countries are also experiencing the same kind of demographic and economic problems with a resulting emigration to western European countries as well as to Canada, Australia and the United States.

THE RECEIVING COUNTRIES

The United States is not alone in this; other nations face a similar immigration challenge. The issue is particularly sensitive in western Europe, in part because their fertility levels are already so low that population is decreasing; in part because some of these nations are culturally homogeneous and are not accustomed to receiving large numbers of newcomers from other parts of the world.

With the rebuilding of western Europe after World War II and with its economic rebound in the 1960s, the demand for labor intensified. Most European countries did not experience a prolonged baby boom as did the United States and Canada. Labor shortages became critical as the economic boom persisted. Importing temporary workers was the apparent solution. Workers came from Turkey, Yugoslavia, Italy, Portugal, Algeria, and Tunisia. From former colonies such as Surinam, Indonesia, Pakistan, and the West Indies came thousands more. They settled in the Netherlands, West Germany, Switzerland, France, United Kingdom, Sweden, and elsewhere. Then the oil crisis of 1973 put an end to the need for additional foreign labor. Although family reunification continues, little additional labor migration is allowed. Nevertheless, by the end of 1985, immigrants accounted for 10.7 percent of all employment in the West German manufacturing industry and for 30.5 percent of the Swiss. Their share of manual work is much higher, for example, 27 percent of all assembly and assistance workers in engineering, 25 percent of all chemical workers, and 24 percent of metal manufacturing workers in Germany.[8]

The United Kingdom began limiting immigration from its former colonies with passage of the Commonwealth Immigration Act of 1962, which for the first time placed restrictions on migration from Commonwealth countries. The Immigration Act of 1971 severely restricts the immigration of Commonwealth citizens in favor of "patrials," persons — almost all of them white — who were either born or naturalized in Britain or who have at least one grandparent who was. Since its passage, immigration of Commonwealth citizens from Asia, Africa, and the West Indies has dropped dramatically.

Neither Germany nor Switzerland consider themselves to be "immigration countries." After 1973, immigration was almost completely ended, except for family reunification. Germany, of course, accepts fellow Germans from eastern Europe, but they are automatically granted citizenship and are not considered immigrants. Switzerland has, on occasion, considered expelling the foreign population, which comprises almost one-third of its labor force. All such initiatives were defeated.

France has always thought of itself as an immigration country and has a tradition of assimilating foreigners into French culture. However, movements from North Africa as well as sub-Saharan Francophone Africa have become so large that a not inconsequential proportion of the population expressed support in the 1986 Parliamentary elections for the candidacy of Jean-Marie Le Pen — an outspoken candidate of the far right, who blamed immigrants for taking away jobs and causing crime and campaigned on the slogan "two million immigrants equals two million unemployed."

Even in northern Italy, which has relatively few immigrants, a growing number of incidents involving Africans, Arabs, and even southern Italians have been noted. Italy, which has been a homogeneous society for centuries, is now becoming multiracial. Suddenly, in moments of economic difficulty, a defensive mechanism, the Le Pen phenomenon, is unleashed.[9]

Canada is one of the few advanced countries which espouses a policy of accepting limited numbers of immigrants to assure that its population will not decline in the future. Thus, immigrants are accepted for demographic as well as other reasons. There too concern is being expressed about the increasing number and proportion of newcomers from Asia, Africa, and Latin America and the Caribbean. As recently as 1977, 27 percent of all immigrants to Canada came from Asia and some 18 percent came from Latin America and the Caribbean. Today, a significant majority come from Third World sources.

Never in history have more people desired to move almost anywhere on this planet if their lives could be improved. Over 40 years ago, the noted demographer, Kingsley Davis, wrote these prophetic words which, interestingly, closely resemble the later remarks attributed to Prime Minister Boumedienne. Davis wrote:

> The nationalistic control of migration has led to a peculiar world situation. Demographically the potential migration pent up in today's world is enormous. . . . Certain backward, primarily agricultural regions are glutted with people and are showing signs of even greater glut in the future, while other areas, primarily industrial, are casting about for means of increasing their birth rates. Between the two kinds of areas the differences in level of living are fantastic. What more natural than to expect the destitute masses of the underprivileged regions to swarm across international and continental boundaries into the better regions? . . . One wonders how long the inequalities of growth between major regions can continue without an explosion that will somehow quickly restore the balance.[10]

The pent up demand for migration is far greater today than it was when Davis wrote these words. It remains to be seen if the balance will be restored; and if so, in what manner.

The receiving nations are in this together. All are experiencing very low fertility and some immigration. But as matters now stand, any new restrictions by one country simply mean that another country will become the recipient of those immigrants now shut out of their country of first choice. The United Kingdom's restrictive laws of 1962 and 1971 illustrate this point. Potential immigrants from Jamaica, Trinidad and Tobago, and Barbados, for example, simply changed their plans. The United States and Canada replaced Great Britain as their destination point.

The time is rapidly approaching when the western European nations, and in particular the emerging European Community, as well as Canada, Australia, New Zealand, and the United States should get together on a regular basis to plan their immigration policies in concert. There is an urgent need for joint action by all countries concerned to assure an equitable answer to this increasingly crucial question.

CONCLUSION

The second population explosion is here. Realistically, there seems to be no way in which most developing countries can accommodate the massive growth that will take place over the next few decades. Yet it is not in the best interests of the United States (or other industrialized receiving countries) to serve as a "safety valve" for this overpopulation. Doing so only serves as a disincentive for the sending countries to address their own population problems. The numbers are awesome and those who advocate having open borders should be aware of the momentum for population growth present in the sending countries.

It would be far better for all concerned, and certainly more humane, if the United States and other receiving countries would concentrate on giving ample family planning assistance to all countries who request it. However, even this is not sufficient. Family planning assistance in and by itself cannot solve the immediate problem of overpopulation. Massive economic assistance must also be forthcoming from all industrialized nations if these countries are to survive and begin to show promise of some improvements in the quality of life of all their people.

NOTES

1. Bob Reiss, "The Melting Pot," *Potomac Magazine, Washington Post*, 17 July 1977, 27.

2. Marjorie Miller, "Despite New Laws, U.S. Still a Lure in Mexico," *Los Angeles Times*, 21 August 1989, 1.

3. Alfonso Sandocal Arriaga, "Perspectivas y retos para el ano 2000," *Demos* 2 (1990): 4.

4. United Nations, *International Migration Policies and Programs: A World Survey* (New York: United Nations, 1982).

5. International Labor Office, *Economically Active Population — 1950-2025* (Geneva, 1986).

6. Leon F. Bouvier and David Simcox, "Population Change in Meso-America: The Tip of the Iceberg," *Population and Environment* (Spring 1989).

7. Douglas S. Massey and Felipe Garcia-Espana, "The Social Process of International Migration," *Science* 237 (August 1987): 737.

8. Goran Thernborn, "Migration and Western Europe: The Old World Turning New," *Science* 237 (September 1987): 1185.

9. Tullia Zevi, as quoted in Alexander Stille, "A Disturbing Echo," *Atlantic Monthly* (February 1989): 20.

10. Kingsley Davis, *Human Society* (New York: Macmillan and Co., 1948), 592.

Conclusion

The United States has grown from 4 million inhabitants in 1790 to 254 million today and may surpass 388 million within another 60 years — all because of changes in demographic behavior. The United States, once demographically young, is now aging. Once overwhelmingly populated by persons of European ancestry, the United States is on the verge of becoming a region with no ethnic majority — all because of demographic behavior.

A close relationship has been noted between the shifts in population growth and the economic demands of society — whether in America or in Europe. Some two centuries ago a demographic revolution of momentous importance — the "demographic transition" — took place in most of what is now the industrial world. The thousands of years of infinitesimally slow growth where birth and death rates were both very high came to an end. A new era of high though falling fertility and rapidly declining mortality was inaugurated. The resulting rapid growth fit the labor intensive needs of the Industrial Revolution also just getting under way in that era. Indeed, population growth was so rapid that a significant number of Europeans emigrated to the Americas and elsewhere where the innovations of the Industrial Revolution were put into practice. The demographic behavior of that era was just what was needed to fuel the Industrial Revolution that changed the world.

By the 1970s fertility rates had fallen substantially and growth was once again low in most developed countries. Again such demographic behavior fit into the post-industrial era with its shift from labor to capital intensive economies. The demographic transition was complete. The advanced nations had returned from rapid growth because of falling death rates to slow growth but this time because of falling birth rates.

Today a new demographic revolution is emerging; we are beyond the demographic transition. This new revolution is marked by population decrease in some countries as death rates surpass birth rates. As the early stages of the demographic transition matched the demands of the Industrial Revolution, this new demographic revolution may fit the needs of the as yet unnamed post-high-tech era of the twenty-first century. The rapidly increasing reliance on computers and robots may mean a lessened demand for human labor. In such a situation, growing numbers of people will no longer be prized. Rather, the abilities of finite numbers of people will be more meaningful.

In numerous European countries population decrease is already occurring yet economic growth continues. In 1965, West Germany registered a natural increase of 366,300 people, the result of an excess of 334,000 births over deaths among the native German population and of 32,300 births over deaths among immigrant workers. But by 1975, natural increase had turned negative. Deaths among the indigenous population exceeded births by 235,600, whereas surplus births among immigrants rose to 99,000. Thus, immigration and natural increase among immigrants were the only source of demographic increase in West Germany in that year. Even a reunified Germany exhibits natural decrease. In 1988, there were 8,000 more deaths than births in East and West Germany together. Similarly in France, the total population increased by 11 million people between 1950 and 1975; almost two-thirds of that increase was due to immigration and one-third to natural increase.[1] Since 1975 just about all growth, if any, in such countries has come from immigration and the natural increase among these newcomers. The resident populations now are most likely to exhibit negative growth — that is, more deaths than births.

The United States is not as far along the path to negative growth as its European counterparts. The momentum from the baby boom assures continued numerical increases for a few more decades, with or without immigration. However, of all the demographic variables, immigration is becoming the prime contributor to population growth. Within a few decades, all growth will come from immigration. The question for the United States as it prepares to enter the twenty-first century is this: Are current levels of immigration in the national interest? The following section of this book addresses this question.

NOTES

1. Thomas J. Espenshade, "Population Replacement and Immigrant Adaptation: New Issues Facing the West," *Family Planning Perspectives* 19, no. 3 (1987): 115.

PART II

WHY LEVELS OF IMMIGRATION SHOULD BE LIMITED

Introduction

During the 1990s immigration levels will reach historical highs. With the new and less restrictive legislation just passed, the 10 million mark will easily be reached and surpassed. If refugee admissions are expanded as has been suggested by some advocates and if illegal immigration is not curtailed, that number could go as high as 15 or even 20 million.

Such massive numbers cry out for the question: is immigration of this magnitude good or bad for the American society — its social structure, its economy, its culture, its environment?

Advocates of increased immigration, and even of open borders, are found in academia, in business circles, among certain ethnic advocacy groups, and among politicians ranging the entire spectrum from Radical Left to Reactionary Right. Some of their arguments follow:

• Immigrants do not take jobs away from American citizens, particularly American minorities. It is argued that immigrants produce more, not fewer, jobs for such minorities. Some actually boast that more immigrants attract or keep minimum wage industries, such as garment factories, in the United States which would otherwise have located offshore.[1]

• The only way the United States can remain competitive with economic competitors such as Japan and Germany, is by having a growing labor force. That can only be accomplished through more immigration. "All that the U.S. need do to sharply increase the rate of advance in its technology and its industrial capacity is relax its barriers against the immigration of skilled creators of knowledge."[2]

• New immigrants, regardless of their numbers, will rapidly assimilate into American society as did their earlier counterparts. "Cultural integration has never been difficult among American immigrants in the past and there is no reason to suggest that it is not occurring today."[3]

• The United States is on the verge of imminent population decline and only through high levels of immigration can the nation avoid such a perceived calamity.[4]   Furthermore, population growth is not related to growing environmental hazards.   It is only because American have unprecedented amounts of disposable income that the nation's quality of life is deteriorating so rapidly.[5]

Careful examination of these claims suggests otherwise.   Large-scale immigration produces at least four problems.

First, unskilled immigrants compete directly and indirectly with disadvantaged American workers for jobs, making it harder to solve the problems of the underclass.   Skilled immigrants fill positions in the medical field, for example, thereby allowing the medical institutional structure the luxury of delaying educating prospective American physicians and nurses for such positions.

Second, the availability of many unskilled immigrants encourages low-wage and low-tech industries to expand, when the United States should be developing a high-tech economy to compete in the global marketplace.   The major challenge posed by labor market trends is a looming mismatch between workers and jobs: tomorrow's work force will be more disadvantaged, but new jobs will require workers to have more skills.   To avoid a labor market nightmare of workers not qualified for the jobs that are available, the United States should increase its investment in education and training its citizens and reduce admissions of immigrant workers who face difficulty in succeeding in an ever-more sophisticated economy.

Third, while it is true that earlier immigrants did eventually adapt to American society, adaptation occurred only after considerable hostility between the new immigrants and the resident population.   Furthermore, this successful adaptation occurred in large part because immigration was drastically curtailed for some three decades, beginning in the late 1920s.   This is not the case today.   Continued high levels of immigration could result in a drastically different, and feuding, kind of nation in the twenty-first century.

Fourth, despite claims to the contrary, the population is growing, more rapidly than any other advanced nation.   While some of the burgeoning environmental problems besetting the United States result from more affluence, increasing numbers of people also contribute to the problem.

These are the four points discussed in detail in this section: (1) Limiting immigration can assist in solving the problem of America's underclass; (2) Limiting immigration will help the United States remain economically competitive; (3) Limiting immigration will allow time for new immigrants to adjust culturally to American society; (4) Limiting immigration will allow the nation to attain a reasonable population size and will contribute to easing the impact of more people on the nation's environment and infrastructure.

Interestingly, there are no simple "Liberal-Conservative" positions on this issue.   At first glance, it appears that liberals favor more immigration and conservatives less. Yet, the *Wall Street Journal* is the media's strongest advocate for opening the borders. The reactionary Sen. James Eastland held up restrictive legislation in the United States Senate for decades when he chaired the Judicial Committee.

In fact those favoring increased immigration can be found on both sides of the ideological divide. The documented liberals say that

> ours is a rich and generous nation, we have room for all, let them come. And let them stay, say the conservatives; a large, cheap, frightened, docile, surplus labor force is exactly what the economy needs. Put some fear into the unions: tighten discipline, spur productivity, whip up competition for jobs. The conservatives love their cheap labor; the liberals love their cheap cause.[6]

Similarly, those in favor of limiting immigration can also be found on both sides. Some reactionaries argue for limiting (and even ending) immigration for racial reasons. On the other hand, labor unions have traditionally favored limiting immigration as have others concerned with the well-being of American minorities and the poor. Some environmental organizations too favor limiting immigration so as to limit population growth. In 1958, John F. Kennedy commented: "There is, of course, a legitimate argument for some limitation upon immigration. We no longer need settlers for virgin lands and our economy is expanding more slowly than in the nineteenth and early twentieth century."[7]

On this issue, many people find themselves sleeping with strange bedfellows!

The United States stands alone as the only major industrial nation which is admitting large numbers of immigrants as it prepares for the twenty-first century. In the past, the nation confidently expected to absorb these newcomers, so that both the immigrants and the United States benefitted. However, past experience is not always the best guide to the future effects of immigration.

NOTES

1. Ben J. Wattenberg and Karl Zinsmeister, *The Comparative Advantage of the First Universal Nation* (Washington: The American Enterprise Institute, 1989), 12; Julian Simon, *The Economic Consequences of Immigration* (Cambridge: Basil Blackwell, 1989), 208-223.

2. Simon, *Economic Consequences*, 184.

3. Wattenberg, *Comparative Advantage*, 7.

4. Wattenberg, *The Birth Dearth*, 21-25.

4. Wattenberg, *The Birth Dearth*, 21-25.

5. Wattenberg, *The Birth Dearth*, 129.

6. Edward Abbey, "Immigration and Liberal Taboos," *One Life at a Time Please* (New York: Henry Holt, 1988), 42.

7. Lamar Smith, "Immigration hurts native-born," Readers' Forum, *Washington Times*, 20 April 1990.

4
Immigration, the Underclass, and the Labor Market

The United States faces a mismatch between workers and jobs. Tomorrow's workforce will be more disadvantaged, but the new jobs available after 2000 will require more skills. How can the United States avoid "a projected highly unskilled and functionally illiterate labor force . . . [which] will cause a crisis in the American labor force and the economy?"[1] The best remedy is to minimize the number of disadvantaged workers. This means that the United States must redouble its efforts to educate and train its own disadvantaged workers for the service sector jobs that are and will continue to be available.

At the same time, there is widespread discussion of labor shortages. The 1990 Economic Report of the President called for increasing skilled worker immigration to deal with impending U.S. labor shortages, noting that during the 1990s attention will shift "away from worries about the supply of jobs that have haunted us since the 1930s, and toward new concerns about the supply of workers and skills."[2] The current Economic Report emphasizes that the challenge for the 1990s will be to find enough qualified workers to fill available jobs.

How does immigration affect this picture of jobs for skilled workers that cannot be filled and underclass Americans who cannot find jobs? The easy short-term solution to the vacant jobs dilemma is to import workers who have the needed education and training; in this way, business is maintained without expensive adjustments. The alternative is to enlist business in the effort to upgrade American workers by sending the signal that immigration will not be the easy answer for labor-short employers. Instead, business will have to become an active and effective partner in upgrading the workers left behind.

Immigration will play a key role in determining how the economy will adjust to slower labor force growth. An optimistic projection for the decades ahead is that a worker-hungry economy will absorb the women and minority workers who have traditionally suffered unemployment and underemployment; in this sense, the 1990s represent a unique opportunity to shrink the number of unemployed and underemployed Americans. The pessimistic picture is an economy unable to compete successfully in the global marketplace because too many American workers lack the basic skills needed to fill the jobs available. These frustrated workers may become a welfare burden and a source of unrest.

Immigrants were about one-third of the 20 million net new workforce entrants in the 1980s, and their availability contributed to the reshaping of the labor market and the economy which occurred in immigration-affected industries and areas. The availability of unskilled immigrants in southern California, for example, made Los Angeles a major low-wage manufacturing center despite high and rising housing prices, and these immigrant workers contributed to the expansion of lawn and garden services and the proliferation of car washes and other service industries that depend on low-wage workers.

The availability of unskilled immigrants promoted the expansion of low-wage industries which employ both immigrant and American workers. Such new jobs and new businesses are counted in economic statistics and contribute to the rapid population and economic growth of the areas in which the immigrants are concentrated. All new jobs and businesses which are created satisfy a consumer need; if affluent and time short homeowners want a lawn-mowing service, such businesses will be created and there will be more jobs for both immigrants and natives. The decision to hire a lawn service instead of mowing one's own yard depends in part on the cost of the service, which in turn depends on the wages of gardeners. Thus, the number of lawn-service jobs depends directly on the wages of unskilled workers; if a wave of unskilled immigrants brings low-wage workers into affluent areas, then there will be more lawn and other service jobs created.

Society has made some value judgments which deliberately reduce the number of jobs. Prohibiting the employment of young children, for example, makes it difficult for businesses such as carpet weaving to emerge in the United States; in this case, society decided that there should be fewer jobs today in order to educate tomorrow's workforce.

Society has been more ambivalent about creating and preserving businesses and jobs that exist primarily because an adult immigrant workforce is available. The availability of often illegal maids and gardeners during the 1980s contributed to the creation of maid and gardener jobs in affluent homes, but the Immigration Reform and Control Act (IRCA) of 1986 sent a signal that Americans who want to employ service workers in their homes must employ persons legally authorized to work in the United States. IRCA's treatment of agriculture, by contrast, illustrates more ambivalence about immigrant workers and U.S. jobs. Under IRCA, farmers who argued that they would go out of business without immigrant workers were able to gain continued access to those workers in a way that has not encouraged them to reduce their dependence on such workers.

Preserving jobs which exist because low-wage immigrants are available is a contentious issue because there is no agreement on the minimum standards for a job in the United States. There is some agreement that a job worth doing is a job which pays at least a minimum wage and offers a safe work place. Society often adds other restrictions which may increase the costs of doing business enough to reduce the number of jobs, such as demanding that employers pay unemployment insurance and social security taxes to support jobless and retired workers. However, when a business which pollutes the environment threatens to shut down rather than install pollution control equipment, a debate over jobs versus the environment often ensues.

These examples illustrate the ambiguities inherent in the trade-off between more and better jobs. It is easy to create more jobs, but much harder to create both more and better jobs. During the 1980s, the United States worshipped the Holy Grail of more jobs, and was less concerned about whether the new jobs created offered decent wages and working conditions. In Europe, by contrast, fewer new jobs were created, but wages and productivity rose faster than in the United States. The United States workforce will grow more slowly in the future than it did during the 1980s, giving the nation the opportunity to stress the quality rather than the quantity of new jobs created.

POPULATION AND LABOR MARKET TRENDS

The labor market matches employees and employers. The labor market determines who finds work and who remains unemployed, what wages and salaries are earned, and also the social status of a person, since the status of a fire fighter differs from the status of a janitor.

The United States and other industrial societies strive to have labor markets in which all people who want to work can find jobs. Most people 16 and older are in the workforce unless they are in school, caring for young children, disabled, or retired. In order to estimate how large the labor force will be, the population in future years and the percentage of the population that seeks employment must be projected.

LABOR FORCE PROJECTIONS

The size of the labor force depends first on the population aged 16 and older. If current demographic trends continue, this population would increase from 192 million in 1990 to 215 million in 2000, 263 million in 2020, and 313 million in 2050. Clearly, the number of people available to work will continue to grow.

Only a fraction of the population is in the labor force, either employed or looking for work. About 66 percent of the population 16 and older is in the workforce today, and 68 percent are expected in 2000. The overall labor force participation rate is expected to fall after 2000 as the workforce is aging and older workers are less likely to be employed or looking for work. Table 4.1 indicates that the labor force will continue to grow for the next 60 years. The labor force increased by 20 million between 1980 and 1990, and is expected to increase by almost as much during the 1990s, but only by 18 million between 2000 and 2020. The female share of the labor force should stabilize at 45 percent.

The U.S. workforce will continue to grow as new entrants — young people, housewives who decide to work for wages, and immigrants — more than replace retiring workers. However, the characteristics and skills of these new workers raise the specter of a labor market mismatch. Anglo men are about 45 percent of the 1990 workforce and they will be about half of the exits from the workforce in the 1990s, but they will be only 9 percent of the net additions to the workforce in the 1990s. Most of the additional workers will be from traditionally disadvantaged groups: minorities and immigrants.

The age composition of the workforce will also change. The most remarkable change is the projected more than doubling of the older workforce (55-64) between 1990 and 2020. By the latter year that group will account for 1 in 6 workers, versus 1 in 12 today. The number of younger workers, by contrast, will be relatively stable. The teenage workforce, for example, will rise to about 10 million in 2000 and then remain at that level for the next 50 years.

The workforce aged 25 to 34 will shrink during the 1990s, and then increase and surpass its 1990 level by 2020. These workers are an important backbone of the economy. The projection of a declining pool of young and mobile workers explains some of the fears of labor shortages in the 1990s. Employers who became accustomed to a baby boom generation of young employees willing to make sacrifices for their careers may have to adjust to a baby bust generation that is less flexible.

The ethnic composition of the labor force is also changing. In 1990, about 78 percent of the people in the workforce were Anglos. Their share will decline to 74 percent by 2000 and to 66 percent in 2020. Within 30 years, Latinos will surpass Blacks as the largest minority in the workforce: in 2020,

Table 4.1 — Projected U.S. Labor Force: 1990-2050

	1990	2000	2020	2050
Population 16 years and older (millions)	192	215	263	313
Civilian Labor Force (millions)	127	147	165	185
Female (%)	44.3	46.3	44.7	44.4
Ethnicity (%)				
Anglo	77.7	74.2	65.8	54.0
Black	11.4	11.7	12.6	13.2
Latino	7.7	9.6	14.3	21.6
Asian	3.2	4.5	7.3	11.2
Age and Ethnicity (%)				
16-19 Years (million)	8	10	10	11
Anglo	77.2	72.9	64.2	55.0
Black	11.4	12.4	12.4	12.7
Latino	8.8	11.1	17.3	23.4
Asian	2.6	3.6	6.1	8.9
25-34 Years (million)	37	35	40	43
Anglo	75.2	70.9	62.1	50.9
Black	12.8	12.5	13.5	12.6
Latino	8.9	11.3	16.7	23.8
Asian	3.1	5.3	7.7	11.7
55-64 Years (million)	11	13	24	25
Anglo	82.4	80.4	74.3	59.6
Black	9.0	8.8	10.6	12.0
Latino	5.6	6.6	9.5	17.7
Asian	3.0	4.2	5.6	10.7

Source: Basic Projection.

Latinos will be 14 percent of the U.S. labor force, Blacks 13 percent, and Asians 7 percent. These ethnic labor force shares contrast sharply with those of 1990; when Latinos were 8 percent of the workforce, Blacks 11 percent, and Asians 3 percent.

The changing ethnic composition of the workforce will be most noticeable in the 25 to 34 age group. These prime-aged workers, about 30 percent of the

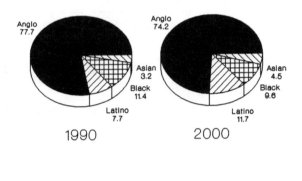

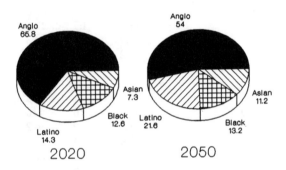

Figure 4.1 — U.S. Labor Force, 1990-2050 (Basic Scenario)

1990 workforce, will change from one-fourth minority in 1990 to over one-third minority in 2020 and one-half minority in 2050. The shrinking number of such workers during the 1990s makes it important to ensure that all receive the education and training needed to be productive contributors to tomorrow's economy.

If current demographic trends continue, Latinos and Asians will comprise ever larger proportions of the total workforce in future years. For example, the Latino labor force will increase by over 3 million in the 1990s and the Asian workforce will grow by 2 million, largely because of immigration. Between 1990 and 2020, over three fourths of the net growth in the U.S. labor force will come from increases in the number of Latino and Asian workers. A slow growing, aging, and increasingly diverse workforce will pose a challenge for the twenty-first-century economy, insofar as training and adaptation are concerned.

LABOR FORCE AND LABOR MARKET CHANGES

The United States has already experienced changes in the pace of the labor force growth and changes in the composition of the labor force. Since World War II, the baby boom generation was born, filled schools in the 1950s and 1960s, joined the workforce during the 1970s, and entered middle age in the 1980s and 1990s. The labor force and society had to accommodate this tidal wave of additional workers while also adjusting to larger numbers of working women. The baby bust which followed the baby boom after the mid-1960s meant that there were fewer children to care for. Smaller families, in conjunction with changing attitudes and more service sector jobs, made women a larger fraction of the workforce.

During the 1970s, the labor force became younger and included more women. These changes had enormous impacts on American society. Working women reinforced the shift from an industrial to a service economy and women were available to be service workers. The entry of baby boom youth into the workforce during the 1970s kept unemployment high despite rapid job growth, and governmental attempts to reduce this unemployment contributed to inflationary pressures.

In the future, a slower growing, aging, and more diverse workforce will also have significant effects on American society. Some employers will have to introduce more technologies which save labor, such as self-service gasoline stations and automated banking. An aging workforce is less mobile, so there may be labor shortages in one area and surpluses in another. But the changing ethnic composition of the workforce may be the biggest challenge of all: will society be able to educate and find good jobs for the growing number of Latinos, Blacks, and Asians who have fared so unevenly in the labor market in the past?

In 1947, the workforce included almost 60 million people, the unemployment rate was under 4 percent, and about 56 percent of the adult population was employed. Forty years later, the workforce doubled to 120 million, the unemployment rate jumped by 50 percent, and a much larger share of the adult population was employed despite more young people enrolled in college and earlier retirement. Put another way, during the past 40 years, the workforce has grown much faster than the population despite work-reducing trends in education, retirement, and affluence which would have led observers after World War II to expect that a smaller proportion of adults would be working today.

This labor force growth was due to more married women deciding to work after they had children; to baby boom adolescents born in the 1950s entering the workforce in the 1970s; and to the 1970s and 1980s surge in immigration. These trends led to extraordinary U.S. labor force and employment growth in the 1970s and 1980s.

Four major changes have occurred in the U.S. labor market since World War II. First, the United States has emerged as the world's premier job-creating machine: no other industrial country has created so many new jobs so fast. Second, real or inflation-adjusted wages rose rapidly in the 1950s and 1960s, but wages stagnated in the 1970s and 1980s. Rapid job growth and stable wages help explain the debate over the fate of the middle class: the incomes of such families rose during the 1970s even though wages were stable because married women entered the workforce. However, middle-class families in which both parents work cannot earn even more in the 1990s unless wages rise. Middle-class families who lament that they have more money but a lower quality of life than their parents are reflecting the fact that families today have to devote more hours to work outside the home in order to have real incomes that are comparable to those earned in the 1950s and 1960s.

Wages have not risen in the 1980s because of the third change: slow productivity growth. Generally, wages rise with productivity growth: workers become more efficient, their wages rise with this increased efficiency, but prices do not. During the 1950s and 1960s, productivity rose by about 2.5 percent annually, so that real wages could double every 30 years and not cause inflation. Productivity growth slowed in the 1970s and so did the increase in real wages.[3]

Unions continued to push up wages in a few industries despite the productivity slowdown, but the internationalization of the economy, an anti-union climate, and the deregulation of major American industries soon stripped American unions of most of their power to raise wages.

Rapid job growth, stable wages, and the gradual demise of unions are linked to the fourth labor market trend, the changing composition of the workforce, i.e., what people produce (goods or services) and who the workers are (men or women, immigrants or natives). The labor market absorbs new workers into the economy and helps American workers to switch from one part of the economy to another, as from agriculture to industry. Since World War II, the labor market helped women, baby boom teens, and immigrants to find jobs, and it shifted workers from agriculture and manufacturing into the service sectors of the economy.

The American economy will continue to offer jobs in service industries to a slower growing and aging workforce increasingly comprised of women and minorities. These new service sector jobs will usually require higher skill levels than current jobs, especially in the rapidly-growing health and business services sector. The nation faces the challenge of avoiding a labor market problem of square pegs and round holes, or new jobs for which there are no workers coupled with workers who cannot find jobs.

The mismatch fear arises from U.S. Department of Labor projections that many new jobs will require a post-secondary education.[4] New jobs reflect a balance which includes jobs which exist today and tomorrow (school teachers), jobs with more workers tomorrow than today (computer programmers), and jobs with fewer workers tomorrow than today (farm workers). The overall number of new jobs or the net growth in jobs is expected to be about 1.5 million annually during the 1990s, and the mismatch fear arises from the shrinking number of jobs available for persons with little education and the growing number that require a college education.

About ¼ of the 112 million persons employed in 1986 were in administrative, professional, and technical occupations which usually require a college education. During the 1990s, some jobs will disappear while others are created, but on balance, the number of jobs will increase. Occupations which require more education will expand their shares of all jobs, while the number of jobs in occupations requiring a high school education or less will shrink in the expanding economy. Of the additional jobs expected to be created by 2000, half are projected to require a college education or more, and only 14 percent will require a high school education or less. Such projections mean that the one-third or more of the high school students who drop out of school before graduation will be competing for a shrinking pool of unskilled jobs. If they are joined in the quest for jobs by unskilled immigrants, the surplus of workers at the bottom of the labor market will be aggravated.

If job growth by occupation is compared to the current distribution of workers by race, the potential labor market mismatch is apparent. Blacks and Latinos are under-represented in the industries and occupations expected to add jobs at the fastest pace. Conversely, they are over-represented in slow-growing or declining industries and occupations. These employment projections highlight the need for minority youth to be educated and trained for tomorrow's jobs or face a future filled with unemployment and frustration.[5]

IMMIGRANTS AND THE UNDERCLASS IN THE LABOR MARKET

The United States underclass is growing just when the number of unskilled jobs available to bring them into the mainstream economy is shrinking. There is no official definition of the underclass or "ghetto poor" as sociologist William J. Wilson prefers[6]: it is usually described as persons who are persistently poor and who live in urban areas with other persistently poor people. Economist Ronald Mincy includes in the underclass everyone living in areas with concentrations of welfare households, female-headed families, teenage high school dropouts, and fathers who work less than half the year. According to this definition, the United States underclass included 2.5 million mostly Black and Hispanic residents of 880 neighborhoods in 1980, a tripling of the 1970 underclass.[7] The underclass swelled during the 1980s despite rapid job growth, suggesting that there are new pockets of poor Americans who are divorced from labor market and economic trends.

Defining the origins and dimensions of the underclass problem could implicitly help to identify solutions for underclass persons, but there is no agreement on "the process and mechanisms that create, maintain, or overcome the conditions and consequences of persistent and concentrated urban poverty."[8] The factors which have been suggested to explain why the underclass arose and persists range from international economic competition to discrimination to immigration. One explanation highlights the shift from blue-collar to white-collar jobs; New York City, for example, lost a net 172,000 blue-collar jobs between 1970 and 1980 but added a net 264,000 white-collar jobs.[9] This loss of blue-collar entry-level jobs in urban areas eliminated a traditional job ladder for poor youth to work their way out of the ghetto. Without such a ladder into the mainstream economy, poor youth may be encouraged to get involved in drugs and crime, further isolating themselves in the underground economy.

There are both supply and demand explanations for the persisting underclass. Supply explanations center on the rising expectations of unskilled and poor urban residents. As the expectations of American workers rise, immigrants get the unskilled jobs available. Demand explanations note that some unskilled jobs have become less attractive as remaining employers of unskilled workers hire part-time workers and persons with temporary contracts at or near the minimum wage. Such employers offer a career of a lifetime minimum wage job with few promotion opportunities to residents who have underground or drug economy alternatives and their lottery-like prospects of a huge payoff. Regardless of which combination of factors best explains the origins and growth of the underclass, it is clear that socio-economic developments have produced a large group of poor people who are increasingly isolated from mainstream America.

Studies of America's poor developed a pessimistic ring during the 1980s, as exemplified by Charles Murray's book *Losing Ground*,[10] which argued that governmental efforts to help the underclass to escape poverty were misguided and instead increased the dependence of poor people on government assistance programs. Many students of immigrant economic progress, by contrast, highlighted the upward mobility of persons who arrived in the United States with little but achieved much. Few studies have examined the link between immigration and the underclass, largely because no one can ever know what would have happened to the underclass if there had been no immigration. Econometric studies which examine the effects of immigrants on poor Americans generally find that the arrival of immigrants does not have measurable effects on Black workers, but such studies cannot deal with Blacks who did not move to Los Angeles because of competition from immigrants or

Blacks who did not move to Los Angeles because they were not recruited by employers satisfied with immigrants.

Advocates of increased immigration cite such studies as "proof" that immigration does not hinder the wages or job opportunities of the native-born, particularly Blacks. In his most recent book, George Borjas states: "The methodological arsenal of modern econometrics cannot detect a single shred of evidence that immigrants have a sizeable adverse impact on the earnings and employment opportunities of natives in the United States."[11] Regarding the impact on Black Americans, Borjas writes:

> It is often argued that Blacks are the one group whose economic progress is most likely to be hampered by the entry of immigrants into the United States. Perhaps the most surprising insight provided by the recent econometric evidence is that *no* study finds any evidence to support this claim.[12]

In his recent book, Julian Simon endorses this position: "Taken together, the empirical studies . . . suggest that general immigration causes little or no unemployment at large, even in the first year or two; the same is true of low-income Hispanic immigration even among groups most likely to be 'displaced' by them."[13]

These cold econometric models are just that — cold statistics. They miss the entire sociological point. Historically, the most recent immigrants allowed earlier arrivers to move up the socio-economic ladder — a sort of social capillarity. One would expect that unskilled immigration would result in economic progress among Black Americans. Unfortunately that has not been the case, in large part due to the long history of discrimination and the resulting low educational attainment among many Black Americans. The nation's concern should not be with whether immigration affects Black wages and employment; the concern should be concentrated on how to raise the overall socio-economic status of Black Americans. Immigration has not accomplished that goal. Is it not time to try something else like reducing the level of immigration?

The link between poverty and immigration is indirect and complex. The availability of immigrant workers without options makes it unnecessary for employers to upgrade the jobs they offer in order to attract the poor Americans whose expectations have risen. As long as the immigrant seamstresses keep arriving, there is little pressure on employers to upgrade sewing jobs, to develop flexible work schedules, to develop new sewing technologies, or to move sewing operations overseas.

If immigrants affect the quality and quantity of jobs available, then immigration policy plays a special role in determining what effects labor force trends have on the American underclass. Most immigrants enter the workforce, and they tend to be concentrated at the extremes of the occupational ladder. Some are scientists and engineers who are successful in the U.S. labor market, but most are unskilled. Indeed, "recent immigrant waves are not as successful in the U.S. labor market as earlier waves."[14] They settle in poor neighborhoods, seek unskilled jobs, and often have an easier time finding such jobs than poor Americans. Employers sometimes prefer to hire the immigrants: even though they may not speak English, the newcomers are likely to be grateful for what to them is a high wage job. The American workers who are available for such unskilled jobs, by contrast, are likely to be dissatisfied with the low wages and lack of advancement opportunities.

It is easy to understand why immigrants in such situations can be seen as poor but virtuous, while Americans are seen as poor and pathological. As the immigrants succeed, sympathy for the American underclass declines. Thirty years ago President Kennedy argued that the United States only needed to create a full employment economy to provide jobs for poor Americans: the conventional wisdom was that a rising tide would lift all boats, rich and poor alike.

Many Americans do work their way out of poverty, just as they did in earlier decades. But attitudes toward poor Americans have changed. Instead of offering public intervention to create more opportunities for poor American residents, welfare critics argue that welfare programs should be eliminated so as to compel the underclass to be poor but virtuous.[15] These critics fail to note the effects of labor market competition on the aspirations of poor Americans. Some programs to help the poor were undoubtedly misguided, but it is also true that competition from unskilled immigrants makes it harder for the American underclass to lift itself up by its bootstraps.

IMMIGRANTS AND AMERICAN WORKERS

Immigrants are younger than the resident U.S. population, and many are motivated to come to the United States in order to improve their economic status. Within a few years after arrival, the percentage of immigrants in the workforce often exceeds the percentage of Americans in the labor force. In 1980 about 61 percent of all persons 16 and older were in the labor force. Among the foreign-born, this was 64 percent. This higher immigrant labor force participation rate hides the fact that 70 percent of the persons who arrived between 1970 and 1974 were in the workforce in 1980, but only 59 percent of the 1975 through 1980 arrivals.[16] The declining participation rate of immigrants in the 1970s reflects the changing composition of immigrants; refugees, who are less likely to join the U.S. labor force immediately, were a higher proportion of foreign-born persons arriving in the second half of the decade.

Most immigrants wind up in the labor force, but few are screened in order to determine whether their skills are needed in the U.S. labor market. Persons who want to immigrate legally to the United States face a preference system which still favors family unification over workforce needs, despite new legislation that purports to encourage the immigration of skilled workers. Thus, most immigrants enter because they have relatives who are U.S. residents, not because a U.S. employer has shown that there are no Americans available to fill a particular vacant job for which the employer wants to hire an immigrant. In addition to these unifying families, refugees ask to come to the United States and asylees enter the United States and ask to stay without being screened for their labor market effects. Finally, illegal immigrants entered the United States in large numbers in the 1970s and 1980s; they too were not screened for their labor market effects, and over 3 million were legalized under the Immigration Reform and Control Act of 1986.

Over 9 million immigrants came to the United States in the 1980s, but fewer than 4 percent arrived after it was determined that they were needed in the sense that a U.S. employer asked the Department of Labor to certify that there were no American workers available to fill the vacant job for which an immigrant was being requested. Table 4.2 indicates that in the legal immigration system of the mid-1980s, needed workers and their families were less than 9 percent of the almost 600,000 legal immigrants and refugees admitted each year. Slight increases may be noted in the future because of the 1990 legislation.

Immigrants at first blush appear to replicate the United States occupational structure, suggesting that they do not make the economy more or less skilled, but this first impression may be misleading. About 25 percent of U.S. workers were employed in managerial and professional occupations in 1987, and one-fourth of the immigrants arriving in the United States in the mid-1980s reported that they had such occupations in their country of origin.[17] However, a large fraction of the immigrants are in lower-skilled occupations: almost half of the mid-1980s immigrants were operators and laborers, service workers, or farm workers in their country of origin, but only one-third of the U.S. workers had these occupations in 1987. If the 3 million aliens legalized under the Immigration Reform and Control Act of 1986 are added to 1980s immigrants, then the low-skilled group rises to more than half of all immigrants.

The scientists and other professional immigrants at the top of the job ladder generate little controversy because they are relatively few in number, sometimes screened to ensure that they are truly needed, and integrate quite easily into American work places and communities. What about the immigrants at the bottom of the job ladder? Here controversy reigns supreme.

Three major theories offer explanations of how unskilled immigrants affect

Table 4.2 — Average Annual Immigrant Admissions 1985-1987

Type of Immigrant	Percent of All Immigrants
Immediate Relatives of U.S. Citizens	36.5
Other Relatives	36.0
Needed Workers[1]	8.9
Refugees and Asylees	16.7
Other	1.9
Total (number)	591,078

[1] Includes the worker and his or her family; in 1987, for example, there were about 12,000 third preference or high-skilled immigrants and 11,600 sixth preference or other needed workers admitted.

Source: *The Effects of Immigration on the U.S. Economy and Labor Market*, DOL, 1989, p. 23.

U.S. labor markets. Each sees a different link between unskilled immigrants and the U.S. underclass, and each has a different implication for immigration policy.

(1)   One-for-one displacement assumes that unskilled immigrants and American workers compete for the same jobs, with the immigrants preferred by employers because they are willing to work "hard and scared" for low wages. This theory assumes that, if the unskilled immigrants disappeared, jobs would become available for American workers.

(2) Segmented labor market theories argue that there is little competition between unskilled immigrants and American workers because recent arrivals take only the jobs rejected by American workers.   In this theory, the disappearance of immigrants would force some employers out of business but not open up jobs for Americans.

(3) Triage theories recognize that there is some one-for-one displacement and some segmentation, but triage stresses the flexibility of the labor market. Since labor markets adapt to the presence or absence of unskilled immigrants, fewer immigrants would mean fewer but better jobs for American workers.

The   policy   implications   of   each   theory   are   straightforward.   The displacement theory suggests that restricting immigration will open up a significant number of jobs for American workers. Segmentation suggests that reducing the number of immigrants will have few effects on the American underclass because Americans will refuse the jobs vacated by recent arrivals. Triage theory recognizes that there is some displacement and segmentation, but that the dynamic labor market and economy will adjust to fewer unskilled immigrants by upgrading jobs, automating them, or simply eliminating those jobs which are not worth hiring someone to do at a decent wage.

The triage theory implicitly recognizes that immigration policies shape the labor market, the economy, and society. In other words, the United States can affect how much of a labor market mismatch it faces through its immigration policies.   However, immigration policies are not generally connected to employment policies: the United States recently legalized 3 million immigrants who, on average, had less than a high school education while at the same time a series of reports sounded the alarm that, within a decade, the number of jobs for persons with less than a high school education will shrink.

Waves of unskilled immigrant workers distort labor markets and the economy, producing such paradoxes as high cost-of-living Los Angeles becoming a major low-wage manufacturing center.   However, the links between immigration and employment policies have never been explicit. At the beginning of the twentieth century, U.S. factories and farms could absorb most of the unskilled immigrants who arrived, so that screening immigrants to determine their labor market effects was unnecessary. However, the twenty-first-century economy promises too many unskilled workers for the unskilled jobs which will be available. The United States thus confronts a massive retraining challenge which includes retraining immigrant seamstresses who are made jobless by technology or even lower wages abroad. Given this labor market scenario, does it make sense to continue to admit unskilled immigrants who will have to be retrained in 10 or 20 years?

These common sense arguments against unskilled immigration are often obscured in the sometimes emotional arguments for more immigrants. Immigration advocates argue that unskilled immigrants cannot be hurting American workers because unemployment rates in the southwestern cities which have the most immigrants are as low or lower than rates in eastern and midwestern cities with few immigrants.   Such a static comparison of unemployment rates ignores the fact that the southwestern cities which used to attract unskilled Americans are now sending, for example, Blacks from Los Angeles to Atlanta. Unskilled immigrants often drive unskilled Americans from immigration areas such as Los Angeles, and the underclass which remains tends to drop out of the labor force, making the low unemployment rate deceptive.[18]

Furthermore, as economist Vernon Briggs recently pointed out in reviewing the Borjas monograph *Friends or Strangers*:

The employment data Borjas uses are for SMSAs. An SMSA contains a large central city and, usually, its several adjacent counties, defining a general labor market that transcends narrow political jurisdictions. If foreign-born workers are disproportionately concentrated in the central cities of SMSAs (which they are), the inclusion of the data for adjacent counties will dilute the measurement of their impact in the labor markets of the central cities. . . . Likewise, for the employment effects in industry, he uses broad classifications (e.g., manufacturing) and not the specific sub-classifications (e.g., apparel manufacturing). If immigrant workers are concentrated in only a few sub-classifications, as data shows they are, any adverse effects of immigrant workers on the wages and employment for everyone in the broad industrial classification will be minimized. Hence, the extent of adverse effects on citizen workers is still an open question. Just because significant employment displacement and wage depression were not found by Borjas at his level of analysis does not mean that these effects do not exist.[19]

Immigration advocates also argue that unskilled immigrants benefit the economy because, even though they start at the bottom, they soon catch up to similar American workers. Immigrants with 6th grade Mexican education tend to earn less initially than Mexican-Americans with 6th grade educations, but they work longer hours than the Americans and, after 10 to 20 years, they earn on average more than the American with similar levels of education. This does not mean that the immigrants are "better" than the Americans, or even that they raise the average incomes of Americans. The earnings of some immigrants catch up with the earnings of similar Americans, but if the immigrants and the Americans that they catch up to are poor, then the average income of all Americans falls.

The conclusions of studies of the economic progress of immigrants conflict. The basic idea behind these studies is that immigration is an investment which eventually yields a return, just as going to college for four years means spending money for tuition and books and having no earnings in order to enjoy a higher salary later. An individual's earnings in these models of economic progress make the annual earnings of immigrants and natives dependent on individual characteristics such as years of education, age, and traits such as race or ethnic group and marital status.

The first economic progress models showed that immigrant earnings increased rapidly after their arrival in the United States.[20] Studies which compare the earnings of immigrants and similar natives also come to the conclusion that immigrants who arrived 10 to 20 years earlier have earnings which equal those of similar native-born persons in a base year such as 1980.

The fact that immigrant earnings equal and surpass native earnings suggests that the immigrants have special motivations or work hard, and that the United States generally benefits economically from immigration. The logic of this argument is not compelling. Having immigrants equal and surpass poor

Americans does not make the U.S. economy better off; it merely increases the number of American residents in poverty. Second, there is a problem in generalizing about immigrant behavior on the basis of a snapshot year such as 1970 or 1980. The fact that immigrants arriving in the United States in 1952 earn as much as similar native-born residents in 1970 does not mean that immigrants arriving in 1953 also catch up in 1971. In order to determine whether immigrant earnings equal those of similar native-born persons, a motion picture which tracks immigrants and natives over time is needed, not a series of snapshots.

Recent attempts to simulate a motion picture of immigrant progress generally report that the earlier snapshot findings of immigrant earnings catch-ups were too optimistic. The most extensive attempts to simulate the tracking of a group of immigrants over time report that more recent waves of immigrants do not appear to be catching-up to comparable native-born workers.[21] Once again, it is hard to identify the reasons why more recently-arrived immigrants seem to have a harder time in the U.S. labor market. Immigrant motivation or "quality" could have declined as entry became easier, or it could be that the U.S. economy and labor market have changed in ways which make it harder for post-1980 arrivals to catch up to similar natives in earnings.

Immigrants to the United States generally require a decade or more of familiarity with the U.S. labor market to catch up to similar native-born workers. However, just because Asian immigrants who arrived in the early 1950s had their earnings catch up 20 years later does not mean that Asian immigrants who arrived in the early 1980s will experience an earnings catch-up at the turn of the century. Instead immigrant "quality" may be declining in the sense that it will be two or three decades before the earnings of immigrants approach those of natives, if they ever do.[22]

The final point about the earnings progress of immigrants is perhaps the most important: who are the immigrants catching up to? If most immigrants are engineers, an earnings catch-up, whether it occurs sooner or later, would be regarded as adding a higher-than-average income as well as technical expertise to the U.S. economy. However, if most immigrants are farm workers or laborers, then even if the immigrant earnings catch up to those of U.S.-born farm workers or laborers, this is as a dubious accomplishment in a labor market which promises to be awash in unskilled workers.

IMMIGRANT NETWORKS AND LABOR MARKETS

Most jobs at the bottom of the labor market are found by word-of-mouth, and after one or more immigrants is hired, an immigrant network often establishes itself to deliver new workers quickly to the employer. The employer of low-wage and unskilled workers — a restaurant or hotel, a shoe or furniture manufacturer, or a farmer — typically experiences a high turnover of American workers because the Americans are dissatisfied with the low wages, hard work, and few benefits of these jobs. The immigrants, by contrast, report diligently every day and offer to bring their friends and relatives to the work place and train them. The loyalty and dependability of immigrants makes them a preferred workforce, and employers eager to avoid dealing with unskilled workers turn recruitment and hiring over to the immigrant network.

Once the immigrant network is established, unskilled Americans tend to be bypassed in the scramble for jobs. An ethnic foreman favors the people he knows best, and the language of the work place becomes Spanish or Tagalog. The Americans who show up feel out of place and soon quit, reinforcing the employer's belief that Americans don't want low-wage jobs anyway. The jobs become less and less attractive because the isolated immigrants do not demand and employers do not offer the wage and working condition improvements that are occurring in other labor markets. In this way, the American workers who used to be recruited for low-wage jobs find themselves excluded from them by immigrants.

One effect of such immigrant work place takeovers is to cut the bridge between disadvantaged Americans and low-wage jobs which was once the first step up the economic ladder. A number of observers have lamented the now missing bridge between disadvantaged youth and jobs — Charles Murray argues that this missing job bridge decoupled poor youth "from the mechanism whereby poor people in this country have historically worked their way out of poverty."[23] There is a dispute over how to restore the jobs bridge — whether penalties for crime should be increased, welfare programs scaled back, or the educational system reformed — but no disagreement that the jobs bridge has been weakened for the underclass and should be restored.

Case studies of such immigration networks demonstrate how quickly certain jobs become the property of immigrants. In Los Angeles, many of the unionized Black janitors who once cleaned high-rise office buildings were displaced by Mexican immigrants over a five-year period in the early 1980s. This displacement occurred quickly and indirectly: according to a GAO report, the number of unionized Black janitors in Los Angeles county fell from 2,500 in 1977 to 600 in 1985, even though janitorial employment rose 50 percent because of a building boom.[24] The reason for this displacement of unionized Black janitors in an expanding service industry is that competing janitorial services which employed recent immigrants offered to clean buildings for 25 to 35 percent less because they paid their immigrant workers up to two-thirds less than prevailing union wages.

Immigrants in expanding industries often prevent wages from rising. The luxury hotel industry doubled its capacity in San Francisco during the 1980s, but wages for unskilled hotel workers rose no faster than average because there was an ample supply of them. Similarly, employment in restaurants expanded as affluent Americans ate out more often, and the availability of immigrants helped the full service restaurants to expand as rapidly as fast food outlets and coffee shops.[25] The availability of immigrants in the kitchen helps to create jobs for American waiters and bartenders, but this means that the full service restaurant industry can create "good" jobs for Americans only if it has an immigrant worker subsidy.

THE LOOMING MISMATCH

The U.S. labor force will include more minorities and immigrants in the future, and the economic mobility of these new workers and their children is uncertain in a segmented economy and a polarized labor market. Some observers see a half-full water glass, optimistically predicting that rapid economic growth and slow workforce growth will help immigrants and their children to climb the American economic ladder and increase American competitiveness in the international economy. Others worry that the glass is half empty, that immigrants and disadvantaged Americans will be trapped in dead-end jobs which do not provide the helping hand of training needed to advance in a labor market which needs and rewards knowledge skills. The children of minorities and immigrants, according to these pessimists, are more likely to be high school dropouts or graduates without the basic literacy needed to compete in tomorrow's labor market than the skilled and bilingual workers needed to compete in the international economy. One thing is clear: the occupational profile of immigrants and minorities will have to change if they are going to be represented in proportion to their numbers in the professional and technical jobs of the future.

Most of the workers who will join the workforce in the 1990s are in school today; in addition to these young entrants, housewives may decide to work, older workers may elect not to retire early, and adult immigrants may enter the United States and go to work. During the 1980s, this combination of young entrants, adults who decided to work or to work longer, and immigrants added 20 million people to the U.S. labor force. During the 1990s, the workforce is expected to expand by less than 20 million, even though the population is growing.

Will these entrants to the workforce during the 1990s have the qualities needed to sustain and expand the U.S. economy? Leaders in business, education, and government have expressed fears that the United States is "A Nation at Risk" because many workforce entrants do not have the skills needed to do today's jobs. Many employers report that only 20 to 30 percent of the applicants who want to be clerks or technicians have the basic English and calculation skills needed to operate the computers and monitoring equipment that are common even in entry-level jobs. Business leaders blame the educational system for sending them unprepared workers, and they support educational reforms aimed at raising the basic skills of high school graduates so that new entrants will not have to be retrained in the work place.

Some of the workforce entrants in the 1990s will not have attended American schools; they will be immigrants who enter the United States as adults. These unskilled immigrant workers often experience dead-end jobs in cyclical and declining industries such as garment or shoe manufacturing, construction, or agriculture. In these industries, there are still jobs for unskilled workers, but these jobs pay low wages and offer few chances for advancement. Furthermore, international competition and seasonality cause periodic layoffs, contributing to unemployment and pleas for tariffs and quotas against imports. Unskilled immigrants often want to escape from such jobs and industries, but many are trapped by their lack of English and other skills. If technological breakthroughs, international competition, or a recession lead to widespread layoffs, these unskilled immigrant workers may find few opportunities for upward mobility or even lateral transitions. They risk becoming a lost generation which is used to squeeze a few extra years of production and profits from declining sectors until imports, technology, or changing consumer tastes finally eliminate their jobs.

Because immigrants are clustered at the extremes of the skills spectrum, large numbers of immigrants reinforce inequality in the American labor market. The business services industry, for example, is expected to almost double its employment by 2000, but the occupations involved in this expansion are at the extremes of the skill spectrum. Less than half of business services employment is highly paid research and management consulting, computer services, and advertising; much of the other half is janitorial services, word processing, temporary employment, and security personnel.

CONCLUSION

Many of the jobs currently filled by unskilled American and immigrant workers may be eliminated in the future. Routine data entry and word processing jobs, for example, are being shifted abroad, so that daily airline passenger manifests are entered into computers in the Caribbean, where supermarket cents-off coupons are sorted, and even engineering drawings are completed in India and transmitted by satellite to U.S. companies. If U.S. wages continue to rise, the spread of computers and cheaper communications may push more and more routine jobs overseas. Admitting immigrants in order to retain such jobs in the United States cannot succeed unless U.S. wages fall to developing country levels.

There are two kinds of mismatches possible because so many immigrant workers find jobs that may be eliminated at the bottom of the labor market. The first mismatch involves the fate of immigrant workers buffeted by changes which eliminate or downgrade their jobs. What will happen to the army of immigrant seamstresses who made southern California and New York City centers of garment production in the 1980s if import barriers are removed? If these immigrant women, many of whom entered the United States during the 1980s when they were 20 to 30 years old, become unionized, their unions may fight imports and new technologies. If they remain unorganized, they may face difficulty finding other jobs which pay reasonable wages and do not demand language or numeracy skills.

The second mismatch involves disadvantaged American workers. Economies and labor markets are flexible; they adjust to the presence or absence of additional workers, and they will adjust to the availability of unskilled workers by creating low-wage jobs for some of them. Low-tech garment employment expanded in part because immigrant workers were available; this industry probably would not have expanded without immigrants. It is thus correct to say that the availability of immigrants permitted the low-tech garment industry to expand, creating jobs in the United States. However, without such immigrant workers, a high-tech garment industry might have emerged which employed American rather than immigrant workers. The availability of immigrant workers pushed the garment economy along a losing low-tech rather than a winning high-tech trajectory. The low-tech garment industry can buy a few extra years of survival, but this temporary survival will not help the United States to employ its disadvantaged workers nor will it help the U.S. economy to become more competitive.

The expansion of the low-tech economy because immigrant workers are available makes the United States vulnerable to twin mismatches: the mismatch which occurs when immigrant workers are displaced from low-tech jobs and cannot find re-employment in the shrinking low-tech economy, and the mismatch which results from the preference of expanding businesses for unskilled immigrants rather than disadvantaged American workers. Both mismatches threaten to frustrate a generation of immigrant and disadvantaged American workers and aggravate the problem of retraining them to avoid a widening skills gap in the twenty-first century.

NOTES
1. Augustus Hawkins, statement in hearing before the Subcommittee of Investment, Jobs, and Prices of the Joint Economic Committee, Senate Hearing 100-78, April 1988, iv.

2. Alan Murray, "Bush Sees Labor Shortage, Looks Abroad," *Wall Street Journal*, 7

February 1990), 2.

3. In the mid-1980s, output per worker rose 3 percent annually in the restructured manufacturing industry, but only 0.6 percent per year in the non-manufacturing service sector, where 80 percent of Americans are employed.

4. U.S. Department of Labor, *Projections 2000* (Bureau of Labor Statistics, 1988).

5. Leon F. Bouvier and Vernon Briggs, *The Population and Labor Force of New York* (Washington: Population Reference Bureau, 1988), 57-58.

6. "How to make anti-poverty politics popular," *The Economist*, 27 April 1991, 23.

7. Ronald Mincy, *Wall Street Journal*, 9 May 1989, B1.

8. Robert Pearson, "Economy, Culture, Public Policy, and the Urban Underclass," *SSRC Items* (June 1989): 23.

9. Ibid., 25.

10. Charles Murray, *Losing Ground: American Social Policy, 1950-1980* (New York: Basic Books, 1984).

11. George Borjas, *Friends or Strangers* (New York: Basic Books, 1990), 81.

12. Ibid., 87-88.

13. Simon, *Economic Consequences*, 251.

14. Borjas, *Friends or Strangers*, 115.

15. Murray, *Losing Ground*.

16. U.S. Department of Labor, *The Effects of Immigration on the U.S. Economy and Labor Market* (Washington: U.S. Dept. of Labor, 1989), 25.

17. Ibid., 27.

18. Thomas Muller and Thomas Espenshade, *The Fourth Wave: California's Newest Immigrants* (Washington: Urban Inst.), 65.

19. Vernon M. Briggs, Jr., "The Declining Competitiveness of Immigrants — Review: George J. Borjas' *Friends or Strangers: The Impact of Immigrants on the U.S. Economy,*" *Scope* (Summer, 1990): 7.

20. U.S. Department of Labor, *Effects of Immigration*, 159-67.

21. Borjas, *Friends or Strangers*, 115 ff.

22. George Borjas, *International Differences in the Labor Market Performance of Immigrants* (Kalamazoo: Upjohn Inst., 1988).

23. Charles Murray, *Wall Street Journal*, 15 May 1985, 34.

24. *Illegal Aliens: Influence of Illegal Workers on Wages and Working Conditions of Legal Workers* (Washington: GAO, PEMD-88-13BR, 1988), 40-41.

25. Thomas Bailey, "A Case Study of Immigrants in the Restaurant Industry," *Industrial Relations* 24 (Spring 1985): 205-221.

5
Immigration and
Economic Growth

Population changes affect the trajectory or development of the economy as well as the evolution of the labor market. Immigrants contribute to economic growth when they find U.S. jobs, earn wages, and become consumers or when their capital and entrepreneurship creates new jobs and businesses. The number and characteristics of immigrants determine their influence on the economy. If most immigrants are unskilled workers, the economy will expand in a manner which absorbs large numbers of such workers. On the other hand, if U.S. immigration policies favor the entry of Cuban or Korean entrepreneurs, then immigration will be associated with new business startups.

Current immigration policies, by permitting the entrance of so many unskilled immigrants, encourage the creation of unskilled jobs and promote labor-intensive economic development. In this sense, immigration policy is a type of industrial policy which in the 1980s steered the economy mostly in a low-tech direction. Most of the nine million immigrants who arrived in the 1980s had less than a high school education. The entry of so many unskilled immigrants contradicted government research and development and tax policies to promote and sustain a high-tech economy that is competitive in the global marketplace. While the 1990 legislation will permit more skilled workers to enter, the number of unskilled immigrants is also expected to rise.

The effect of the 1980s immigration is evident when comparing the performance of the U.S. economy with economic trends in Europe and Japan. The United States had rapid employment growth during the 1970s and 1980s, but wages and productivity grew slowly. In Europe and Japan, by contrast, new jobs were created at a slower pace but wages and productivity in these areas rose faster than in the United States.

THE MORE VERSUS BETTER JOBS TRADE-OFF

The immigration policies of the 1980s created more U.S. jobs. However, the U.S. also can create jobs with less immigration. The U.S. can even create more jobs for unskilled workers: for example, eliminating minimum wage laws would increase the number of jobs for unskilled workers. If more adolescents dropped out of school, fast food outlets might have more jobs. These examples demonstrate that creating more jobs is not the only goal: there is a trade-off between more jobs and better jobs.

However, the United States has not yet developed a consensus on the minimum standards for a job. For example, the United States is the only major industrial society in which the minimum wage, which applies to only a small fraction of the workforce, is permitted to fall to less than half of the average manufacturing wage because of arguments than an even lower minimum wage will create more jobs for unskilled workers. There is a consensus that children should be prohibited from working too much because they need to be educated to be productive workers as adults.

Immigration policies also affect the number of jobs, and a large number of unskilled immigrants has economic effects similar to encouraging teenagers to work instead of remaining in school: there are more jobs in the short-term, but there is slower economic growth in the long-run. Importing immigrant farm workers helps to keep food prices down, but leaves the United States with disadvantaged workers if wages are low, and with displaced workers if the immigrants are replaced by machines.

Unskilled immigrants are not necessary for rapid economic growth. The continued availability of unskilled immigrants eventually slows economic growth by encouraging the United States to maintain or develop businesses which are not competitive internationally or which can be maintained only on the backs of disadvantaged workers.

When our forebears arrived, the United States had a frontier to settle, railroads to build, and factories to staff, so that most unskilled immigrants found jobs quickly. But a history of large-scale immigration and rapid economic growth does not guarantee that future waves of unskilled workers will ensure continued economic growth. The economy has changed, and the unskilled immigrants arriving today, while employable, may not be strategically useful for the high-tech economy the United States needs to compete internationally.

Immigrants play a special role in economic growth, but it is a changing role. Just because the United States accepted unskilled immigrants and grew economically in the past does not mean that immigration is necessary for economic growth today, as demonstrated by the booming economy of non-immigrant Japan. Similarly, the fact that immigrants have made and continue to make important scientific discoveries in the United States indicates that some immigrants provide vital new seed; such highly-trained immigrants should be favored in the United States selection system, not displaced in the immigration queue by unskilled immigrants.

POPULATION GROWTH AND ECONOMIC GROWTH

Economies grow by increasing their physical quantities of people and capital or raising the productivity of people and capital. The productivity of people and capital rises when their "quality" improves: the quality of people goes up with education, and the quality of machines increases if new versions implement the latest technologies.

In earlier periods of large-scale immigration, the United States grew by increasing its physical quantities of people, land, and machinery. Each new family that began to farm in frontier areas bought equipment and sold the food that it did not need to live on, thus raising the U.S. GNP. Settling the frontier affected both the quantity and the quality of farming, the major economic activity during the 1800s. For example, wheat yields rose as settlers spread into the Great Plains because the new land being farmed was more productive than the exhausted soil along the eastern seaboard. After the frontier was settled, immigrants no longer raised productivity and GNP by farming the frontier, but they did raise the productivity of machinery in factories by staffing them around the clock. In this way, the productivity of machinery increased because it was used for more hours, and the price of industrial goods fell for both immigrants and natives.

History provides limited guidance to determine how immigration policies will affect economic growth in the future because both the immigrants and the economy have changed. The immigrants of the early 1800s were settling frontier areas. Succeeding waves of immigrants were primarily unskilled and semi-skilled workers, and so were most American residents. There were few labor or safety laws to protect the workers flocking into the nation's factories, and long hours of work under unsafe conditions for low pay were common. The economy grew, and a handful of industrialists became wealthy, and unions and the federal and state governments began by the 1920s to establish minimum workplace standards to protect both American and immigrant workers. Economic growth and these labor standards improved the lives and incomes of all Americans, immigrants and natives alike.

Today both the immigrants and the economy are different. The immigrants to the United States have changed from being a group of unskilled workers to a two-tiered group of highly-trained professionals and unskilled laborers, just as the economy has changed from one which advertised simply for workers to an economy which asks for either computer technicians or farmhands. A majority of Americans have at least some post-high school education, but today's immigrants are either more educated or less educated than the average American. At the unskilled end of the labor market, one result of the 1980s wave of immigrant workers is the revival of street corner or day labor markets. Immigrants gather outside a fast food outlet or convenience store at 6 or 7 AM, and employers drive up to shouts of "how many" or "how much do you pay." Bargaining and hiring in a babble of tongues is accomplished in less than a minute, and the new employees drive off to an unfamiliar work site with an unknown employer. Not surprisingly, abuses of workers in such situations is common. Worker productivity is often low, and workplace accidents are common. The unskilled immigrants work hard, but their employers cannot communicate easily with them and do not expect to employ the immigrants long enough to train them.

Most labor markets are more structured. Job applicants must usually submit applications and certificates, be interviewed and tested, and then work on probation before they become regular employees. Investing in selecting and training employees seems to increase productivity. One reason why Japanese manufacturers operate in the United States more efficiently than U.S. firms is that they invest so much more in selecting and training employees.

Raising productivity or enabling people to do their jobs better and faster is the key to economic growth today. The sources of productivity gains are disputed, but all agree that an educated workforce with modern technologies is more productive than a workforce with little education and few modern machines. Economists disagree on exactly which government policies raise productivity fastest, but all agree that increasing the number of educated workers spurs productivity growth.

Productivity growth slowed during the 1970s and 1980s, and this slowdown in economic growth was soon translated into smaller annual increases in incomes. The failure of rising productivity to generate more of the nation's economic growth has spawned debate over what is wrong with the American economy. The winds of international competition are shifting the U.S. economy away from its worldwide dominance for several reasons. The American people do not save nor invest enough, the federal government and trade deficits are too big, and a decade of debate has not put the U.S. economy back on the path toward economic strength.

Discussions about the decline of the U.S. economy are long on descriptions of the problem but short on solutions. The description of a short-run oriented economy is now familiar: Americans would rather spend than save, and this failure to consider the future has produced mountains of consumer, business, and government debt. The U.S. government, for example, borrowed about $20,000 per family of four during the 1980s to finance an unbroken string of deficits. Most of this deficit spending went to pay for defense and fixed obligations, not to construct an efficient economy for tomorrow. As a consequence, the United States faces a "third deficit": in addition to the trade and budget deficits, physical and educational infrastructures have fallen into disrepair, and they will be expensive to fix. Similarly, educational reforms have failed to keep secondary school students competitive with students abroad.

Immigration is not usually added to this list of problems. Low savings rates and high deficits cannot continue indefinitely, but some people believe that high levels of immigration can continue for another century. Immigrant workers did not cause the U.S. economic problems, but large numbers of unskilled immigrants aggravate the search for solutions to economic problems, productivity, and the type of growth which occurs.

IMMIGRANT WORKERS, PRODUCTIVITY, AND ECONOMIC GROWTH

Much of the economic growth which occurred during the 1970s and 1980s has been low quality and unsustainable growth. The United States cannot continue to rely on fast-food outlets and convenience stores for new jobs; sustainable long-term economic growth requires that productivity-increasing investments be made in industries in which the United States has a long-term comparative advantage. These industries include knowledge and computer-intensive sectors, such as finance and insurance, and high-tech manufacturing, such as aerospace. The goal of such world class industries is "total flexibility" — high quality, customized goods at mass production prices. The United States will continue to offer a relatively large number of unskilled low-tech jobs in industries which range from hospitals to hotels, but the number of such jobs should not be increased artificially by a wave of unskilled immigrants.

Immigrants play a relatively small but important role in the U.S. economy. Most American businesses hire American workers. There are well over 120 million workers employed by over 7 million U.S. businesses; perhaps 5 million of these workers are unskilled immigrants who arrived in the 1980s. Although it is often alleged that many hotels, restaurants, or farms would go out of business without unskilled immigrants, the relatively small number of immigrant workers makes it clear that most of the 260,000 workers hired each day are American workers. What the availability of immigrant workers does is to divert attention from long-term solutions to the problem of bad jobs. Instead of investing in a new technology to clean hotel rooms or pick fruits and vegetables, businesses dependent on immigrant workers invest in the political process to assure continued access to such workers.

Immigrant workers are associated with a handful of businesses in a few areas. American workers in the 1950s filled jobs such as cleaning hotel rooms, working in restaurant kitchens, and picking fruits and vegetables. As American workers came and went, hotel and restaurant operators and farmers developed various strategies to cope with worker turnover. Some jobs were eliminated by machines or the shifting of production overseas; some employers raised wages and improved working conditions enough to attract and retain their American workforce. However, if immigrant workers were available, as Braceros — Mexicans admitted each year to the United States to do farm work during the 1950s — were once available to southwestern farmers, many businesses turned to them.

Unskilled immigrants soon became essential workers in the eyes of the owners of certain businesses. Instead of the cost and uncertainty of labor-saving machines, or dealing with American workers who complained about low wages and poor working conditions, many immigrants willingly accepted prevailing wages and working conditions. For a low-wage business in which controlling labor costs that are 30 to 60 percent of total costs is the difference between profits and losses, such an availability of workers is a godsend. Low-wage employers got the same dependability and worker referrals enjoyed by businesses such as IBM, but without raising wages or improving working conditions.

SUBCONTRACTING AND WORKER DISPLACEMENT

Immigrant networks promote a certain type of business expansion. Businesses which have a reliable supply of low-wage workers can expand more easily than those that face workforce turnover and uncertainty. In this way, unskilled immigrants indirectly displace American workers by permitting their employers to expand faster than employers who hire higher-cost Americans.

The competitive process by which immigrants indirectly displace Americans can be illustrated by examining subcontracting. In many businesses, low-wage operations are performed by subcontractors; in this way, the low-wage workers who clean offices or rooms do not appear on the regular payroll of a bank or hotel. There is a great deal of competition in the shadowy world of subcontracting, and labor law violations are common. Contractors minimize complaints about such violations by knowing and controlling their workforces.

Low-cost contractors expand on the backs of immigrants, while their higher-cost competitors who hire American workers simply disappear. Such a competitive process occurred in California agriculture in the early 1980s. The nonprofit organizations which tried to stabilize seasonal farm worker employment for Americans were driven out of business by lower cost labor contractors who hired recent immigrants.[1]

Lemon harvesting in Southern California provides an illustration. Lemon harvesters are paid about 90 cents to pick a 20-pound box of lemons, and the landowner pays an additional overhead charge to cover payroll taxes and employee benefits. Even though payroll taxes and equipment costs have increased, overhead charges fell during the 1980s as a proliferation of contractors replaced employers who hired unionized and settled workers. This labor market transformation occurred quickly. In 1979, about 80 percent of the 5,000 lemon harvesters in the Ventura area were settled local workers and union members; a decade later, there are no union members picking lemons. Today most of the harvesters are recent immigrants.

Contractors survive and sometimes prosper on paper-thin margins by cheating on payroll taxes, charging workers for jobs, transportation, and housing, and otherwise attempting to make profits despite the squeeze on overhead charges. The beneficiaries of this immigrant-contractor system are major landowners; if wages rose, the value of the orchards they own would fall. Consumers do not benefit from low-cost lemon picking because marketing regulations force about half of the picked lemons to be diverted into dish soap and other industrial uses so as to limit the supply of fresh lemons, thereby keeping lemon prices high.

Lemon harvesting also illustrates a more pernicious effect of unskilled immigrant workers; their availability slows productivity growth. Lemon growers had become dependent on Bracero harvesters. When the Bracero program ended in 1964, growers improved their employment practices, mechanized the harvest, and developed dwarf trees to eliminate the ladders which made picking jobs unattractive to Americans. However, as unskilled immigrants again became available in the 1970s, these productivity-improving efforts lost steam; growers began to believe that unskilled immigrants would always be available, so they stopped funding productivity-increasing research. Instead, they lobbied for continued access to immigrant workers.

For a time, there were no noticeable effects. The recent immigrants who worked "hard and scared" actually picked lemons faster than the disadvantaged Americans who had filled in for Braceros. But wages which are low by U.S. standards are not low enough to compete with wages in developing nations. Lemon harvesters earning $4 to $5 hourly in California are still too expensive to compete with harvesters who earn $4 to $5 daily in Spain and Israel, and lemons from these countries began to enter the United States. In this sense, an abundance of unskilled workers bought a few more years of viability for the obsolete hand-harvesting method of picking lemons in the United States.

This story of an abundance of unskilled immigrants encouraging an American business to resist costly labor-saving innovations that eventually weaken its competitiveness can be retold for many industries in the 1980s. Instead of investing profits in research, low wages are translated into profits that raise land values but do not generate productivity-increasing technologies. Employers get spoiled by the ready availability of workers. When the food industry recently reviewed its response to the nationwide debate over perceived labor shortages, many commentators lamented the extraordinary human resources dilemma facing the industry. Efforts to automate and mechanize were not necessary during years of rapid workforce growth, and few were undertaken. Today, the food industry faces a costly technological catch-up. Throughout the U.S. food system, low wages, few benefits, and only part-time jobs became the rule in the 1980s, so that 50 to 75 percent turnover rates became common.[2] Employers who begin the year with 100 workers in 100 jobs must hire 50 to 75 new workers during the year to remain fully staffed. An industry that can thrive with such a turnover rate may be forced to make a series of catch-up adjustments when faced with fewer people available.

THE DOUBLE-EDGED SWORD OF LOW WAGES

Unskilled immigrants keep wages low and increase profits, but these extra profits do not often turn into productivity-increasing business investment. When wages rise in industrial countries, employers have an incentive to invest in productivity-increasing machinery, increasing worker productivity and lowering consumer prices. Higher profits enable businesses to make productivity-increasing investments, but the availability of low-wage labor deprives entrepreneurs of the incentive to make such investments. As former Secretary of Labor F. Ray Marshall noted in his dissent to the Final Report of the U.S. Select Commission on Immigration and Refugee Policy, "Additional supplies of low-skilled alien workers with Third World wage and employment expectations cannot only lead employers to prefer such workers, it can also lead to outmoded labor-intensive production processes, to the detriment of U.S. productivity."[3]

Unskilled immigrants and low wages are a double-edged sword affecting economic growth. Unskilled immigrants can lower wages and increase profits, but if workers are readily available, firms are discouraged from buying machinery which raises productivity. Low wages, uncertain economic prospects, and high interest rates discouraged productivity-increasing investment in the 1980s despite high profits. Low wages and high interest rates encourage many firms to hire easily laid-off workers instead of committing themselves to buying equipment which must be paid for whether it operates or not. The availability of immigrant workers helps to explain why parts of the American economy remained labor-intensive in the 1980s despite calls for business to raise labor productivity to compete successfully in the global economy.

Some U.S. businesses have been investing in labor-saving production methods because their managers believe that the United States cannot compete with foreign producers on wages. A rubber company president asserted that "We'll never have labor rates [in the United States] comparable to [those in] developing countries . . . we've got to out-innovate or out-automate the world if we're to have a chance of competing."[4] High and rising real wages can be an incentive for businesses to invest in labor-saving and quality-increasing innovations; German manufacturers have pursued this high wage and high quality strategy successfully in the 1980s. But there is a minority of American businesses whose owners depend on immigrant workers. They believe that "cheap labor" will always be available, they fail to plan for higher-cost labor in the future, and then they echo agriculture's lament that higher wages or immigration reforms will "put us out of business."

SELF-EMPLOYED AND SKILLED IMMIGRANTS

Few fourth-wave immigrants are self-employed. Korean, Cuban, and Indian immigrants are the well-known exceptions who often buy or begin marginal businesses with capital from their families or relatives. The explanations for such self-employment patterns are sometimes cultural, such as the Chinese and Jewish traditions of entrepreneurship; and sometimes related to labor market circumstances, as when a concentration of immigrants needs bilingual middlemen to deal with the larger community; and sometimes economic, as when immigrants with capital and business skills earn more being self-employed until they learn English and acquire credentials recognized in the United States. Immigrant self-employment declines as the immigrants become integrated into the U.S. economy.

The effects of immigrant self-employment on U.S. workers are hard to ascertain. Most U.S. and most immigrant businesses are small, and the immigrant-owned businesses are distinguished by their tendency to employ immigrants from their country of origin. Mexican immigrant businesses tend to hire Mexican immigrant workers and businesses started by Korean immigrants tend to hire Korean immigrant workers. There are many explanations for this immigrant-hiring-immigrant strategy.[5] If the immigrants become self-employed in part because of language difficulties, they will favor hiring fellow immigrants with whom they can communicate. Similarly, if the capital to open the business or the customers on which the business depends are an ethnic community, the immigrant business will rationally favor immigrant employees to reward the community for the capital and patronage it provides. In such ethnic enclave situations, the immigrant business, workforce, and customers become something of a closed circle which has only limited contacts with larger community suppliers and governmental authorities.

Immigrant businesses in ethnic enclaves are often praised for their entrepreneurial spirit which sometimes revives areas in economic decline. But there is a darker side to immigrant self-employment. Self-employed persons and businesses are more likely to avoid taxes, and their small size and informal record-keeping make enforcement of tax and other laws difficult. Businesses started by immigrants may favor and hire recent immigrants from their country of origin for loyalty and language reasons, irrespective of anti-discrimination laws. New arrivals may also be favored because they are vulnerable in the U.S. labor market. Most farm labor contractors in the southwestern states, for example, are Mexican immigrants who hire more recent arrivals from Mexico; they favor such workers in part because they are easier to "control" as newcomers are not likely to form or join a union, complain to labor law authorities, or demand better wages and benefits. In some ethnic enclaves, recent immigrant employees are protected by "reciprocal obligations and responsibilities" in the sense that, even if the immigrant business violates labor or other laws, employment conditions are within the norms of that community.[6] However, in less cohesive immigrant communities, more established immigrant businesses exploit new arrivals without fearing social ostracism.

What about skilled immigrants? Polls in the *Wall Street Journal* report that three-fourths of U.S. employers have or expect skilled worker shortages, although most of these employers do not have a plan to keep the skilled workers they already have.[7] Some employers think that Congress should get immigrants for them. Should immigration policy be modified to make it easier for employers to import the nurses and engineers that they need? Or should easing immigration barriers be linked to policies which require employers who want skilled immigrants to first train and retrain Americans? The 1990 immigration legislation addresses some of these questions. It remains to be seen what its effect will be.

In 1987, about 25 percent of all U.S. workers and 25 percent of the mid-1980s immigrants were in professional and managerial occupations. The most important occupations among the 30 million workers with managerial and professional occupations include teachers (12 percent), engineers (6 percent), and nurses and accountants (5 percent each). The professional and managerial workforce increases by about 500,000 annually, and about 57,000 or 10 percent of these additional professional workers are immigrants.

The perceived skilled worker shortage issue illustrates the more basic dilemma of labor-motivated immigration. Employers and societies can adjust; they do not need to import additional skilled workers. Importing skilled workers makes it possible to avoid adjustments or to make less costly adjustments, and the United States has not been able to achieve a consensus on which industries and occupations should have the easiest access to immigrants and thus face lower adjustment costs. For example, should farmers get easier access to immigrant workers than hospitals have to immigrant nurses? Skilled worker immigration raises the same adjustment questions raised by unskilled immigration, but it arouses less opposition because skilled immigrants are more likely to achieve above average U.S. incomes.

DOES THE AMERICAN ECONOMY NEED UNSKILLED IMMIGRANT WORKERS?

Large numbers of unskilled immigrant workers push the economy along an unsustainable economic path. Instead of preparing the United States to compete in the global marketplace, such workers prop up declining industries which then lobby for protection from imports. A few extra jobs and a few more years of operation are bought at too high a price. Immigrant-dependent businesses such as garment manufacturers sometimes win protections and subsidies, forcing consumers to pay higher prices, or the business fails and the displaced workers must be retrained.

The basic projections outlined in Part I assume that future net immigration will be 950,000 per year. About 570,000 of these new arrivals will join the workforce each year, and if current trends continue, a significant majority will be unskilled workers. The U.S. economy does not need to import that many unskilled workers during the 1990s. With fewer unskilled immigrants, the economy will adjust: there will be more automation in manufacturing and services, more mechanization in agriculture, and fewer unsustainable industries. On the other hand, if immigrant workers are readily available, productivity-increasing innovations will lag in immigrant-dominated industries, causing both the economy and society to become more segmented and isolated. Industries such as aerospace which must compete against high-wage firms abroad will march ahead with productivity-increasing innovations, while immigrant-dependent farm and factory owners will continue to argue that they cannot compete with foreign producers and must be protected from the international economy.

Although economies adjust to the presence or absence of additional workers, it is easy to ignore this common sense truth. Because economies adjust to the resources available, it is hard to take seriously predictions that there will be labor shortages in the years ahead. Most past predictions of labor shortages have been wrong and based on this book's projections, it is clear that current "doomsday" lamentations about future shortages are also incorrect.

ECONOMIC ADJUSTMENTS TO SLOWER LABOR FORCE GROWTH

Americans gained an appreciation for how the economy adjusts to changing prices and wages by experiencing the adjustments to rising energy prices during the 1970s. Rising energy prices meant smaller cars and fewer trips as well as the development of more efficient engines and alternative fuels. It is easy to assert that the economy will adjust and even to predict how it will adjust to rising prices and wages, but it is hard to determine just how fast or how costly the adjustment process will be. Higher wages for unskilled workers will force more adjustments on some firms and businesses than others. For example, labor-intensive businesses such as restaurants, hotels, and other service establishments that employ a high-proportion of minimum-wage workers may have to raise their prices if there are fewer unskilled workers. Consumers might go to restaurants less often if prices are raised, so the number of jobs may decrease. In this way, a labor shortage solves itself by pushing up wages and setting in motion a series of adjustments which solve the labor shortage problem.

Understandably, many labor-intensive businesses do not welcome a decline in the ample supply of unskilled workers to which they became accustomed in the 1980s. Instead of making adjustments that might reduce their profits, these employers complain that raising wages will aggravate inflation, that their businesses cannot adopt new technologies to save labor, and that the only choice is to maintain a large pool of low-wage workers or watch their restaurants and farms go out of business.

Behind every story of persisting labor shortages there is a more complex reality. Persistent complaints of farm labor shortages involve a small group of southwestern growers, most of whom produce fresh fruits and vegetables for distant markets. Instead of subdividing large tracts of land so that such labor-intensive crops are produced by farm families, or growing several crops so that hired workers can be employed for longer periods, or developing machines to harvest fruits and vegetables, these growers have become accustomed to immigrant workers being readily available to hand-pick their crops for 2 to 6 weeks at the minimum wage. Furthermore, a century of Chinese, Japanese, Filipino, and Mexican immigrants have convinced many farmers and their Congressional representatives that picking crops under the sun is a job fit only for unskilled immigrants.

The reality of farm labor shortages is more complex. The crown jewel of U.S. agricultural economy is typified by Iowa corn and hog farms; these farmers who feed a hungry world are mostly American citizens, not immigrants. These farmers are so productive that there are too many of them. The simultaneous surplus of American farmers and shortage of American farm workers says far more about lagging wages, working conditions, and technologies in fruit and vegetable agriculture than it does about the special abilities of immigrants to do farm work.

Similar complexities are behind complaints of shortages of nurses. Nurses' wages represent about 25 percent of health care costs, and during the 1980s, nurses' wages rose slowly but health care costs rose rapidly. If nursing wages continue to rise during the 1990s, health care costs will probably rise as well, but the experience of the last decade shows that it is not rising wages alone which spur health care cost increases. Nurses are in short supply because their wages are relatively low given their training; they face a short labor ladder which means that their promotion opportunities are limited; and their workload in many hospitals has increased. There are enough trained nurses to fill today's vacancies, but hospitals would have to make adjustments to wages, schedules, and workloads to persuade more of them to return to nursing. It is easier to recruit immigrants for urban nursing jobs than to begin making the costly adjustments necessary to get American nurses.

Labor shortage complaints usually include grains of truth. Adjustments are costly, and not all businesses will survive adjustments that include rising wages or new investments. However, the loss of low-wage jobs as the pool of entry-level workers shrinks is only half the story. Makers of labor-saving machinery would create new jobs as they rushed to make the dishwashers and other productivity-increasing equipment needed because unskilled workers are not available. Since jobs making dishwashers pay better than the job of washing dishes, average wages would rise as dish washing jobs disappear.

As labor markets begin to tighten, the response of employers to fewer workers indicates that the U.S. economy and labor markets have enough "wiggle room" so that productivity increases and economic growth can continue even as workforce growth slows. If hotels, restaurants, and hospitals realized that a bottomless reservoir of workers is not available, they would adjust. Metropolitan hospitals, for example, typically offer a bonus of $200 or more to each new nurse referred. In addition, some employers have redesigned their personnel policies to reduce turnover. Fast food outlets which rely on adolescents began to test a variety of strategies to reduce turnover, including changing their uniforms, offering tuition aid, and improving kitchen air-conditioning.

Raising wages helps businesses to recruit new workers and to retain current employees, and many employers in low-wage service industries have done just that. The federal minimum wage has become increasingly irrelevant in urban areas where jobs outnumber workers, so that fast food restaurants pay almost twice the minimum wage in some cities.

These initial adjustments to the shrinking pool of low-wage workers requires significant attitude changes by managers. When unskilled workers were readily available, the strategy was to make jobs "idiot proof" and to treat workers as interchangeable pieces of equipment: "When they stop being productive, we'll just bring in somebody new." The worker participation programs designed to involve employees in management typically exclude janitors and other unskilled workers because, in the words of one manager, "The people at that level need less incentive because the amount of thinking they put into the job is less." One major hotel chain reported that "the only qualification to hire somebody (during the 1980s) was that they were breathing."[8]

The shrinking pool of unskilled workers can make such management attitudes outdated and expensive, especially in service industries which obtain premium prices for high quality service. The initial adjustments to fewer unskilled workers are scattered and uneven, but most involve changing management attitudes and developing programs for unskilled workers that are already common for higher-paid workers, such as training newly-hired workers, offering them opportunities to advance within the business, and developing health and pension programs to link the worker to the company. Some managers have turned to older workers; there were 3.4 million persons 65 or older employed in 1989, and a February 1990 *Wall Street Journal* poll by Louis Harris estimated that another 1.9 million workers aged 50 to 64 are available to employers willing to accommodate them with part-time and flexible work schedules.

When higher wages and better recruitment policies cannot close the gap between jobs and workers, jobs can be eliminated with technology and better management. The hotel company which was the first employer fined in 1987 under IRCA for knowingly hiring illegal aliens as maids and kitchen workers two years later opened a moderately priced motel chain designed so that a 92-room unit can be operated with only 12 full-time employees, about 13 percent fewer than average. The Sleep Inn chain saves on labor by having smaller rooms to cut cleaning times and sophisticated computers to eliminate room keys.

Service industries can automate many of the jobs which once seemed to defy automation. McDonald's has developed a grill that cooks hamburgers on both sides at once, eliminating the job of flipping hamburgers. Credit cards and self-service pumps have reduced employment in gasoline retailing, just as automated teller machines reduce banking employment. In most industries, necessity is truly the mother of invention when the task is to save labor by automating or redesigning the means of delivering a service.

While some jobs go unfilled today, many workers remain unemployed because they lack basic verbal and writing skills. In cities and areas with low unemployment rates, high school drop-outs and even high school graduates remain unemployed because they do not have the basic skills and motivations that employers want. Employers are reaching deeper into the queue of available workers, thus widening opportunities for traditionally disadvantaged workers, but many of the unqualified workers who are hired are quickly fired or quit.

Instead of relaxing the constraint of fewer workers which is encouraging American business to change its policies toward unskilled workers and to automate, the United States should continue to encourage adjustments to fewer unskilled workers. Our major European and Asian trading partners are adjusting to slower labor force growth with technology and management changes; the United States should not stand alone as the only industrial country trying to replenish its entry-level workforce with unskilled immigrants.

Even if the United States were to choose a future which includes large scale unskilled worker immigration, many production processes will still be mechanized or disappear in the United States, since other countries will mechanize and Americans will turn to cheaper imported goods. For example, the United States does not *have* to automate its automobile factories, but if it does not, American car buyers will switch to lower cost and higher quality Japanese cars produced in automated factories. Some Americans lament the mechanization of farm production, but without tractors and combines they would buy bread made with mechanically-harvested Canadian or Argentina wheat.

THE LABOR SHORTAGE DEBATE

As a nation of immigrants, the United States has a history of importing the people or the human capital that it needs. But the economy has changed so that it makes no sense for the United States to continue importing large numbers of unskilled immigrants. Importing unskilled immigrants, as the United States did in the 1980s steers the economy in a losing low-tech direction.

A major motivation for turning once again to immigration in order to satisfy America's human capital requirements is the prediction that there will be shortages of labor in the years ahead. Yet, such will clearly not be the case, as this book's projections show. A decade of economic growth may have blinded forecasters to recessions and unemployment. However, much of the discussion in academia and among policy makers suggests that the United States fix in law a new and higher level of immigration designed to head off labor shortages. The 1990 legislation presumes to do just that and the end result will be net immigration of close to 1 million people annually. This represents a doubling of recommended immigration levels in just one decade. In 1981 the U.S. Select Commission on Immigration and Refugee Policy endorsed 450,000 to 500,000 immigrants annually after reviewing the American tradition of an open society, and economic foreign policy, social, and environmental factors.

Raising immigration above these levels seems unwise. The 1980s level of immigration led to rapid job creation and an unsustainable type of economic growth, but this high level of immigration has not put the U.S. economy on a high-tech trajectory. High levels of immigration did not cause low-tech growth in the 1980s, but absorbing immigrants did aggravate the problem.

The much cited *Workforce 2000* report of the Hudson Institute[9] does not mention immigration among its six challenges for the twenty-first century, which include integrating Blacks and Hispanics into the workforce, improving the schools, reconciling the needs of women, work, and families, increasing the flexibility of an aging labor force, improving productivity, and stimulating economic growth around the world.

The curious omission of immigration among these challenges and the assumption that current or higher levels of immigration will have at worst benign effects on U.S. workers reflects the failure to appreciate just how fast the population is growing and changing. Suppose, for example, that net immigration remained at its 1980s level of 750,000 annually. Within 30 years, the labor force would be 24 percent larger, and most of the additional new workers would be traditionally disadvantaged workers. This means that continued workforce growth — and the 1990 legislation will expand net immigration to perhaps 950,000 per year — will aggravate the challenge of raising productivity and integrating disadvantaged workers into the workforce. It makes more sense to begin to solve persisting workforce and productivity challenges at the lower levels of immigration recommended in the early 1980s than to endorse the higher levels that the U.S. Congress has recently approved.

The United States is developing a dual labor market and economy. The United States has some of the world's best trained workers and some of the worst pockets of underclass poverty among industrial societies. Similarly, the United States has both world-class industries that dominate competitors elsewhere and lagging businesses which barely survive despite low wages.

The American economy still retains enormous strengths. It remains the world's largest market linked by a common currency; larger than the new European Community and twice the size of Japan's economy. Many American workers are as productive as their counterparts abroad, and businesses which range from American Express in travel services to Boeing airliners are world leaders in their industries. These economic strengths permitted the United States to go on a buying spree in the 1980s that was financed by foreigners who lent us the money to buy cars and trucks, microwave ovens, and VCRs.

The buying binge will probably end in the 1990s, when the economy must once again return to earning additional consumer goods the old-fashioned way, by raising productivity. But it may be harder to get back on the fast track economic growth path in the 1990s because of the policies of the 1980s. Deficit spending during the 1980s will limit the ability of the government to raise taxes adequately or borrow money to educate and train workers for twenty-first-century jobs; businesses diverted from productivity concerns by takeover fever may find it harder to compete internationally; and consumers interested more in spending than saving may be reluctant to make the sacrifices necessary to integrate disadvantaged newcomers into American society.

When painful choices have to be made during the 1990s, there will be appealing arguments that the status quo can and should be maintained in areas which range from government deficits to high immigration. Indeed, the Congress and the administration addressed both issues in 1990 and the result was continued massive deficits and increased levels of immigration. However, these arguments for maintaining the status quo assume that fundamental problems never have to be resolved. It is true that foreigners may continue to finance deficit spending, but most Americans believe that the government tendency to overspend must eventually be tamed.

High immigration can also continue, but high immigration will compound economic trajectory problems. Suppose net immigration rises to 1.5 million annually, a level higher than the almost one million per year of the 1980s but still a lower immigrant proportion of the population than the United States had in the early 1900s. At such high immigration levels, the labor force would jump from 127 million in 1990 to 175 million in 2020 and 218 million in 2050. If the immigrant composition is unchanged, most of the almost 100 million new workers added over the next two generations would be unskilled immigrants.

What would happen if immigration was reduced?   Lower levels of immigration translate into slower workforce growth.   Net immigration of 350,000 annually, for example, translates into a workforce of 150 million in 2020, or 15 million fewer than under the basic scenario. Yet, between 1990 and 2020, with this lower level of immigration, almost 1 million new workers would still be added annually.

The United States has more immediate control over immigration that it does over fertility and life expectancy. Which level of immigration should it choose? During the 1950s and 1960s, net immigration was about 250,000 annually. During the 1970s, net immigration rose to 500,000 annually, and during the 1980s, net immigration jumped to about 750,000 annually, when legal immigrations, refugees and asylees, newly-legalized illegal immigrants, and the continuing stream of illegal aliens are included. That overall number should rise to 950,000 in the 1990s.

The labor market and economy do not need large numbers of unskilled immigrants to prosper; such immigrants are more likely to hurt rather than to help both American workers and economic growth in the twenty-first century. Immigration levels should be reduced to satisfy the humanitarian, economic, foreign policy, and other goals of immigration in an open society.

CONCLUSION

The debate over future labor shortages or surpluses is closely related to the question of what kind of economy and society Americans want. Some proponents of unskilled immigration assume that *all* jobs offered by employers should be filled: Political scientist Michael Piore says that the jobs taken by unskilled immigrants ". . . are critical to the functioning of an industrial society . . . any wholesale attempt to end the migration is, therefore, likely to be exceedingly disruptive to the operation of society and to the welfare of various interest groups within it."[10]

But many of the jobs filled by immigrants are artificial as they would disappear if wages rose slightly. If the government opens the border gates to admit more unskilled immigrants, thus creating and preserving unskilled jobs, then Americans should ask whether the resulting economic activity is worthwhile.

An example might help to illustrate the tradeoff between immigration and socio-economic policies. Most of the 80 million U.S. homes are cleaned by their occupants, so that there are relatively few housecleaning jobs despite the large number of houses. Vast numbers of workers in Latin America would be eager to clean American houses for $2 an hour or less, so the United States could create perhaps 10 million additional housecleaning jobs. The underlying reality — more or less clean houses — would be unchanged, but the availability of low-wage immigrant workers would create additional low-wage jobs. The Americans who used to clean their own homes would have more time available for work or leisure if the immigrant cleaners were available, but if the immigrant workers disappeared and cleaning wages rose to $4 or $5 hourly, many might revert to cleaning their own houses again, shrinking the number of jobs and U.S. GNP. Middle-class Americans might be better off with the immigrant cleaners, but the additional immigrant cleaning jobs are artificial in the sense that they would disappear if low-wage immigrants disappeared.

Cleaning homes illustrates the tradeoff between the number of jobs and the kind of society we want. The United States can create additional cleaning jobs by having a class of helots available who are willing to work at low wages. If the cleaners remain in the United States, they are the truly disadvantaged, willing to do dirty work but unable to better themselves economically without threatening their jobs. In this case, importing large numbers of Third World immigrants also means importing the Third World characteristic of having servants for the privileged.

What would happen if the jobs which depend on the availability of unskilled immigrants disappeared? All inevitable adjustments are costly, but policies which promote necessary economic adjustments are in the nation's best long-term interest. Blacksmiths argued correctly that the automobile would eliminate their jobs, but Americans would be much poorer today if the nation had remained a horse and buggy economy to protect blacksmiths.

An extreme example of adjustments to labor shortages comes from reactions to the Black Plague in fourteenth-century Europe. Between 1348 and 1350, from 35 to 65 percent of Europe's population died, usually within three days of contracting the disease. Labor became scarce and wages rose, so the first response of landowners in England was to enact laws which froze wages and prohibited peasants from migrating to higher-wage urban jobs. These laws to prevent economic adjustments did not prevent real wages from tripling, and these higher wages encouraged English landowners to switch from labor-intensive grain production to raising sheep. Wool production stimulated the development of water power in mills that turned wool into cloth, and England switched from being an importer of cloth before the Black Plague to being an exporter of cloth.[11]

Eliminating low-wage jobs does not mean that there will be massive unemployment or even that industries will disappear. During the 1930s, there were 7 million U.S. farmers. Today, one-third as many farmers produce twice as much food and fiber. A business which sheds jobs and adopts productivity-improving technologies is more likely to survive in a dynamic economy than a business which resists productivity improvements. Recognizing that immigrant workers will for a time work at wages low enough to compete with imports, some have suggested that the United States should continue to import unskilled workers in order to avoid pleas from business for tariffs, quotas, and other protections from imports. However, low-wage immigrants will not be enough to help sunset industries. Many of the industries clamoring for protection from imports, such as shoes and apparel, already employ large numbers of unskilled immigrants. A policy of importing workers to avoid inevitable adjustments is often self-defeating. Helping an industry to survive without making adjustments usually guarantees that there will be vulnerable jobs and businesses asking for protection in the future.

Does the United States need large numbers of unskilled immigrants? The answer is no: large numbers of unskilled immigrants will generate more jobs and faster economic growth, but an economic trajectory shaped by unskilled immigrants will not yield the high productivity jobs and businesses necessary to compete internationally. An immigration policy which promotes adjustments to a high-wage and high-productivity economy promises sustainable economic growth while maintaining the American heritage of equality and opportunity for all.

NOTES

1. R. Mines and P. Martin, "Illegal Immigration and the California Citrus Industry," *Industrial Relations* 23 (1984): 139-149.

2. The United Food and Commercial Workers Union reported that its 800,000 members in retail food jobs (1989) were 70 percent full-time and 30 percent part-time during the 1960s; today, these proportions are reversed. (Larry Waterfield, "Shrinking Working Pool Threatens Food Industry," *The Packer*, 27 May 1989, 1A, 6A)

3. F. Ray Marshall, as cited in *Final Report of the Select Commission on Immigration and Refugee Policy*, Appendix B (Washington: Government Printing Office, 1981), 365.

4. *Business Week*, 15 July 1985, 56.

5. Alejandro Portes and Robert Bach, *Latin Journey: Cuban and Mexican Immigrants in the United States* (Berkeley: University of California Press, 1985).

6. Demetrious Papademitrious and Thomas Muller, *Recent Immigration to New York: Labor Market and Social Policy Issues* (Washington: National Commission for Employment Policy, 1987), 51.

7. "Total Jobs Keep Rising Despite Many Layoffs and Talk of Recession," *Wall Street Journal*, 24 March 1980.

8. Jolie Solomon, "Managers Focus on Low-Wage Workers," *Wall Street Journal*, 9 May 1989, B1.

9. Hudson Institute, *Workforce 2000* (New York: Hudson Institute, 1987).

10. Michael Piore, "Illegal Immigration to the U.S.: Some Observations and Policy Suggestions," in *Illegal Aliens: An Assessment of the Issues* (Washington: National Council for Employment Policy, 1976), 26.

11. Charles Maurice and Charles Smithson, *The Doomsday Myth* (Palo Alto: Hoover Institution, 1984).

6

Immigration and Cultural
Adaptation

Social and economic issues are not the only arguments for lowering immigration, also to be considered are the cultural adjustments that must be made by residents and newcomers alike.

Some form of interaction necessarily follows whenever one group migrates into an area already inhabited by another group. Both must adapt to a new situation. Humankind has been faced with the challenges of group adaptation ever since migration began thousands, if not millions of years ago. In America, some form of adaptation has taken place whenever a new group of immigrants has arrived. This process is again occurring and will be repeated as long as immigration to the United States persists.

CULTURAL ADAPTATION PROCESSES

Residents and newcomers alike must adjust to a new situation that results from group interaction. At one extreme, cultural separatism, the newcomers are socially isolated from the resident group either through their own volition or through segregationist practices by the host group. The slave-free person relationship exemplifies cultural separatism, as does that between the dominant American society and religious groups like the Amish. At the other extreme, cultural amalgamation, a new society and culture results from massive intermarriage between the two groups. The racial blending in nineteenth-century Latin America which led to the emergence of mestizos is an example of cultural amalgamation.

Between these extremes are pluralism, assimilation, and the so-called "melting pot." In pluralism, the society allows its constituted ethnic groups to develop, each emphasizing its particular cultural heritage. Assimilation assumes that the new groups will take on the culture and values of the host society and gradually discard their own heritage. Following the seminal study by sociologist Milton Gordon, cultural assimilation (or acculturation), where a subordinate group takes on many of the characteristics of the dominant group, is distinguished from structural assimilation, where that subordinate group gains access to the principal institutions of the society.[1]

In the melting pot, the host and immigrant groups share each other's cultures and in the process a new group emerges. Consequently, melting pot differs somewhat from pure assimilation, although some scholars treat them almost synonymously. While early advocates of the melting pot theory encouraged newcomers to "assimilate" into American society, the society they envisaged was not intended to be totally dominated by Anglo-Saxons, but rather, was a new society formed by the blending of the various groups, albeit with strong Anglo-Saxon influence.

Throughout American history, immigrants as well as residents have had to adjust to each other; a process of cultural adaptation was necessary if the society was to survive.

THE FIRST IMMIGRATION WAVE

Before Independence in 1776, ethnic groups were likely to maintain separate cultures and languages. Some settlers of English ancestry were unhappy with this cultural diversity. Benjamin Franklin, for one, was concerned lest his beloved Pennsylvania become "Germanized." "This Pennsylvania will in a few years become a German colony; instead of their learning our language, we must learn theirs, or live as in a foreign country."[2]

A new feeling of nationalism came with Independence. No longer was there a built-in tie with England. The separation from England infused the definition of nationality in the United States with a distinctive political ideology. New citizens were expected to give their allegiance to a set of political principles, as well as to a government. Participation in the Revolutionary War legitimized the claims of the non-English Europeans to a full share in the new nation and by 1790 the United States was truly a mosaic of peoples, though overwhelmingly western European.

If Jefferson, Adams, and Franklin had had their way, the United States would have a "Great Seal" that reflects the American people's diverse national origins. Their proposed design, submitted to the Congress in August 1776 featured "a shield that was divided into six parts, each with its own ethnic emblem. . . . Among the seal's other elements: a motto, 'E Pluribus Unum'

(Out of Many, One)."[3] Eventually Congress approved another design. *E Pluribus Unum* remained, but now the seal referred to the states in the union and not to the several nations which the new Americans had left.

Despite the diversity already present in the American population, the English segment clearly dominated. Low immigration also contributed to increased cultural homogeneity in the early decades of the Republic. Languages other than English gradually faded from use.

By 1840, the nation had established its own identity, separate from that of England. Nevertheless, much of what was English was preserved, language in particular. By 1840, the United States was a white, predominantly Protestant nation. Blacks comprised some 20 percent of the population but most were still enslaved and the remainder were culturally separated from the Anglo-American population.

THE SECOND IMMIGRATION WAVE

Many second-wave immigrants were either Catholic or Jewish and came mainly from Ireland and Germany. By 1850 Catholicism was the largest Christian denomination in the land — 7.5 percent of the population. In many large cities, Catholics were rapidly becoming the majority.

During this period when such changes were occurring, native-born Americans began displaying their ambivalent feelings about immigration. No restrictions had been placed on anyone desiring to enter — an "Open Door" policy had been in effect since Independence. Some Americans became suspicious of newcomers, especially those who differed from themselves — such as Catholics and Jews, Chinese and Mexicans. There was a widespread belief that immigrants were taking jobs from the native-born Americans. All these concerns led to the formation of societies to "protect" Americans against immigrants.

On the east coast, anti-immigrant feelings were strong. On the west coast, anti-Chinese feelings intensified. By the 1870s, Chinese immigrants were viewed by other workers as major competitors for jobs. They were willing to work anywhere, under most conditions, for low wages. As a result they became the victims of anti-Chinese rioting as well as many discriminatory state laws, particularly in California.

Cultural adaptation was not as simple a process in the 1840-1890 period as it had been earlier. Then, the non-English European groups had assimilated into the Anglo-American population. After 1840, different types of immigrants entered the country. Catholics and Jews threatened the Protestant domination of the country; Asians and Mexicans entered (or were annexed) in what some considered to be alarming numbers. The latter two groups, as well as the Blacks after the end of the Civil War, were deliberately prohibited from entering the mainstream of American culture; a clear example of cultural separatism.

By the 1880s, while those of Anglo-Saxon ancestry remained solidly in power, new groups were joining them — groups that worshipped differently, and in some cases, were of different racial background. The ethnic mosaic was becoming more diverse.

THE THIRD IMMIGRATION WAVE

A majority of the immigrants arriving after 1880 came from eastern and southern Europe and most were either Catholic or Jewish; many were poor and illiterate, even in their own language. The illiteracy rate among adult Italians who migrated between 1899 and 1909 was 46.9 percent; for Jews 25.7; Poles 35.4; Slavs 24.3.[4]

The movement of Blacks out of the agricultural south into the industrial north was not international. Yet it has many of the same characteristics and helps describe the increasing heterogeneity in northern cities around the turn of the century. Migration out of the south began slowly after 1865. At first some of the newly freed slaves headed for the Great Plains where land was thought to be available. But "though the federal government possessed over one billion acres of public land which it generously doled out to European settlers, railroads, and other special interests, almost none was made available for black settlement."[5] The movement out of the south gradually intensified and soon shifted directions. Between 1890 and 1930 some 2 million Blacks left the rural south for the major cities of the north and the midwest. There they found themselves in direct competition with the new immigrants from southern and eastern Europe.

Despite the tremendous demands for manual labor in the industrial north in the latter part of the nineteenth century, Blacks were deliberately kept out of this employment stream. Had it not been for racial discrimination, the North might well have recruited southern Blacks after the Civil War to provide the labor for building the burgeoning urban-industrial economy. Instead, northern employers looked to Europe for their sources of unskilled labor. Thus while northern industry absorbed tens of millions of European immigrants in the decades that followed the Civil War, "a color line barred the employment of black labor until the supply of white labor had been exhausted. . . . Once again blacks paid the price and carried the burden of the nation's need for cheap and abundant cotton."[6] This was not to be the last time that Blacks would be economically deprived because of new waves of immigrants.

World War I changed these conditions. With so many of the new immigrants in the armed forces, the industrialists finally turned south for workers for their factories and mills. It was only then that the massive Black movement out of the south truly began.

Together these diverse streams — whether from southern and eastern Europe, from Asia, or from the nation's own southern states — contributed to the creating of yet another image of America. It also called out for a new mode of cultural adaptation. No longer were Anglo-Saxons as numerically dominant as previously, although they ruled politically and economically. The ethnic mosaic was changing more rapidly than ever as the number of southern and eastern Europeans increased in the east and midwest; Asians and Hispanics increased their numbers in the west and southwest and Blacks moved out of the agricultural south into northern cities.

ASSIMILATION VS. PLURALISM

At the beginning of the twentieth century, the Anglo-American majority favored the total assimilation of the new European groups into an Anglo-dominated society. (It was taken for granted — indeed, it was ordered — that Mexicans, Asians, and Blacks would remain culturally separate.) Cultural pluralism and even the melting pot were adamantly opposed. Theodore Roosevelt felt nothing but disdain for the hyphenated American and Woodrow Wilson declared that: "Any man who thinks himself as belonging to a particular national group in America has not yet become an American."[7]

ASSIMILATION

"Americanization" was in full vogue in the early decades of the twentieth century. It was assumed that all new European immigrants would become, indeed would want to become, "Americanized." Anglo-conformity was to be encouraged from all the new immigrants.

> The ideal [Americanization] was one of full assimilation of all immigrant groups to a common national type, so that ethnicity would play a declining role in individual consciousness, groups would not be formed around ethnic interests, 'hyphenated Americans' would be a thing of the past, and the United States would be as homogenous in its Americanness as the nations of the old world were once in their Englishness, their Frenchness.[8]

CULTURAL PLURALISM

Aligned against total assimilation were the cultural pluralists who urged a new type of nation in which the various national groups would preserve their identity and their cultures, uniting as a world federation in miniature.[9] Horace Kallen argued vehemently against assimilation and the melting pot, convinced that if the course of cultural pluralism were followed: "the outlines of a possible great and truly democratic commonwealth become discernible. Its form would be that of the federal republic; its substance a democracy of nationalities, cooperating voluntarily and autonomously through common institutions in the enterprise of self-realization through the perfection of men according to their kind."[10]

MELTING POT

The "melting pot" theory was a compromise between the extremes of cultural pluralism and total assimilation. The 1907 play, "The Melting Pot" by Israel Zangwill brought the idea to the attention of many people. But historian Frederick Jackson Turner probably did more than anyone to popularize the concept. In his discussion of the frontier in American history, Turner pointed out that, "The frontier promoted the formation of a composite nationality for the American people. . . . In the crucible of the frontier the immigrants were Americanized, liberated, and fused into a mixed race, English in neither nationality nor characteristics. The process has gone on from the early days to our own."[11]   Later Turner added: ". . . the tide of foreign immigration . . . has risen so steadily that it has made a composite American people whose amalgamation is destined to produce a new national stock."[12]

In one sense, the melting pot is a form of assimilation in that the emphasis is on the formation of an American culture; nevertheless, its determination not to overemphasize Anglo-conformity makes it a different type of assimilation than that advocated by the "Americanization" movement.

> Distinctive of the melting-pot ideology was the emphasis . . . on a fusion of cultures, rather than the wholesale acceptance by many different nationalities of the culture of a single one of them. But still the basic idea of assimilation remained: There was to be an *American* culture, however it came about, and immigrants and their children were to accept it, even if they also made some contribution to it.[13]

RECENT PATTERNS OF CULTURAL ADAPTATION

As we look back over the past century to assess how the cultural adaptation process among persons of European ancestry developed, it is clear that the pressures to "Americanize" everyone to Anglo-conformity through total assimilation did not entirely succeed. Most European groups retained some semblance of ethnicity over the years while at the same time adapting to new surroundings.

Neither has cultural pluralism been particularly successful among European immigrants and their descendants, despite efforts on the part of some of its advocates to maintain ethnic identities. In recent decades serious attempts have been made to revive some form of ethnic pride. Michael Novak has argued strongly for such a movement.[14] If cultural pluralism means that various groups maintain cultural and structural separatism from each other thus creating the possibility of also maintaining cultural patterns different from those of the "host" society, then the evidence suggests that this form of cultural adaptation has not succeeded among most Americans of European ancestry. Such cultural pluralism has become what Herbert Gans has referred to as "symbolic ethnicity."

> [It] can be expressed in a myriad of ways, but above all . . . it is characterized by a nostalgic allegiance to the culture of the immigrant generation, or that of the old country; a love for and a pride in a tradition that can be felt without having to be incorporated in everyday behavior.[15]

By the 1980s, the melting pot had worked quite well for immigrants from southern and eastern Europe, structurally as well as culturally. The melting pot may be working in a different way than had been anticipated. In addition to different groups acting increasingly alike, a new population is in the process of forming — the "unhyphenated Americans."[16] In addition, the power elite, historically almost exclusively White Anglo-Saxon Protestant, is being replaced by one in which persons of non-WASP heritage are commonplace.[17]

It has taken some two or three generations for the melting pot to "come to a boil." By mid-twentieth century major changes began to occur among Americans of European ancestry. In corporate business, a second-generation Italian-American, Lee Iaccoca, reached the top. In higher education, the late A. Bartlett Giamatti, served as president of Yale University and later became Commissioner of baseball. John Brademas, of Greek parentage, served as president of New York University. Today, both the advisor to the president, John Sununu, and the majority leader of the U.S. Senate, George Mitchell, are of Arab background.

In the 1968 election, both major parties offered second-generation American vice-presidential candidates, Muskie of Polish parentage, Agnew of Greek parentage. Among those mentioned as potential candidates for the nation's presidency in 1988 were second-generation Italians, Greeks, and Basques. Most important was the fact that to most people it didn't matter. Who would argue that Michael Dukakis is not as American as George Bush?

The situation was quite different in 1930 if the reply of President Herbert Hoover to a mild letter of criticism from then Congressman Fiorello LaGuardia is an example.

> It seems to me, a Republican, that you are a little out of your class, in presuming to criticize the President. It strikes me as impudence. You should go back to where you belong and advise Mussolini on how to make good honest citizens in Italy. The Italians are predominantly our murderers and bootleggers. . . . Like a lot of other foreign spawn, you do not appreciate this country which supports you and tolerates you.[18]

Exaggeration is an ever present danger. While the melting pot has worked admirably among Americans of European ancestry, islands of dissent are still noted. Often these are subtle as in remarks about Governor Dukakis' patriotism in the 1988 election campaign exemplified by questions raised by country singer, Loretta Lynne, about the "Americanness" of a person with such a funny name. In the minds of a few, some hesitancy remains about accepting "ethnics" as truly American. Yet, the nation has come a long way, within its majority population of European ancestry. As Stephen Thernstrom has remarked: "What is surprising — indeed, rather amazing — in global perspective, is not the diversity but rather the speed and thoroughness with which these groups blended together and became absorbed in a common national culture."[19]

Since its birth, the nation has been trying to define some coherent relationship between the universalistic sentiments of the Declaration of Independence, which established a nation based on principles rather than on ethnicity, and the fact that the majority group, the original settlers, dominated while other groups faced discrimination and prejudice. The Civil Rights Act of 1964 and the Immigration Act of 1965 determined that the initial principles should prevail over any lingering attachment to the original founders of the republic.[20] Or as Robert Christopher puts it, there has been a "de-Wasping of America's power elite."[21]

Comparisons of the Third and Fourth Waves

Although almost one century separates them, the third and fourth waves of immigrants to the United States have interesting similarities. Both are large. Both movements led to protests and intergroup conflict. Numerous disturbances resulted from the new immigration from eastern and southern Europe during the early 1900s. In recent years, conflict has emerged between the newest immigrants from Latin America and Asia and residents in a number of places. In these conflicts, the argument is always the same. Among other things, the perception is that these "newcomers" are taking jobs away from Americans or are lowering the hourly wages for said jobs.

Both movements have resulted in legislation that curtailed at least some portion of the immigration. The Quota Laws of the 1920s were a direct result of the so-called "New Immigration" of the 1890s and the early 1900s. The laws' purpose was to reduce the numerical impact of southern and eastern European immigration and to maintain Anglo-American dominance. The 1986 Immigration Refugee Control Act's purpose was to reduce, if not end, illegal immigration into the nation.

Differences are also to be found between these two immigration streams. These differences help explain the success of the melting pot for the third wave and why the cultural adaptation of the fourth wave may be both different and more difficult than that of its predecessor.

Considerable intermarriage occurred among European-origin ethnic groups in the second and third generations. Among Irish Catholics, 70 percent had non-Irish spouses by the mid-1960s; among Polish Catholics, it was about 60 percent; among Jews in the 1970s, one-third had married a non-Jew. In recent marriages, generally 2/3 to 3/4 of Italians married non-Italians. Only about 20 percent of Italian men born since 1950 have chosen wives with all Italian parentage, while another 10 to 15 percent have chosen wives with part-Italian ancestry.[22]

> By the 1980s, two decades after some of the most prestigious sociological gurus in the United States had proclaimed the extinction of the melting pot, Americans in unprecedented numbers were opting to 'melt' in the most basic possible manner — intermarriage with members of ethnic and religious groups other than their own.[23]

The era of the unhyphenated American (of European ancestry) has arrived.

Today, over 80 percent of immigrants come from Latin America and Asia. While interracial marriages are on the increase, they remain a relatively rare occurrence.[24] The possibility of attaining what Philip Wylie once called a "tea-colored" society is hardly within our reach. This is not to say that such a "new America" cannot be attained in the more distant future. Indeed the renowned Black Sociologist, W.E.B. Dubois predicted that, "Some day, on American soil, two world races may give each to each those characteristics both so sadly lack." Dubois called for the maintenance of racial purity only "until this mission of the Negro people is accomplished, and the ideal of human brotherhood has become a practical possibility."[25]

A second difference lies in the change in structural mobility and industrialization. Between 1930 and 1960, the overall status of occupations rose significantly. It was possible for members of the newer immigrant groups to move upwards without displacing someone else. It was not a zero-sum game.

The earlier wave also coincided with the robust expansion of industrialism in America, based around the cities of the northeast and midwest. Those cities and their factories had a huge appetite for low and semi-skilled labor as America began its glory days as the pre-eminent industrial power. Cities, in particular, functioned as a great machine to integrate millions of foreign arrivals. Entry-level jobs were abundant, wages and living standards rose, and the cities proved to be a springboard to upward mobility for millions of newcomers. Later, the G.I. Bill of Rights made higher education possible for the children of immigrants, resulting in still more upward mobility. The costs were high, yet the overall result was a powerful voyage toward economic progress which carried millions of immigrants into American nationality with all its benefits.[26]

Today, the nation is predominantly a service-based economy, and is in a new era of international competition. Consequently, if the nation is to retain a substantial industrial capacity, it must be through a shift toward the knowledge-intensive sectors in both manufacturing and services, leaving low-wage mass production industries to flourish elsewhere. This does not imply a larger labor force. It does imply a labor force of high educational and skill levels and aspirations. Yet, educational funds have been reduced rather than increased. Today, while some economic mobility is possible, climbing economically and socially appears to be less prevalent than in the early days of industrialization. In a service society, only those with adequate education and appropriate training will qualify for upward mobility. With well over half of future jobs requiring at least some post-secondary education, many of the newest immigrants will simply not qualify. The jobs will be there but the people to fill them — immigrants or minorities — will not be adequately prepared. In the past, a rising standard of living, changes in the structure of the economy that increased the proportion of white-collar and professional positions, and the general prosperity of the cities where most immigrants lived made possible a large measure of social mobility. One cannot be sanguine about the continuation of those trends in the future. The standard of living is stabilizing or falling and American cities are in unprecedented distress. The risk is real that, except for the most gifted and lucky, those who join the society at its bottom ranks will stay there.

Third, at the time of the third wave, individual immigrants (or families) were gradually accepted by residents and they became part of the successful melting pot described earlier. Strong pressure was exerted on the newcomers to become "American." While "Americanization" did not always succeed, it did contribute to a feeling of having to join the mainstream if one were to make it in America. This pressure was especially effective on the second generation, many of whom turned their backs on their parents and ancestral land in an effort to become more "American."

Today, the nation seems to have lost its concern for individuals. The emphasis is on group rights. Indeed, laws now protect minorities from the "sink-or-swim" expectations that encouraged earlier arrivals to adopt the dominant culture or fall by the wayside. "The past decade has seen the emergence of what we have called 'affirmative ethnicity' — government mandated grants of preferential treatment and of special benefits for some individuals, on the basis of their membership in a minority group that is perceived as disadvantaged."[27] Such a concept is appropriate for Black and Native Americans. Compensation must continue to be awarded for three hundred years of oppression at the hands of the Anglo majority. However, group rights should not be applied to new immigrants, particularly in the area of affirmative action.

> It has gone so far in terms of immigration that, in one foreign-relations appropriation bill being considered, there is a section claiming that if aliens can show that they are part of a 'group' of people who could even remotely be persecuted at home, the U.S. attorney-general has to prove that they are not. In this brave new world, aliens have 'rights'; the highest ranking American justice official has 'duties.'[28]

Such an emerging political philosophy is not conducive to the development of a united society.

A final difference between the two immigration waves is particularly relevant. The earlier immigration movement ended in the 1920s. Restrictive legislation, the Depression and war all combined to drastically lower the levels of immigration. These factors contributed to the acculturation and social elevation of the new immigrants and their descendants. The shutting off of the immigration flow made it difficult for ethnic cultures to be maintained. As a result the newcomers were better able to adapt to their new homeland. A continuing influx of European immigrants would have continuously renewed ethnic cultures and sentiments, retarding if not altogether preventing the assimilation of the descendants of the immigrants. The shutting off of the immigrant flow made clear to the second and third generations that their future lay in the new society.[29]

Now legal, and illegal, immigration coming chiefly from Asia and Latin America, and possibly from Eastern Europe and Africa in the future, appears to be unending. Given the increase in the number applying for citizenship every year, and taking into consideration the 3 million persons amnestied as a result of the 1986 IRCA legislation (who in turn may opt for citizenship), immigration to the United States will continue to climb. That climb will be expedited by the 1990 legislation. The "breathing time" afforded the immigrants earlier in this century will not be available to the current waves now entering the country.

Those who favor reducing immigration are often criticized for repeating the fears of early restrictionists. "We've all heard it before" is the cry coming from advocates of increased immigration. Or more specifically:

> The United States has experienced these effects [i.e., impacts of immigration on the society] over and over again from previous waves of immigration. In each case, the wave was accompanied by dire predictions of the economic, political, and social consequences on the United States, only to be contradicted in practice.[30]

The significant differences between immigration waves make it clear that the concerns of 1990 are dissimilar from those of one hundred years ago.

CULTURAL ADAPTATION PROCESSES REVISITED

Can the relative success achieved over the past half a century in the adaptation of third-wave immigrants and their descendants into a new kind of America (a true "melting pot" within the majority population) be duplicated with the current and future mix of racially diverse ethnic groups? The question of how the United States is to maintain a unified country out of peoples from all over the world is one that can never be long ignored. "A dynamic nation whose place in the world, whose sources of immigration, whose self-image constantly changes, must again and again address itself to this great question and ponder what its answer is to be."[31]

It seems unlikely that a repetition of the successful melting pot process will occur given the situation in 1990-2000 as compared to that in 1890-1900. The differences in the economic structure, in the possibilities of inter-ethnic marriages, in the increasing emphasis on group rights, and particularly in the level of immigration are far too great to envision a new interracial melting pot in the foreseeable future. What then are alternative options?

Hopefully cultural separatism is a thing of the past. Yet there are those who would favor such a process. A few Hispanic irredentists dream of a new Spanish-speaking southwest as a way to take back demographically what the United States took militarily some 140 years ago. It is undeniably true that Mexican-Americans in the Southwest feel at home there in a way that cannot be said, say, of the Irish in Chicago. This becomes evident when, after discussing the immigration question with even the most moderate Mexican-Americans, one is invariably reminded that "we were here first," or "this was our land and you stole it from us."[32] Or as James Michener's mythical character, Senorita Enriqueta Muzquiz put it,

> What is happening is simple in process, glorious in effect. We are quietly reclaiming the land which Santa Anna lost through his insane vanity. Vast areas which are rightfully Mexican are coming back to us. No battles . . . no gunfire . . . no animosities, simply the inexorable movement of people north. The Anglos still control the banks, the newspapers, the courts, but we have the power which always triumphs in the end, the power of people.[33]

And there are always a few segregationists who would dearly love to keep all the races separate and "in their places." Indeed, the 1980s have witnessed a growth in the intensity of such bigoted behavior. In his novel, *Bluebeard*, Kurt Vonnegut describes the feelings of some Americans:

> The darkest secret of this country, I am afraid, is that too many of its citizens imagine that they belong to a much higher civilization somewhere else. That higher civilization doesn't have to be another country. It can be the past instead — the United States as it was before it was spoiled by immigrants and the enfranchisement of blacks.[34]

Neither is the total cultural assimilation of the new minority groups, i.e., the complete surrender of immigrants' symbols and values and their absorption by the core culture, a realistic goal. Soon there may be no majority in which to assimilate! In fact, the English are no longer the numerical majority of the Anglos in the United States — indeed, they are far from it.[35]

The racial and ethnic identity consciousness that has emerged from the Civil Rights and immigration legislation of the 1960s (reinforced by the 1990 legislation) together with the growth of large enclaves of new immigrants in certain parts of the country precludes any substantive assimilation into the dominant culture of the nation. Furthermore, there is considerable doubt as to whether the newer groups desire total assimilation and even whether the current majority favors it.

The choices lie between cultural pluralism and a new mode of adaptation called pluralistic assimilation. Whatever direction the nation follows will determine the kind of America that will evolve in the twenty-first century.

A benign form of cultural pluralism has long been part and parcel of American life. Ethnic enclaves are still present in large cities. Diverse religious and cultural holidays remain on the calendars of many Americans.

However, cultural pluralism took on a different meaning in the 1960s. European ethnic groups began to clamor for "rights" similar to those that had been bestowed on Black Americans. To some people, "cultural pluralism implies the conscious pursuit of a national order in which Americans find their identity primarily as members of ethnic and/or religious blocs and only secondarily as individuals engaged in carving out a position in the general society."[36]

A harder-edged version of cultural pluralism is currently in vogue. The focus is on a contention that the United States is a compact between what some are beginning to lump together as a "Euro-American" population and a limited set of minority groups, made up principally of African-Americans, Native Americans, Asians, and Hispanics.[37] Portes and Bach argue that this form of cultural pluralism stems from the discrimination suffered by immigrants to the United States. "It emphasizes the experience of immigrant groups, which, though acculturated to dominant values and norms, have been rebuffed in their attempts to seek entrance into the core society. . . . The rejection experienced by immigrants and their descendants . . . constitutes a central element in the reconstitution of the ethnic culture."[38] The immigrants then rely more and more on in-group cohesiveness and cultural reassertion as the only effective means to counter social discrimination.

From this argument, one could conclude that if these immigrants had been accepted by American society, rather than shunted aside as was the case, assimilation would have been more successful. Furthermore,

> a pluralism based on systematic inequalities is inherently unstable because ethnic groups at or near the bottom of the social ladder have little reason to endorse the ethnic status quo. On the contrary, groups aspiring to class mobility are typically forced to adopt strategies that are designed to advance their class interests, but at the same time, whittle away at the pluralist structure.[39]

Indeed, these social inequalities are pluralism's very lifeblood.

Too often, Americans confuse the fact that we are a pluralistic nation with acceptance of cultural pluralism. America is pluralistic in the sense of having many religions and ethnic groups represented in its population. Nevertheless it has constantly striven to achieve overall unity in its basic interests and ideals. E Pluribus Unum succinctly describes the "ideal" American nation. If cultural pluralism was but a supplement to these common interests and ideals, it would be totally appropriate. However, cultural pluralism, as presently conceived, argues for the primacy of the homeland language and culture. Indeed, as the late Theodore White commented, "Some Hispanics have . . . made a demand never voiced by immigrants before. That the United States, in effect, officially recognize itself as a bicultural, bilingual nation."[40] Such cultural pluralism is not the most attractive direction for the nation to follow as it strives for more unity rather than disunity.

PLURALISTIC ASSIMILATION

The challenge to America is to find a way to assure that all its residents, of whatever background, have equal access to all avenues to success and in the process adapt to American culture while contributing to its ever changing content. At the same time, all its residents, of whatever background, must have the choice of maintaining their own subculture within the broader American society. As the nation gradually becomes more multiracial, it is particularly important that a form of cultural adaptation be accepted that takes the best of cultural pluralism and assimilation while at the same time maintaining the American culture and assuring its acceptance by all.

Sociologist J. Milton Yinger and historian John Higham have both addressed this issue and have suggested new forms of adaptation that would take into account pluralism as well as assimilation. Yinger feels that some sort of integration that falls short of assimilation may be the right compromise.[41] Higham's "pluralistic integration" does not eliminate ethnic boundaries but upholds the validity of a common culture.[42] However, neither Yinger nor Higham examine the possibility of a truly multiracial society where no one group clearly predominates. Pluralistic assimilation, while derived from these earlier models, looks at a truly multiracial society.

Neither Yinger's group integration, nor Higham's pluralistic integration, nor pluralistic assimilation will appeal to the most militant champions of a particular ethnic group, nor will they satisfy those rationalists for whom all ethnic feelings are prejudices to expose.

Nevertheless, pluralistic assimilation might be appropriate if the goal of the society is to be united insofar as possible given the population's composition. All groups are assimilated, both culturally and structurally, into the already diverse mainstream American society. This is not "Anglo-conformity" nor even "White American conformity." This is really "assimilation among" rather than "assimilation into" and reflects the changing demographic picture and the fact that in the future no one ethnic group will dominate. It is a "New Americanization." The inclusion of structural assimilation suggests that all groups will have equal access to power, whether economic or political. Pluralistic, on the other hand, reflects the fact that the society is no longer dealing with ethnic groups of the same race. These multiracial groups may maintain their identity at the same time that they become "assimilated" into the mainstream American society.

Some form of pluralistic assimilation may have been implied in Franklin's first version of the shield for the nation. Recall that his shield represented the six European peoples who comprised the white population of the new nation. In that context, *E Pluribus Unum* was a recognition that the survival of the new government depended on its ability to forge a nation from a population in which ethnic diversity was the norm.[43]

The approaches of two prominent Black politicians illustrate the difference between cultural pluralism and pluralistic assimilation. Rev. Jesse Jackson is a prime example of cultural pluralism in action. In his campaigns, racial differences are identified and the "Rainbow Coalition" represents cultural pluralism. On the other hand, the current governor of the Commonwealth of Virginia, L. Douglas Wilder, exemplifies pluralistic assimilation. In his campaigns, almost no reference is made to race. Jackson campaigns as a Black American; Wilder campaigns as an American who happens to be Black.

The success of Japanese-Americans, despite the horrors of internment during the second World War, provides us with a working model of pluralistic assimilation. While gradually becoming assimilated, culturally and structurally, into the mainstream society, they remain an identifiable racial group, though some interracial marriages are occurring. Perhaps part of their success can be attributed to the fact that immigration from Japan has dwindled to about 4,000 per year in the 1980s thereby easing the adaptation process. It would, of course, be naive to conclude that prejudice against Japanese-Americans is nonexistent. Indeed, it is increasing. Pluralistic assimilation is an on-going process and its eventual success will require the cooperation of all groups. Nevertheless, the very fact that Japanese-Americans are cited as an example of the achievement of a "New Americanization" is evidence of the powerful integrative forces at work in American society.

Numerous factors must be present if pluralistic assimilation is to succeed. These will be discussed in a later chapter. First and foremost, however, levels of immigration must be substantially reduced. Only in this way will the newest immigrants gradually become part of twenty-first-century American society as white ethnic minorities became a part of the majority soon after the end of the third wave of immigration.

CONCLUSION

"Pluralistic assimilation," "forms of interaction," "cultural assimilation," "the melting pot theory," "cultural amalgamation," and "group integration" are examples of jargon no doubt endearing to the hearts of some sociologists who can devote hours to splitting hairs on the true meaning of each term.

Basically, these terms reemphasize the fact that whenever one person or group moves into an area inhabited by another person or group, both must adapt to a newly defined situation.

The early colonists made contact with the Native Americans and somewhat later with the Africans imported as slaves. No assimilation occurred and the three racial groups remained socially and culturally separate. The latter part of the first wave of immigrants came primarily from France and northern Ireland. Assimilation into the dominant English society was relatively straightforward.

The second wave, coming from Germany and Catholic Ireland, created a few problems. Jews and Catholics were not always welcomed by the resident Anglo-Saxon Protestants. Yet these groups eventually assimilated into a more broadly defined Anglo-dominated society.

The third wave, coming from eastern and southern Europe, proved to be even more troublesome. These newcomers were mostly Catholic or Jewish and many spoke no English. Furthermore, many of them "looked different." Pure assimilation no longer worked; rather, some kind of melting pot became the predominant mode of adaptation. This is an ongoing process.

In all three instances the availability of jobs relevant to the needs of the era, some intermarriage between host and immigrant groups, an emphasis on individual abilities, and a temporary reduction in immigration all contributed to the relative success of the adaptation process. But what stands out even more is that the greater the physical and social differences between the host group and the immigrant group, the more difficult the process of adaptation. So with each new wave, cultural adaptation has become more and more difficult for both, the hosts and the immigrants. Indeed, for non-whites — Native-Americans, immigrants and their descendants from Africa, Latin America, and Asia — various levels of cultural separatism were imposed.

This does not bode well for the adaptation of the fourth wave of immigrants and provides one reason why pluralistic assimilation may be the most desirable mode of cultural adaptation for the future. It reflects the increased difficulties involved given the greater differences between hosts and minorities. There has been a gradual change in the mode of adaptation followed over the past two centuries. It moved from complete assimilation, to assimilation within religious boundaries, to the melting pot, and now perhaps to pluralistic assimilation, or possibly to a mode of cultural pluralism that borders on separatism.

One has to be an unbridled optimist to hope for the success of pluralistic assimilation within the next few decades. The road to pluralistic assimilation will not be smooth. American society has always been of two minds on immigration. Part of it proudly proclaims that it is a nation of immigrants and recites those glorious words of Emma Lazarus at the foot of the Statue of Liberty; part of it remains suspicious about immigrants. Do they take jobs away from Americans? Do they want to become Americans? In recent years, a well intended "compassion fatigue" has emerged among many Americans who have concluded that "enough is enough." Then too the ever present racism that seems to have increased in intensity during the 1980s must be addressed.

If pluralistic assimilation is to succeed, levels of immigration must be reduced. Without some reasonable limits on immigration, future cultural adaptation could easily regress into the more negative forms of cultural pluralism or cultural separatism.

NOTES

1. Milton Gordon, *Assimilation in American Life* (New York: Oxford, 1964), ch. 3.

2. As cited in Leon F. Bouvier, *Immigration: Diversity in the U.S.* (New York: Walker and Co., 1988), 19.

3. Willi Paul Adams, "A Dubious Host," *The Wilson Quarterly*, New Year's 1983, 102.

4. Thomas J. Archdeacon, *Becoming American: An Ethnic History* (New York: The Free Press, 1983), 152.

5. Stephen Steinberg, *The Ethnic Myth: Race, Ethnicity, and Class in America* (Boston: Beacon Press, 1981), 199.

6. Ibid., 200.

7. As cited in Adams, "A Dubious Host," 110.

8. Glazer, *Ethnic Dilemma*, 335-36.

9. Randolph S. Bourne, "Trans-National America," *Atlantic Monthly* 118 (July 1916): 35.

10. Horace M. Kallen, *Culture and Democracy in the United States* (New York: Boni and Liveright, 1924), 124.

11. Frederick Jackson Turner, *The Frontier in American History* (New York: Henry Holt, 1920), 22-23.

12. Ibid., 190.

13. Richard D. Alba, *Italian-Americans: Into the Twilight of Ethnicity* (Englewood Cliffs: Prentice-Hall, 1985), 6. See also Gordon, *Assimilation in American Life*, ch. 5.

14. Michael Novak, *The Rise of the Unmeltable Ethnics* (New York: MacMillan, 1971).

15. Herbert J. Gans, "Symbolic Ethnicity: The Future of Ethnic Group Culture in America," in H.J. Gans, et al., eds., *On the Making of America: Essays in Honor of David Reisman* (Philadelphia: University of Pennsylvania Press, 1979), 193.

16. Stanley Lieberson, "Unhyphenated Whites in the United States," in Richard Alba, ed., *Ethnicity and Race in the USA: Toward the 21st Century* (London: Routledge and Kegan Paul, 1985), 179.

17. Christopher, *Crashing the Gates*, 17.

18. As cited in E. Digby Baltzell, *The Protestant Establishment: Aristocracy and Caste in America* (New York: Vintage Books, 1964), 30.

19. Stephan Thernstrom, "Comment," *Journal of American Ethnic History* 5 (1985): 77-78.

20. Glazer, *Ethnic Dilemma*, 127.

21. Christopher, *Crashing the Gates*, 17.

22. Lieberson, "Unhyphenated Whites in the United States," 179; Richard D. Alba, ed., *Ethnicity and Race in the USA: Toward the 21st Century* (London: Routledge and Kegan Paul, 1985), 149.

23. Christopher, *Crashing the Gates*, 18.

24. "As of 1981 more than ⅓ of the marriages by third-generation Japanese-Americans were with Caucasians. And according to political scientist Andrew Hacker, the number of marriages between whites and Asian-Americans generally increased by more than 70 percent in the ten year period ending in 1986." (Christopher, *Crashing the Gates*, 56.)

25. W.E.B. Dubois, *The Souls of Black Folks* (Greenwich, Conn.: Greenwood Press, 1961), 22; see also John Higham, *Send These To Me* (New York: Atheneaum, 1975), 210-212.

26. Otis L. Graham, Jr, testimony before the Joint Economic Committee of the U.S. Congress, June 1986, 16.

27. Gerda Bikales, *A More Perfect Union* (Washington: Federation for American Immigration Reform, 1982), 104.

28. Georgie Anne Geyer, "Bush was right about the Chinese students," *The Virginian-Pilot*, 1 February 1990, A-15.

29. Alba, *Italian-Americans*, 168.

30. Sidney Weintraub, "Implications of Mexican Demographic Developments for the United States," in Frank D. Bean, et al., eds., *Mexican and Central American Population and U.S. Immigration Policy* (Austin: Center for Mexican American Studies, 1989), 185.

31. Glazer, *Ethnic Dilemma*, 11.

32. Peter Skerry, "The Ambiguity of Mexican-American Politics," in Nathan Glazer, ed., *Clamor at the Gates: The New American Immigration* (San Francisco: Institute for Contemporary Studies Press, 1985), 245.

33. James Michener, *Texas* (New York: Random House, 1985), 1016.

34. Kurt Vonnegut, *Bluebeard* (New York: Delacorte Press, 1987), 179.

35. Stanley Lieberson and Mary C. Waters, *From Many Strands: Ethnic and Racial Groups in Contemporary America* (New York: Russell Sage Foundation, 1988), 42.

36. Christopher, *Crashing the Gates*, 20.

37. Thomas J. Archdeacon, "Melting Pot or Cultural Pluralism? Changing Views on American Ethnicity," *Revue Européenne des Migrations Internationales* 6, no. 1 (1990): 18.

38. Portes and Bach, *Latin Journey*, 25.

39. Steinberg, *The Ethnic Myth*, 256.

40. Theodore White, *America in Search of Itself: The Making of the President — 1956-1980* (New York: Harper and Row, 1982), 367.

41. J. Milton Yinger, "Toward a Theory of Assimilation and Dissimilation," *Ethnic and Racial Studies* 4 (July 1981): 261.

42. Higham, *Send These To Me*, 248.

43. Archdeacon, "Melting Pot or Cultural Pluralism?" 11.

7

Immigration, Population Growth and the Environment

Virtually all discussions in Congress about legal immigration center on questions of *who* this nation should permit to immigrate so as to benefit the nation's labor force. The 1990 legislation, for example, concerned itself with the occupational characteristics as well as the country of origin of potential immigrants. The larger question, of *how many* immigrants are appropriate, was not discussed. Yet, as a result of this legislation, the United States population in 2050 will be about 35 million larger than it would be if such legislation were not passed. This failure to take population growth into account is unfortunate, because the number of immigrants the United States admits is not only a major determinant of future United States population size, but also has significant ramifications for environmental protection.

If current demographic trends are maintained, there will be 388 million Americans in the year 2050. With slight increases in fertility and immigration, there could be 454 million Americans in the year 2050. Looking farther into the future, the range of possibilities becomes even more dramatic: the same scenario that produces 454 million Americans in 2050 leads to 900 million Americans by 2120. Demographers Ahlburg and Vaupel foresee a possible population of 811 million by 2080.

> A U.S. population of 800 million may seem incredible, but the annual average growth rate that produces it runs at only 1.3 percent per year. This is the same as the average annual growth rate that has prevailed in the United States over the last half-century and not too much above the 1 percent average annual growth rate of the last decade.[1]

In other words, the United States could have more people in 100 years than India has today. This is not a welcome prospect.

Public Policy and Population Growth

Public policy in the United States influences fertility in subtle and not-so-subtle ways. State and federal governments fund (or don't fund) family planning clinics; restrict (or don't restrict) the availability of abortion; provide (or don't provide) sex education and population education. In many diverse ways, our national and state governments and the culture in general influence family size decisions. But these decisions remain — and should remain — those of individuals alone. Changes in life expectancy also affect the size of the population. But all agree that life expectancy should be increased for all Americans. Immigration remains the one aspect of domestic population growth that is — in theory at least — regulated by the federal government in the national interest.

With fertility at late 1980 levels (1.8) and net immigration reduced to 350,000, stabilization could be achieved by the middle of the next century at about 316 million; or, with increased fertility and immigration, the United States could be on a course toward a virtually unimaginable one billion Americans.

Thus, immigration policy is a far-reaching means to influence population growth. Goals for U.S. population size should be an essential part of every discussion of immigration policy.

U.S. Population Growth and the Environment

Environmental protection is a matter of widespread concern in the United States and throughout the world. Millions of Americans participated in Earth Day celebrations in spring of 1990. Some three-quarters of Americans consider themselves environmentalists as measured by polls, and membership in environmental groups has been rising dramatically. The political importance of environmental issues can be seen in the extent to which elected officials (and those campaigning for public office) make the claim to be solidly for the environment. Even President Bush proclaims himself to be the "environment president."

Although *domestic* population growth has been far from the public eye since the early 1970s, environmental groups (including the Sierra Club and Population-Environment-Balance for example) have long believed that human population growth is harmful to the environment, and that population stabilization is essential in the long run if environmental goals are to be achieved and maintained.

GLOBAL CLIMATE CHANGE

The drought of 1988, together with the unseasonably warm winter of 1989 made all Americans aware that this warming trend was a possible harbinger of the dreaded "greenhouse effect." Many respected scientists are warning that the greenhouse effect could cause unprecedented disruption to the global environment.

Many gases emitted into the earth's atmosphere (including carbon dioxide, methane, chlorofluorocarbons, and nitrous oxide) are known to trap heat. The concentration of these "greenhouse gases" will continue to increase until significant changes are made in energy use. It is estimated that the earth is already committed to an average temperature increase of 3.5 — 9 degrees Fahrenheit (2-5 degrees Centigrade) before a new equilibrium is achieved. This is an increase without precedent in recorded history.

In order to slow the rate of build-up of greenhouse gases, far-reaching measures must be adopted. Those recommended by the Sierra Club include: (1) a ban on the production and releases of chlorofluorocarbons, which not only contribute to the greenhouse effect but are also the chief culprits in the destruction of the stratospheric ozone layer; (2) a decrease in the use of coal and increase in the energy conservation and the use of renewable energy sources; (3) a halt to the destruction of forest ecosystems and a major program of reforestation; (4) a greatly increased effort to reduce the rate of population growth in each country of the world, with the eventual goal of a stabilized world population size.

Although population growth is more rapid in developing nations, per capita energy use in the United States is so large that even a small rate increase of population growth in the United States results in large increases in energy use — and hence, production of greenhouse gases.

Not only would the United States benefit directly from a stabilization of its own population, but people throughout the world would benefit through reduced United States production of greenhouse gases.

FOOD PRODUCTION

The United States has long been a food exporting nation. Given the demands of many rapidly growing nations of the Third World and parts of Eastern Europe, this is very fortunate. However, with increasing population and growing individual consumption by Americans, surpluses in food production are dwindling rapidly.

In 1972, USDA experts concluded that:

> American agriculture appears capable . . . of meeting the challenges of the year 2000. Even under the most demanding assumptions about food and constraints on technology, food and fiber needs could be met without great difficulty, but would require some increase in prices. . . . If this analysis were continued out to the year 2020, the cost of bringing additional farmland into production could possibly increase food prices substantially.[2]

More recently entomologist David Pimentel testified before the Select Commission on Immigration and Refugee Policy that if soil erosion can be stopped and if the availability of energy at today's relative prices is unchanged, the United States could increase productivity (and thus production) by 25 to 30 percent over the next 50 years.[3]

The United States population will grow by over 35 percent between 1990 and 2040. If this rate is not reduced, either Americans will be eating less well or American farmers will be exporting far fewer food products. To be sure, new agronomy methods may be discovered which will increase productivity beyond Pimentel's estimates. However, this only postpones the inevitable. If the United States population keeps growing, sooner or later food production will be insufficient for export.

Not only will this be harmful for the countries in dire need of food imports, it will also pose problems for the United States trade deficit where food exports help keep that deficit lower than it otherwise would be.

WATER SUPPLY

Water shortage is a large and growing problem in some parts of the nation. This is not a new problem. In 1972, in a report prepared for the Commission on Population Growth and the American Future, Ronald Ridker concluded,

> Growth in population and economic activities during the next half century will force upon us significant expenditures for treatment and storage facilities [of water]; moreover, for a growing number of regions, such investments will eventually prove inadequate. When one takes a region-by-region look at the situation, it becomes clear that the scope for redistribution of water, activities, and people is more limited and difficult to achieve than it might appear at first glance.[4]

Some eighteen years later the problem of adequate water supply remains.[5] Average per capita withdrawal in the United States increased 22 percent between 1970 and 1980. This was less than the 37 percent increase of the previous ten years, but still roughly twice the rate of population growth. In 1985, average water withdrawal by Americans amounted to 1,950 gallons per person, of which 450 gallons were consumed. Americans use about three times as much water per capita as do the Japanese.[6]

Furthermore, water supply is not evenly distributed with the west receiving 30 percent of the fresh water runoff but accounting for 80 percent of the consumption. In California, these problems are compounded by rapid population growth. A report by the National Academy of Sciences says that in order to accommodate the needs of the burgeoning population in California more water will have to be shipped in from someplace else. And that someplace else will be harder, if not impossible, to find.[7]

Regarding water quality, the 1987 Council of State Governments report concludes:

> For the first time we are confronted with water quality problems everywhere. Every state is experiencing contaminated groundwater supplies, unsafe drinking water, and higher costs for maintaining a supply of water to meet growing demand. These problems are a result of modern society and will become more severe with the *growth of population* and the expansion of the man-made environment.[8] (emphasis added)

AIR QUALITY

There is sufficient air for all of us to breathe. However, it does not take a doomsayer to be alarmed at the quality of that air that all of us breathe. About 90 percent of the air pollutants in the United States can be attributed to the burning of fossil fuels. Half of all the air pollutants come from motor vehicles and another 28 percent come from power and industrial plants. Air quality improved during the 1970s in large part due to the passage of the Clean Air Acts of 1970 and 1977. Between 1982 and 1985, however, ambient levels of major pollutants other than lead either remained the same or climbed slightly. These increases are the result of Reagan administration cutbacks in enforcement of air pollution control regulations.

They are also the result of growth. Clearly, clean air cannot be achieved without strong pollution controls on individual automobiles and on emissions from factories. Yet, as many metropolitan areas have discovered, the sheer amount of growth, by putting more automobiles on the road, can erode gains achieved at great cost through emission controls. Fortunately, a new Clean

Air Act was passed in late 1990. However, in order to be successful, a Clean Air Act must also incorporate a plan for population stabilization, not only for the nation as a whole, but also for specific areas with severe air quality problems.

WASTE DISPOSAL

Landfills everywhere are nearing capacity and public opinion opposes "imported waste." All Americans remember the 1988 two-month odyssey of the infamous Islip, Long Island, garbage barge. During that barge's travel it was refused permission to unload its cargo by six states and three countries. Ultimately that cargo was burned in a Brooklyn incinerator. In 1990, Indiana objected strenuously to continued garbage disposal in that state by New Jersey. These episodes illustrate the enormous sewage and waste disposal problems Americans are facing. The United States produces 160 million tons of municipal solid waste per year, nearly 3.5 pounds per day for every man, woman, and child in the nation. With expected increases in population as well as in consumption, the 200 million ton per year mark will be soon be reached. Even without any increases in consumption, that mark will be reached within 20 years.

Problems are greater in large metropolitan areas. Southern California, for example, has already reached its limits for burying garbage: the landfills are full. Sewage problems are equally severe.

> Spills of raw sewage into the ocean off Southern California are becoming commonplace. Fish found in the Santa Monica Bay are not edible due to diseases and contamination. The city of Los Angeles processes most of its sewage at the Hyperion Sewage Treatment plant which is unable to keep up with demands caused by increased population. Because of this, 800 million gallons of only minimally treated sewage spews into the ocean every day.[9]

On the Atlantic, similar problems are emerging as noted by the garbage found on New Jersey shores and elsewhere in recent summers.

The proportion of materials recycled can certainly be greatly improved and waste production can be reduced. Yet even if per capita production of wastes is halved, should the population double, the nation will be even worse off than when it started, because waste production will be back at the same level, with the easy waste-reduction steps already having been taken.

WETLANDS

Far too little attention is being paid to the staggering loss of inland wetlands throughout the United States. "Located away from ocean tides, these are the bogs and swamps that act as nature's sponges. They soak up pollutants, provide breeding grounds and habitat for wildlife including migratory fowl. Without these humble swamps, floods become a far greater menace."[10]

Because choice lands are already developed, draining the nation's inland wetlands to make way for development is increasing despite federal and state laws designed to protect these diminishing wetlands. Over half of the nation's wetlands have been destroyed and at least an additional 300,000 acres are destroyed every year — all for housing and commercial development. Unfortunately, the Bush administration's recent redefinition of "wetlands" will exacerbate the problem.

INFRASTRUCTURE

The infrastructure problems facing the United States are growing. Roads, bridges, water systems, railroads and mass transit are all deteriorating. According to the Report of the National Governors' Association 1989 meeting, the price to bring America's transportation infrastructure into reasonable condition within the next 20 years is estimated to range from $1 trillion to $3 trillion, requiring annual outlays in the range of $50 billion to $150 billion.[11] Roads and bridges are the biggest problems. Over 200,000 miles of the nation's roads are in "poor" or "very poor" shape, and another million miles are rated only "fair." Of the nation's 575,000 highway bridges, 42 percent are structurally deficient or functionally obsolete. In some regions of the country, many bridges have already deteriorated to the point of being safety hazards for the public.

Over the last two decades, traffic has grown five times faster than highway capacity. In the next two decades, congestion is projected to become five times worse. In California, transportation officials fear that it will be virtually impossible for enough new highway miles to be constructed to keep pace with population growth. Similar problems are noted in most of the nation's metropolitan areas as suburbs are extended farther and farther away from the central cities to accommodate the burgeoning population. The result is sprawl development, choked highways and massive traffic congestion. The average speed on Los Angeles freeways, already a very low 37 miles per hour, is projected to drop to 17 miles per hour by the year 2000.

The list of population-related infrastructure problems is almost endless. Consider the nation's crowded beaches and National Parks; consider its deteriorating water and sewage systems; consider its transit system, whether bus, plane or train. "Airports anticipate a 72 percent increase in passenger volume in this decade; by 1997, 33 major airports are expected to experience, cumulatively, 20,000 hours of delays annually."[12]

Population growth worsens each of these problems. All levels of government are struggling to catch up with the needs of growing numbers, and all too often fail to maintain the systems built in the past or to improve them for the future.

Consider too that the added 100 or 200 million Americans will not be equally distributed among the 50 states. Visualize more than 50 million people living in California, at least 25 million in Southern California, compared to 15 million today. Visualize 30 million people living in Texas; another 30 million in Florida, and yet another 25 million in New York, with more than half of them in the New York City metropolitan area. Without any movement to such underpopulated places as the Dakotas and Montana, such regional population concentrations are a distinct possibility if the United States population increases by 100 million or more over the next 60 years.

WORLD POPULATION GROWTH

World population increase is widely recognized as one of the most serious problems facing humankind. Scientist Norman Myers has called the 1990s "the most decisive decade in humankind's history," the "final window of opportunity" to come to grips with the world's population and environmental problems, and protect the habitability of the planet. Myers, in considering how much environmental destruction has already been made inevitable, examines an unusual hypothesis:

> Suppose that in the year 2000, humanity were to be eliminated from the face of the Earth. The in-built inertia of [biological] decline would by then be so great that species would continue to disappear in ever larger numbers, due to 'delayed fall-out processes.' The ecological injury already done would have triggered the irreversible unravelling of food webs, leading to domino-effect extinctions for many decades, even for a whole century.[13]

Imagine the environmental destruction associated with a world population of 10 or 15 billion!

The root of all these problems can be traced at least in part to the incredible rate of population growth on the planet. Just 150 years ago, world population reached one billion. Recently, the 5 billion mark was passed. In the hour or so it may have taken the reader to reach this chapter, 16,000 babies were born while about 6 thousand people died. The world's population increased by 10,000 people.

In 1980, in his farewell message to the nation, President Jimmy Carter addressed the problems of population and the environment:

> There are real and growing dangers to our simple and most precious possessions; the air we breathe; the water we drink; and the land which sustains us. The rapid depletion of irreplaceable minerals, the erosion of topsoil, the destruction of beauty, the blight of pollution, the demand of increasing billions of people, all combine to create problems which are easy to observe and predict, but difficult to resolve. If we do not act, the world of the year 2000 will be much less able to sustain life than it is now. But there is no reason for despair. Acknowledging these realities is the first step in dealing with them. We can meet the resource problems of the world — water, food, minerals, farmlands, forests, overpopulation, pollution — if we tackle them with courage and foresight.

Unfortunately, President Carter's successors have not heeded his warnings.

PROPONENTS OF UNITED STATES POPULATION GROWTH

Concern about *world* population growth is widespread and not seriously questioned. However, a few widely-quoted individuals have argued that, in effect, the United States is exempt from the principle that population stabilization is beneficial. They claim that growth is beneficial for the United States.

This is simply wrong. The United States does not need population increase beyond the 60 million increase that is virtually inevitable. Rather, every expansion of the number of Americans hurts the nation's ability to solve its environmental and other problems. Indeed, environmental scientists David and Marcia Pimentel argue that: "For the United States to be self-sustaining in solar energy, given our land, water, and biological resources, our population should be less than 100 million. . . . However, with a drastic reduction in standard of living, the current population level might be sustained."[14]

Because the average consumption of Americans far exceeds that of any other country, any increase in the number of Americans has a disproportionate negative effect. According to Norman Myers:

> The one billion people at the top of the pile generally do not feature high population rates, but such are their materialist lifestyles — many of them, for instance, consume 100 times as much commercial energy as do most Bangladeshis, Ethiopians, and Bolivians — that in certain respects the additional 1.75 million Americans each year may well do as much damage to the biosphere as the 85 million additional Third Worlders.[15]

Large-scale immigration to the United States helps the few who migrate, but harms the billions who do not. In terms of global warming, waste production, energy use, and many other environmental concerns, citizens of the world can breathe easier when United States population stops increasing. It does not matter whether United States population increase comes from fertility or immigration — ending it helps protect both the world environment and the environment of the United States.

Furthermore it is quite possible that a portion of the very recent increase in fertility may reflect the changing ethnic proportions of the population. As long as these ethnic shares continue to grow, overall fertility will rise. As long as the fertility of minority groups surpasses that of the current majority population, the growing numbers in the minorities will raise the nation's overall fertility.

Let us assume that the current total fertility rates for the four principal ethnic groups in the United States are as follows: Anglo 1.8; Black 2.3; Hispanic 3.0; Asian and Others 2.3. While we cannot vouch for the accuracy of these figures, they are undoubtedly close to the eventual figures for 1990. Let us further assume that shifts in the ethnic composition of the population will be as described in the basic scenario. The Anglo share will fall from 76 percent in 1990 to 65 in 2020 and 54 in 2050 while that for Hispanics will rise from 9 percent to 15 and 22 percent, and others accordingly.

Given these assumptions, the total fertility rate would rise from 2.0 in 1990 to 2.1 in 2020 and 2.2 in 2050 — without any actual increases in the fertility of any one ethnic group, but rather as a result of "shifting shares" in the overall population. Such "small" increases of .01 every thirty years may seem inconsequential. They are not. According to recent Census Bureau projections, the difference between fertility remaining constant at 1.8 and fertility gradually rising to 2.2 by 2050 (while holding mortality and migration constant) amounts to over 63 million by that year![16] A very slight increase in fertility yields massive increases in population size decades later. Given these numbers, it would appear that any end to population growth in the United States is nowhere in sight so long as immigration levels remain high.

CONCLUSION

This brief discussion of the environmental and population problems facing the nation makes it clear that these problems will not be easy to solve. Population growth is a major factor in making solutions to these problems more difficult, and population stabilization would go a long way toward making such solutions easier.

Every scenario for America's population future shows substantial population increases. Even our "Low" scenario of low fertility (1.8) and net immigration of 350,000 results in a 60 million increase in the number of Americans before stabilization at 316 million in 2050. So the United States will need to find ways to resolve its energy, air quality, water supply, and infrastructure problems with *at least* 60 million more people driving cars, heating their homes, visiting in parks.

But the real question for Americans is *how many more* Americans are desirable beyond the virtually unavoidable 60 million increase.   The environmental arguments for "limits to growth" are overwhelming in theory. The rationale for rapid population stabilization in the United States is also borne out by the work of those actively trying to solve environmental problems and by the experience of average Americans in their everyday lives.

A population of 900 million Americans is too disturbing to even contemplate.   That is also the case for 454 million Americans, or even 388 million. The nation's goal should be the attainment of population stabilization as soon as reasonably possible.

THE POLITICS OF POPULATION

Despite all the evidence of the need for population stabilization, and despite the fact that many nations in the world have adopted explicit population policies supporting slower growth, American policy-makers have been reluctant to address population issues directly.

In 1970, in the shadow of the 1968 publication of Paul Ehrlich's *The Population Bomb*, the federal government established the first national program to fund family planning clinics.[17]   In 1973, the United States Supreme Court legalized abortion throughout the nation.

A Presidential Commission on Population and the American Future concluded in 1972 that "in the long run, no substantial benefits will result from further growth of the Nation's population, rather that the gradual stabilization of our population through voluntary means would contribute significantly to the Nation's ability to solve its problems."[18]   The Commission came down squarely in favor of the two-child family. Immigration was then about 400,000 per year, and the Commission recommended "that immigration levels not be increased and that immigration policy be reviewed periodically to reflect demographic conditions [i.e., population growth] and considerations."[19]

In 1972, United States fertility fell below the "replacement level" of 2100 children per 1000 women and has stayed below until today. As the 1970s progressed, it became clear that immigration policy offered the greatest opportunity for public policy action towards a national population policy, and that large increases in immigration posed the greatest challenge to population stabilization. To whatever concerns policy makers may have had about the political consequences of the fertility implications of a population policy were added concerns about tackling the issue of "how many immigrants."

Federal legislation declaring a policy of population stabilization has been introduced into every Congress for the past decade, but has never garnered much attention. Now may be the most opportune time for the discussion of population policy, in the context of development of overall immigration goals.

TOWARD A NATIONAL POPULATION POLICY

Developing a national population policy means adopting an explicit goal for population size. The most reasonable population policy — and in fact the only inevitable one — would be the adoption of a year and a population level as a target for population stabilization; i.e., an end to population increase.

Now is the time for a broad national discussion of such a population goal. With population stabilization, one of the major components of the nation's environmental problems would be resolved. In addition, as discussed earlier, the rest of the world could breathe easier, knowing that rampant United States consumption of resources and creation of pollution would be more easily abated.

NOTES

1. Ahlburg and Vaupel, "Alternative Projections," 645.

2. A. Barry Carr and David W. Culver, "Agriculture, Population and the Environment," in R. Ridker, ed., *Population, Resources and the Environment* (Commission on American Growth and the American Future, Washington: Government Printing Office, 1972), 193-94.

3. David Pimentel, testimony before the Select Commission on Immigration and Refugee Policy, 1980.

4. Ronald Ridker, *Resource and Environmental Consequences of Population Growth in the United States: A Summary* (Commission on American Growth and the American Future, Washington: GPO, 1972), 221.

5. Water withdrawal must be distinguished from water consumption. Withdrawal involves taking water from a groundwater or surface water source and transporting it to a place of use. Consumption occurs when water that has been withdrawn is not available for reuse in the area from which it is withdrawn. (G. Tyler Miller, *Resource Conservation and Management* [Belmont: Wadsworth Publishing Co., 1990], 185.)

6. Kenneth R. Sheets, "War Over Water: Crisis of the Eighties," *U.S. News and World Report*, 31 October 1983, 7.

7. As cited by Dawn Glesser Moore, testimony before the Subcommittee on Census and Population of the Committee on Post Office and Civil Service, U.S. House of Representatives, 12 April 1988, 3.

8. Kenneth Cole, "Clean Water: National Issue, Regional Concern," in *States' Summit '87: Issues and Choices for the 1990s*, Council of State Governments Annual Meeting, Boston, December 1987, 8.

9. Moore, testimony, 19.

10. Neal Peirce, "Breakthrough for Wetlands: EPA's Reilly Lobbies a Maryland Law," *The Virginian-Pilot*, 22 May 1989, A-7.

11. As cited in David Broder, "On the Roads Again: Governors in the Lead," *Washington Post*, 8 August 1989, 12.

12. George Will, "Congealed in Traffic," *Washington Post*, 11 March 1990, B7.

13. Norman Myers, "People and Environment: The Watershed Decade," *People* (London) 17, no. 1 (1990): 17.

14. David Pimentel and Marcia Pimentel, "Land, Energy and Water: The Constraints Governing Ideal U.S. Population Size," *The NPG Forum* (1990): 5.

15. Myers, "People and Environment," 19.

16. U.S. Bureau of the Census, *Projections of the Population of the United States, by Age, Sex, and Race: 1988 to 2080*, 16.

17. The co-sponsors of this legislation in the House of Representatives were long-time population activist James H. Scheuer (D-NY) and a little-known relatively new Congressman from Texas, George Herbert Walker Bush.

18. Commission on Population Growth and the American Future, *Population and the American Future* (Washington, DC: Government Printing Office, 1972), 50.

19. Ibid., 40.

Conclusion

Four arguments for reducing the level of immigration to the United States have been offered in this section. Both, long-time residents and newcomers, would be better off if immigration levels were limited.

With less immigration, the nation's underclasses would benefit. Many recent immigrants fall into this social category. With less competition for entry-level jobs, these newest immigrants as well as other minorities who share this unfortunate status would at least have a better opportunity to move out of poverty.

With less immigration, it would be necessary for the nation to innovate its factories and farms to compete on a level playing field with its twenty-first-century competitors, particularly Japan and the new European Community. This would mean higher wages and better jobs for all — including the immigrants themselves.

With less immigration, the nation would more easily maintain its cultural heritage and its new residents would more easily learn the English language and culture, so important for success in the United States.

With less immigration, the nation's infrastructure as well as its environment would improve as growth would be limited. The National Parks would be less crowded as would the highways and public transit facilities. An end to population growth might even be in sight.

Despite these many obvious advantages, limiting, though not eliminating, immigration is offensive to some Americans. For example: "Immigration policy for the United States cannot be correctly determined by a population policy which is concerned with opportunity possibilities for one nation. Immigration policy would better be conceived in the context of a world survival concern and an opportunity concern not limited to the United States."[1]

As long as the world consists of nation-states, such a position is totally irresponsible. One can only speculate on the untold millions of people who would migrate to the United States and other advanced nations if immigration policies were only concerned with "world survival." The end result would be poverty throughout the planet.

The words of the nineteenth-century English political philosopher, Henry Sidgwick, are more appropriate: "Immigration can be restricted as soon as failure to do so would interfere materially . . . with the efforts of government to maintain an adequately high standard of living [and it should be added, environmental quality] among the members of the community generally — especially the poorer classes."[2]

That is precisely the point of this book, while realizing of course that immigration to the United States is in fact "restricted." The nation does not have open borders, although leaks are found in many places, and increasingly the possibility of open borders is discussed. Rather, the number of immigrants allowed to enter should be reduced so as to maintain an adequately high standard of living and reduce, if not end, poverty.

NOTES

1. Msgr. Nicholas Dimarzio, testimony presented before the Sub-committee on Census and Population of the Committee on Post Office and Civil Service, U.S. House of Representatives, 12 April 1988, 33.

2. Henry Sidgwick, *Elements of Politics* (London: MacMillan, 1881), 296-7.

PART III

CHALLENGES FOR THE FUTURE

Introduction

The demographic behavior of millions of individuals, here and elsewhere, will pose serious challenges for twenty-first-century America.

Two such demographically-driven challenges are particularly relevant and are discussed in this section: changing ethnic composition and pluralistic assimilation.

Four arguments have been cited for reduced levels of immigration. The changing ethnic composition of the nation is NOT one of them. Americans proudly proclaim that the so-called "American Creed" of liberty, equality, justice and fair opportunity is for everybody. If this is true, then ethnic or racial identity should be irrelevant. To be sure, the "American Creed" is an ideal that is seldom followed. Therein lies the challenge that emerges from the dramatic shifts in the racial composition of the United States population.

These demographic shifts will affect every American institution. Education, being so important to the future well-being of the nation, will be particularly affected. Americans must be made aware of these shifts and how they will impact on the lives of everyone.

The concept of pluralistic assimilation was introduced earlier. Pluralistic assimilation is a far more suitable mode of adaptation than cultural pluralism if the nation is to maintain a unified identity and culture. If pluralistic assimilation is to eventually succeed, reductions in immigration are necessary. Such limitations are merely the *sine qua non* factor. Much more needs to be accomplished if pluralistic assimilation is to become the prime mode of cultural adaptation in the twenty-first century.

If the United States is to maintain its unity and its position of leadership in the world of the future, it must address and accept the fact that it is on the verge of becoming the world's first truly racially heterogeneous industrialized nation. Given such a demographic development, it must move also towards a form of pluralistic assimilation if that unity is to be preserved. These are the twin themes of this section of the book.

In the final chapter the politics of immigration are examined. Limiting immigration is frowned upon in some segments of American society and for widely diverse reasons. As a result few people dare become involved in examining the impacts of immigration on all aspects of the society. In this chapter, recommendations are made regarding immigration policy that hopefully will lead the United States towards the twenty-first century unified and qualified to compete internationally.

8

The Heterogeneous Nation

In his famous book, *American Dilemma*, written almost fifty years ago, social scientist Gunnar Myrdal concluded:

> Mankind is sick of fear and disbelief, of pessimism and cynicism. It needs the youthful, moralistic optimism of America. But empty declarations only deepen cynicism. Deeds are called for. If America in actual practice could show the world a progressive trend by which the Negro became finally integrated into modern democracy, all mankind would be given faith again — it would have reason to believe that peace, progress, and order are feasible and America would have a spiritual power many times stronger than all her financial and military resources — the power of trust and support of all good people on earth. *America is free to choose whether the Negro still remains her liability or becomes her opportunity.*[1]

Almost fifty years later, the issue remains unresolved. Indeed, the issue has become more complex. Rather than Negro, one should include all minorities: Black, Latino, Asian, Native American. For the United States, this may be THE challenge of the twenty-first century.

THE SHIFT IN POPULATION COMPOSITION

High levels of immigration, relatively low fertility, and increased longevity are combining to produce a twenty-first-century America that will be both older and more diverse than ever before in the nation's history.

If current demographic trends persist, that is to say, if fertility remains fairly low, if life expectancy increases slightly, and if net immigration is about 950,000 annually, the majority Anglo group, now representing about three-quarters of the population, will comprise just over half of that population by the middle of the twenty-first century. The Latino group will surpass Blacks before 2020 and comprise 22 percent of the nation's population by 2050 while the Black share will be about 13 percent. The proportion held by Asians too will grow — from 3 percent in 1990 to 11 percent sixty years later.

These projections are not cast in stone. The 1990 legislation could result in more immigration than assumed. Furthermore, movements out of certain European countries could expand. But regardless of the demographic path the nation follows, increased diversity lies ahead. The United States is inexorably on its way to becoming a society with no one predominant group. In California, Texas, and New York, within 25 years no single group will comprise a majority.

The enormity of this challenge to the nation cannot be denied. Never before has any racial group voluntarily and peacefully relinquished its dominant status in a modern industrial nation-state. The United States has been criticized in some quarters for its racial and ethnic diversity. Japan proudly boasts of its homogeneity, implying that American heterogeneity is a source of some of its problems.[2] Yet, the United States is rapidly becoming more diverse than ever.

These racial shifts are a matter of great concern to some Americans. From the far right, Louisiana state representative David Duke, a former leader of the Ku Klux Klan, wants to end immigration so as "to see this country remain the way it is . . . with the kind of population mix we now have."[3] From the far left, Black historian Manning Marable asks: "What will happen when the white American population becomes a minority? Will they still permit 'one man, one vote'? Stop a second before you answer the question. You might say, 'Of course.' But you will see it — a demand to rethink or rechange the political process in this country."[4] Will American apartheid emerge or will all minorities become involved in the political, economic, and social aspects of American life? Clearly, the imminent shift in composition presents challenges never before faced by the United States.

Many Americans are uncomfortable discussing population heterogeneity. For a long time it was seldom mentioned in political or even academic circles except by extremists from both ends of the political and academic spectrum. Only recently have moderate voices begun to discuss it.[5] Indeed, the very mention of the changing racial composition of the United States population can leave one open to charges of racism. Following the publication of *The Birth Dearth* in 1987, some commentators labelled its author, Ben Wattenberg, racist for having brought up the issue of future changes in the racial composition of the nation.[6]

This reluctance to face up to the issue and examine its advantages and disadvantages is unfortunate. The American people must be informed of the dramatic shifts that are presently taking place in racial composition. They must be prepared to play an appropriate role in this new America that is evolving.

Should fertility levels be raised so as to diminish the racial shifts taking place? Absolutely not. The resulting population size would be intolerable. Should immigration levels be reduced so as to minimize these shifts? Absolutely not. Racial shifts, per se, are not a problem.

This book argues strongly for reducing levels of immigration on other grounds; it is concerned solely with numbers. Too many immigrants, irrespective of origin, contribute to high rates of population growth that contribute to more environmental degradation. Too many immigrants, irrespective of origin, make it difficult for pluralistic assimilation to occur. Too many immigrants, irrespective of origin, discourage technological innovations and foster less competitiveness. Too many immigrants, irrespective of origin, postpone the day when America's under-classes can finally uplift themselves.

The United States has undergone significant ethnic though not racial shifts in the past. These caused serious problems but the nation eventually benefitted from them as the new immigrants contributed to the growing society. So too the current and future shifts may be equally beneficial.

The twentieth century was the "Atlantic Century." International power was concentrated in Europe and the United States. In the United States, numbers and power were concentrated on the Atlantic coast. The nation benefitted from the growing heterogeneity of its European-origin population. The United States had become a "European" nation — it was no longer an extension of the United Kingdom. For most of the twentieth century, the nation looked north to Canada and east to Europe for its trading partners and political allies.

Today, economic power is shifting from the Atlantic to the Pacific. In the United States it was not until 1980 that the center of population crossed the Mississippi River moving westward. Internationally, the cities of the Pacific Rim — Los Angeles, Sydney, and Tokyo — are taking over from the old, established cities of the Atlantic — New York, Paris, and London.[7] As the twenty-first century, sometimes referred to as the Pacific Century, arrives, now may be the most opportune time for the United States to cast its eyes and interests increasingly towards Asia and Latin America while not neglecting Europe and Canada.

Europe is no longer considered the center of the universe. As U.S. Secretary of State John Jay commented prophetically two centuries ago: "The Mediterranean is the ocean of the past, the Atlantic the ocean of the present, the Pacific the ocean of the future." Symbolically, as well as demographically, California has replaced New York as the largest state and Texas is not far behind. Population growth in Latin America and economic growth in Japan and the newly industrialized countries of Asia together with the economic potential of China suggest that economic power as well as numbers are moving to the Pacific.

The world is becoming more and more internationalized in communication, in commerce, in industry. An emerging multiracial, though culturally unified, United States conveniently located between, on one hand the European Community and the newly democratic nations of eastern Europe, and on the other hand the growing economic giants of Asia and the massive populations of Latin America, should be ideally suited for the challenges of the twenty-first century. The United States, comprised of significant proportions of people descending from European, Asian, Latin American and African sources, would most certainly be at the center of the universe and become the world's first truly universalistic nation. A Temple University scholar, Molefi Asante, recently commented, in somewhat anticipatory fashion: "Once America was a microcosm of European nationalities, today America is a microcosm of the world."[8]

To repeat; there is nothing improper about increased ethnic and racial diversity. The nation can benefit from such diversity as the world itself becomes smaller. Yet failing to realize that the massive levels of immigration that cause such diversity seriously tax the society would be like the proverbial ostrich with its head in the sand.

The road to success in the melting of various European ethnic groups in the white America of today was not paved with roses. Violence often erupted between ethnic groups as each sought to improve their lot in their new homeland. A more peaceful era eventually arrived but it was not before considerable conflict had ensued, and after levels of immigration had subsided. Such a peace is still elusive among the races that inhabit the nation. America remains a racist society and, indeed, Black-White relations appear to be degenerating rather than improving. Latinos and Asians, too, have long suffered discrimination at the hands of White Americans.

Latino and Asian groups will grow rapidly in future years. Already, tension has appeared among the nation's racial groups in places as disparate as Lawrence, Massachusetts; Miami, Florida; Biloxi, Mississippi; and more recently, in the Mt. Pleasant section of Washington, D.C.

Will White Americans peacefully accept their new status as "just another subgroup"? One does not have to be a bigot to feel embattled when witnessing the declining numerical proportion of his or her group. Will Black Americans accept the new competition from Latinos and Asians? Will they feel that their historical demands for equality might go unheeded given the growth of the newer minorities? Will Asians and Latinos adapt peacefully to each other in those many locations where they share territory? Already fights breakout intermittently between Cambodian and Latino students in Stockton, California. In New York City, Blacks boycott Korean convenience stores and Bensonhurst becomes a point of bitter conflict between Blacks and Whites.

To remain sanguine about the possibilities of conflict among the nation's groups as they interact and compete for advantageous position in the economic and social system would be both naive and stupid. If the United States does not solve its racial problems, the emerging diversity will be an impediment to the unity of the nation. If, however, a solution is found, the United States of the twenty-first century will be the model of unity for the world.

The nation will continue to age. By mid-twenty-first century, half of the population might be under 40, compared to half under 32 today. The number of individuals over 65 could reach 76 million, compared to 30 million today. Those elderly people will be overwhelmingly Anglo. However, working Americans of that period, whose taxes will be needed to support the elderly, will come from far more diverse backgrounds. The possibilities of inter-generational as well as inter-racial conflicts cannot be ignored.

Interestingly, the label of "ageist" is seldom attached to those concerned about the aging of the society and the problems that may emerge, in marked contrast to the labelling of "racist" to those concerned about the shifts in the nation's racial composition. Yet both shifts are inevitable, stemming from past as well as current demographic behavior. There is nothing wrong with an aging society; there is nothing wrong with a more ethnically diverse society. But the residents of the nation must be alerted to these changes.

SELECTED SOCIAL INSTITUTIONS

Racial and ethnic shifts influence and will continue to influence all of the nation's institutions. Reference was made in an earlier chapter to the changing composition of the labor force. The impact of racial and ethnic shifts on education is so strong that the next chapter will be devoted to this issue. These shifts will also pose new challenges for political, religious and health institutions, among others.

POLITICAL INSTITUTIONS

Throughout its history, the United States has witnessed an ongoing shift in the relative political power of its immigrants and their descendants. A new group arrives and settles in a specific area. As its numbers grow the group's political strength increases. At first, it cannot elect its own to positions of power; rather, the group joins one political party in order to receive certain benefits. With increasing numbers, some members of the group eventually win elections, usually with the overwhelming support of their own people. If the group becomes economically successful, it may eventually disperse and the homogeneous ethnic voting block dissipates. Then, when one of the ethnic group runs for political office, he or she does so, not as a member of a particular ethnic group, but as an American.

It was not until the mid-1920s that non-Anglo-Saxon immigrants and their descendants began to play an important role on the national political scene. As the rate of naturalization increased, more and more of these new Americans became potential voters and ethnic voting blocs became commonplace.

The ethnic Americans, roughly defined as immigrants from eastern and southern Europe, wholeheartedly joined the Democratic party at the national level in the 1920s. This was attributable, in no small part, to the election of Alfred E. Smith to the governorship of New York in 1920. Interestingly, while Smith was considered the epitome of the Irish-Catholic politician, he was a product of Italian, German, Irish Protestant and Irish Catholic grandparents. In 1928, Smith received the presidential nomination of the Democratic party. Although he lost the election, Smith was able to cement the party's hold on the various ethnic minorities and this was further reinforced with the election of Democrat Franklin D. Roosevelt as President in 1932.

Through the first half of the twentieth century, this pattern became established. The Democrats could rely on a substantial majority of Catholic and Jewish votes and the not mutually exclusive vote of most ethnic Americans. Protestants and long time residents of Anglo-Saxon ancestry were more likely to claim allegiance to the Republican party, except in the South, where Democrats reigned supreme.

Blacks, those few allowed to vote, remained loyal to the Republican party, the party of Abraham Lincoln, from Emancipation in 1863 to 1932 and the election of Roosevelt. Since then, they have been the most loyal of all Democrats.

By the middle of the century, the various immigrant groups, together with their descendants, had made considerable strides towards attaining political equality with other Americans. In Chicago, Bohemian-born Anton Cermak was elected mayor in 1931. In New York City, Fiorello LaGuardia, an Episcopalian of Jewish and Italian parentage, became mayor in 1933. By the late 1940s and 1950s Jews served as governors of New York and Connecticut and Italians held that position in Massachusetts and Rhode Island.

The historical hold of White Anglo-Saxon Protestants on most of the important political positions was weakening. However, the highest office in the land, the presidency, remained their exclusive domain until the 1960 election of John F. Kennedy, a third-generation Irish Catholic. After 1960, religious affiliation lost much of its meaning in the political process. For example, when William Miller was nominated as the vice-presidential candidate by the Republicans in 1964, almost no mention was made of the fact that he too was Irish Catholic.

The period since the end of World War II has marked the coming of age of white immigrants, politically speaking. This growth in strength was not limited to the Democratic party. As an ethnic group moves up the social and economic ladder, it sometimes becomes more Republican. The elections of the 1980s saw a majority of the ethnic votes go to Ronald Reagan and George Bush. Only the Blacks remain overwhelmingly committed to the Democratic party. Among Americans of European ancestry, the era of ethnic bloc voting has apparently come to an end.

Black Americans have gradually gained political power, particularly in places where they are the majority. It is only very recently that Black politicians have been elected to high office in areas where Blacks do not predominate. The 1989 elections of L. Douglas Wilder as governor of the Commonwealth of Virginia, and David Dinkins as mayor of New York City may indicate that Black Americans are coming of age politically.

The newest Latino and Asian immigrants have not as yet come of age, politically speaking, though their influence is felt in some areas of the nation. As their share of the population increases, that influence should grow. However, numbers of people must be translated into citizens who must register and who, in turn, must actually vote, if an ethnic group is to wield any political clout.

Over half of all foreign-born residents counted in the 1980 census were naturalized citizens, but only 29 percent of Latin Americans and 23 percent of the Mexican-born were naturalized. Few Mexicans become naturalized when they become eligible. The average rate of naturalization is one-tenth that of other immigrants' naturalization rates, and this pattern has hardly changed in recent years.

According to Census Bureau figures, 57 percent of all voting age citizens indicated they had voted in the 1988 election — the lowest figure ever recorded by that agency. Only 52 percent of Blacks said they had voted. Among Latinos 29 percent indicated doing so. The Anglo turnout was 59 percent. These surveys invariably yield higher proportions who said they voted than actually did so. Thus, the voter turnout among Latinos, in particular, was probably closer to 25 percent.[9]

The Latino population is not exhibiting a proportional share in voting prowess. However, once Latinos do register to vote, they are nearly as likely to do so as other Americans. It is estimated that 60 percent of registered Latinos voted in the 1988 presidential election.

The Latino concentration in just a few states automatically increases their political muscle. In 1980, the six states with the largest Latino populations — California, Texas, New York, Florida, Illinois, and New Jersey — accounted for 173 of the 270 electoral votes needed to win a presidential election. Given the changes in population distribution since 1980, together these states will account for 181 electoral votes in the 1992 election.

But even in these states the large proportion of Latinos who are not citizens has diluted their potential political strength. In 1986 about 43 percent of all voting-age Latinos in Florida were not citizens. According to one estimate, more than half of California's Latinos were not citizens in 1986. Latinos constituted 19 percent of all California adults, but only 11 percent of the state's citizens in 1986.[10]

The growth of the Latino population in the United States is not being ignored by the major political parties. Bloc voting may be a thing of the past among European-ancestry ethnic groups but both parties would like to claim a substantial share of the Latino vote. A majority of Latinos identify with the Democratic party; less than 10 percent identify themselves as Republicans and about 20 percent as Independents.[11] However, Latinos increasingly support candidates on the basis of issues and personality rather than party affiliation like most other citizens. For example, in 1980 Ronald Reagan received 25 percent of the Latino vote. In 1988, George Bush received about 30 percent of that vote.

Latinos are a diverse group. While Puerto Ricans and Mexicans are likely to vote Democratic, Cubans are likely to vote Republican. According to Univision, a Spanish-language TV network, Cuban-Americans make up 53 percent of all registered Republicans in the Miami area, and 8 percent of Florida's total Republican voters. However, in Texas, Latinos, mostly Mexican-American, account for about 25 percent of the Democratic vote. An estimated 75 percent of Latino Texans voted for the Democratic presidential candidate in 1988.[12]

The local and state impact of Latino votes can thus be of considerable importance. Miami has a Cuban-American mayor who defeated the former mayor who was of Puerto Rican origin. In 1986, Florida elected its first governor of Latino background, Robert Martinez. The closeness of this political race suggests that were it not for "bloc voting" by the Cuban community, Martinez would not have been elected.

The nation now has a number of Latino elected officials. Both New Mexico and Arizona have had Latino governors. In addition to Miami, San Antonio, Denver, and 15 other cities with populations exceeding 30,000 have or have had Latino mayors. Of the 535 members of Congress, 11 are Latino, all in the House of Representatives and all but one (from Miami) Democrats.

Asians present a vastly different political picture. The diversity among Asians is enormous; there is no common language nor are all Asians of the same racial background. Furthermore, such a large proportion of Asian immigration is so recent as to preclude any insights as to their political leaning and participation. A substantial majority of Asians living in the United States are not citizens yet.

Among the earlier immigrants from China, Japan, and the Philippines, interest in politics has not been very strong. The Chinese and Japanese were barred from becoming citizens for many years. The internment of Japanese-Americans in concentration camps during World War II further postponed any political activity by that group. Although surveys are few, some evidence suggests that Asians vote less frequently that Whites or Blacks. A 1986 study of southern California voters showed that only 30 percent of eligible Asian voters registered, compared to 80 percent of Whites.[13]

There is no indication of any strong loyalty to either political party on the part of Asians. Few have held high political offices. California was represented by Republican Senator S.I. Hayakawa for six years and there are two Japanese-American members in the House of Representatives from California. In addition, the secretary of state in California, from 1987 to 1991, was of Chinese ancestry. In Hawaii, Senator Inouye is of Japanese background as is Congresswoman Mink. Senator Akaka is Hawaiian.

Although there is yet little evidence of political activities on the part of Asians, their geographical concentration suggests that their participation could prove important in the future. Asians are clustered in just a few states. At the 1980 census, nearly 59 percent lived in California, Hawaii, and New York, and only four other states had 100,000 or more: Illinois, Texas, New Jersey, and Washington. Except for Asian Indians, California has the highest proportion among the six largest Asian American groups, especially Filipinos (46 percent) and Chinese (40 percent).[14] These data are based on the 1980 census. Massive shifts have occurred since then.

Given the history of ethnic political power, the next phase in that process may well concentrate on various Asian ethnic groups in particular sections of the country. With rapidly growing numbers, with a fairly well educated population, one would expect increased political participation on the part of these newest immigrants; one would also expect increased recruitment efforts on the part of the major political parties.

The remarkable shifts taking place in the composition of the population of the United States are bound to have momentous impact on the political structure of the nation. If Latinos increase their voting participation, if Asians become more involved in the political process, if Blacks continue to gain political power, the nation will witness a remarkable revolution in its governance. Within a few decades the newest Americans, as well as Blacks, will undoubtedly play an increasingly important role in American politics.

Even if voting participation does not increase among certain groups, their sheer numbers will influence the political process. California, Texas, and Florida are expected to continue growing rapidly over the next few decades. To a great extent, this growth will come from immigration. After the reapportionment following the 2000 census, these three states are expected to gain 7 seats over their 1992 level in the U.S. House of Representatives. Some of these new seats will undoubtedly be held by members of the newer minorities.

Earlier, it was argued that pluralistic assimilation is the ideal mode of cultural adaptation for an increasingly diverse nation. It is in the democratic political process that pluralistic assimilation can develop. However, pluralism should not be exaggerated while assimilation is minimized. If future candidates for political office campaign as "ethnics" or as "minorities," that could bring about a resurgence of ethnic bloc voting and all that implies. If pluralistic assimilation is to be successful, the "assimilation" must be emphasized rather than the "pluralistic."

The newest citizens can contribute a great deal to the nation's polity. But the nation must remain a community of Americans, pluralistic in ethnic composition, but unified in maintaining and improving its democratic political system. The 1988 political candidacy of Michael Dukakis marked the true coming of age of the so-called "ethnic Americans." The campaign of Jesse Jackson in 1988 was perhaps a harbinger of the future when individuals of every race and creed will feel they can be elected president of the United States. Only then will all Americans have come of age politically.

RELIGIOUS INSTITUTIONS

A recent study predicts that if current demographic trends continue, the nation's Muslim population will be larger than the Jewish population "possibly by 2000, definitely by 2015."[15] According to demographer John Weeks, "it is probably reasonable to assume that, as of 1988, the Moslem population of the United States was somewhere between 1.5 and 6 million."[16] The Islamic Renaissance Center estimates that there are between 6 and 7 million Islamics in the United States, including many Blacks.[17]

The decennial census has never inquired into residents' religious affiliation. Therein lies the quandary for anyone attempting to determine the religious composition of the United States population. The only available statistics come from surveys taken by private organizations such as religious bodies. Yet the role of religion in American life must be examined, as it has been and will continue to be an important part of the cultural adaptation process of the American people.

Religion and ethnicity are closely related. In some instances they are inseparable. For example, we often speak of Anglo-Saxon Protestants, Irish Catholics, Russian Jews and Greek Orthodox. Most Latinos are Catholic; most Blacks are Protestant. Filipinos are overwhelmingly Catholic, while most other Asians belong to various Eastern religions such as Buddhism, Hinduism and Confucianism. These relationships between religion and ethnicity reflect the fact that many of the nations from which immigrants came have one predominant religion.

The relation between religion and ethnicity is so strong that a "triple melting pot" analogy was used to describe the assimilation process that took place earlier in this century among majority Americans.[18] At that time it was found that while inter-ethnic marriage was increasing, few people were marrying outside their faiths. By 1950, some social observers felt that religious affiliation had become more important than ethnicity as a means of self-identification on the part of many White Americans. With increasing intermarriage, ethnic identity was losing some of its meaning; for many, religious identity replaced ethnicity.

Today, Protestants comprise about 65 percent of the nation's population; Catholics 25 percent; Jews a little less than 2 percent; Moslems, probably about the same. The remaining 6 percent are either members of other religious bodies or do not adhere to any religion. Catholics are by far the largest single Christian denomination (53 million) with Baptists second (28 million), and Methodists third (14 million). If the middle range estimates of the Muslim population in the United States referred to earlier are accurate, they outnumber both the Episcopalians and the Unitarians.

Changes in immigration patterns will affect these proportions in future years. Differences in fertility by religion among Americans are not great. The variations between Protestants and Catholics disappeared long ago. Jews have slightly lower fertility than other Americans, while Mormons and Muslims have higher fertility. Life expectancy variations among these groups are insignificant. However, differences are significant in immigration patterns. Religious conversions must also be considered.

The two largest sources of immigration to the United States are Mexico and the Philippines. Both are overwhelmingly Catholic and both exhibit relatively high fertility. Of the 12 leading countries of origin over the 1980s, 5 are predominantly Catholic (Mexico, the Philippines, Dominican Republic, Cuba, and Haiti). One is more likely to be Protestant (Jamaica). Four (Korea, China, India, Vietnam) are home to various eastern religions though a substantial minority of Koreans and Vietnamese are either Protestant or Catholic. The twelfth largest source of immigrants is Iran — a Muslim nation. If immigration from Europe picks up because of the 1990 immigration legislation, many of these newcomers may also be Catholic.

In future years, Protestants should increase in number but decline proportionately. Jews may decline in number as well as in shares. Catholics should grow considerably, numerically and proportionately. The possibility that Muslims could surpass Jews fairly soon is real. Finally, rapid growth should occur among Buddhists and Hindus, particularly in California and New York. By the middle of the next century Protestants could comprise only half of the American population, Catholics about one-third, Muslims and other eastern religions as much as 7 or 8 percent, and Jews less than 2 percent.

The impact on the society of such shifts in religious affiliation is difficult to ascertain. Catholics may become the majority in states like California,

Texas and New York. Will the tenets of that church on such social issues as contraception and abortion be reflected by these population shifts? Will anti-abortion movements, for example, gain strength in such important states? It is difficult to answer such questions given that the composition of the Catholic population itself should change dramatically in the future.

By the year 2000, almost 30 percent of the approximately 80 million American Catholics may be Latino and Latinos may well comprise 40 percent of all American Catholics by the middle of the next century. If we add Filipinos, Haitians, some Vietnamese, as well as perhaps 2 million Blacks, Catholic America may someday be comprised of many minorities, with no single majority. In that sense, American Catholics mirror the nation in diversity. As the American Catholic church becomes increasingly heterogeneous, more demands can be expected from these new minority groups. Some 50 million Catholics will be added over the next half century. Given the continued decline in the numbers of priests, the question of who will minister to these people of such varied backgrounds becomes crucial. Thus, attitudes of twenty-first-century Catholics may vary from those of today.

Conversions to and within Protestantism seem concentrated in the more fundamentalist denominations. These sects are gaining converts at the expense of the mainstream denominations. Will this affect American attitudes on social issues? Finally, the growth in eastern religions should not be minimized. In some parts of the nation, their share could increase considerably. American culture may be influenced by shifts in religious concentrations in a way not even conceived of a few decades ago.

HEALTH INSTITUTIONS

The nation is becoming more diverse; the nation is getting older. Demographic behavior, past and present, is guaranteeing these imminent changes. And these changes are causing strains in the American health care system, a system which has never been either efficient or satisfactory.

Public health, as an American social institution, is affected by two separate demographic trends. One is the increase in the size and life expectancy of the population 65 and over. The other is the increasing proportion of the mother-and-child group that are minorities.

Today, about 30 million Americans are 65 or older. Another 2 million will be added over this decade. At mid-century the number could surpass 75 million. While the total population of the United States should grow by 52 percent over the next 60 years, the elderly population could grow by 142 percent!

With more dramatic improvements in life expectancy, the number of elderly would be even larger. Should life expectancy gradually increase to 88 years by 2080 (about 85 in 2050) individuals 65 and over could number 90 million by 2050.

The share of the elderly who are over 75 is increasing. Today, 43 percent of the elderly are 75 and over. That share will grow to close to half by 2050. The number of "old-old" (75 and over) could increase from 13 million today to 19 million in 2020 and 37 million in 2050. If gains in life expectancy are greater than expected, that share could be as high as 60 percent and the number could exceed 50 million!

Elderly Americans are overwhelmingly of European ancestry. This is particularly true of the "old-old." The enormity of the baby boom assures its continued majority status. Once the baby boom generation begins to die out around 2040, the Anglo share of the elderly population will fall to perhaps 70 percent. It will remain the most "European" of all age groups.

The sheer size and increased age of the elderly population will pose serious challenges for the health services of the nation. The high cost of health care, particularly for the elderly, is a matter of serious concern. The emphasis on tertiary services means that costs can be expected to remain high for some time. Medicare pays only for immunizations against pneumonia and hepatitis B; it does not pay for any other primary prevention and covers only a narrow range of secondary services. Pressure is mounting for a reevaluation of the system to include more preventive measures. These pressures will be exacerbated by the growth among the very old who are more likely to be institutionalized and to require long-term care.

Most elderly people live in households with their spouses. However, with increasing age and the death of one of the marriage partners, such living arrangements are less frequent and institutionalization increases. Today, about 12 percent of Americans 75 and over live in institutions compared to only 2 percent of those between 65 and 74. The demand for institutionalized housing of some sort is bound to increase in future years.

The older people want to live even longer and see health care as the way to do it. This means treatment of chronic disease and this can be very expensive. Medicare was established to help pay for such services. Costs have skyrocketed. The United States now spends nearly 12 percent of its GNP on health care and over one-third of that goes to the elderly.

Then there is the other demographic shift affecting the ethnic distribution of mothers and their children. Over the past two decades an enormous increase has occurred in the proportion of mothers and children living below the poverty line. These people rely on public programs for health care.

The United States has consistently had a higher infant mortality rate (IMR) than most other developed nations. The American rate has fallen significantly since 1900 when it stood at 100 infant deaths per 1000 births. However, the IMR has fallen even more rapidly in other developed nations. In 1968 Lyndon Johnson noted the "shocking fact that, in saving the lives of babies, America ranks 15th among the nations of the world."[19]   By 1990, 17 nations had infant mortality rates lower than the United States.

Considerable variation in IMR is noted by ethnic groups. Babies are more apt to die if their mothers are younger than 20 or older than 34, Black or Latino, unmarried, or poorly educated.[20]   The share of all births to unmarried women is climbing and minorities are increasing their proportion of all births. In 1970, over 80 percent of all births were to Anglo women; by 1980 that share had fallen to 71 percent. Today, only about two-thirds of all births are to majority women. By the turn of the century, births to Anglo women will comprise less than half of all the births in the United States. Unless major improvements occur fairly soon, the IMR might climb as the share of single and minority mothers increases. It is thus critically important that infant deaths be reduced as quickly as possible.

At least three kinds of health services can reduce infant deaths, and all fall into the category of "primary prevention," the very category least likely to be covered by today's health insurance packages. One is prenatal care. It has been estimated that every dollar spent on prenatal care targeted at low-income poorly educated women could save $338 during the first year of an infant's life and perhaps as much as $400,000 during its lifetime.[21]   Child health services can also reduce infant mortality. An estimated one in ten infant deaths are from causes that could have been prevented by child health services.   Finally, family planning programs and abortion reduce infant mortality by enabling women to avoid unwanted childbearing. Unfortunately, the United States health care system is not organized to finance these services.

As a consequence of these two divergent demographic shifts — that is, a rapidly growing senior population and a rapidly diversifying mother-and-child group — there is conflict over health-related spending priorities. Two vastly different segments of the population are both depending on the government to guarantee access to care. One is young and increasingly minority. It needs basic primary health care which is relatively inexpensive. The other is older and overwhelmingly Anglo. It needs tertiary medical and surgical services to remain alive and enjoy a reasonable quality of life.

The conflict is political because pressure is coming from both sides. The elderly are a much more powerful lobby because they vote more regularly than any other group in the nation. But concern is being expressed about the relatively high IMR among minority Americans. High national priority should be assigned to the goal of seeing to it that infant deaths decline and that every newborn has an equal chance to survive to adulthood.

The increasing diversity and age of the nation's people do not augur well for its health facilities or its overall well-being. The nation can plan for its future age-related problems. The nation can also do something about its immigration-related health problems by imposing limits on the level of immigration and establishing more selective standards for these newcomers.

There is still time, though it will be financially and politically expensive. However, does the nation have the will to implement them?

CONCLUSION

The challenges of racial and age shifts will be many. Yet, they are inevitable. Rather than resist these changes, the American public should plan and prepare for them and be enthusiastic about the future. Twenty-first-century America can be a model for the rest of the world. But the words of Gunnar Myrdal continue to haunt the nation. Humankind does need the optimism of America, but "empty declarations deepen cynicism." If the United States can demonstrate to the world that minorities of all races can be assimilated, structurally as well as culturally, while maintaining their identity, all humankind will indeed "be given faith again." It is up to the American people to decide what path to follow: America is free to choose whether minorities will be her liability or her opportunity.

NOTES

1. Gunnar Myrdal, *An American Dilemma: The Negro Problem and Modern Democracy* (New York: Harper and Row, 1944), 1021-22.

2. "What Japan Thinks of Us," *Newsweek*, 2 April 1990, 24.

3. "Duke Shows His True Colors," *Newsweek*, 25 December 1989, 12.

4. Philip Waltzer, "Blacks told to prepare to be majority," *The Virginian-Pilot*, 9 February 1990, D3.

5. William A. Henry, III, "Beyond the Melting Pot," *Time*, 9 April 1990, 28-31.

6. Wattenberg, *The Birth Dearth*, 182-186.

7. John Naisbitt and Patricia Aburdene, *Megatrends 2000: Ten New Directions for the 1990s* (New York: William Morrow, 1990), 178.

8. Henry, "Beyond the Melting Pot," 29.

9. Peter Skerry, "Borders and Quotas: Immigrants and the Affirmative Action State," *The Public Interest* 96 (Summer 1989): 94-97.

10. Rafael Valdivieso and Cary Davis, "U.S. Hispanics: Challenging Issues for the 1990s," *Population Trends and Public Policy* (December 1988): 12.

11. Henry Santiestevan and Stina Santiestevan, eds., *The Hispanic Almanac* (Washington: Hispanic Policy Development Project, 1984), 150.

12. Valdivieso and Davis, "U.S. Hispanics," 13.

13. Howard G. Chua-Eoan, "Strangers in Paradise," *Time*, 9 April 1990, 35.

14. Robert W. Gardner, et al., "Asian-Americans: Growth, Change, and Diversity," *Population Bulletin* 40, no. 4 (1985): 11.

15. Yvonne Y. Haddad, "A Century of Islam in America," *The Muslim World Today* (Washington: American Institute of Islamic Affairs, 1986), Occasional Paper No. 4.

16. John R. Weeks, "Demography of Islamic Nations," *Population Bulletin* 23, no. 4 (1988): 4.

17. Patrick J. Buchanan, "Islam's Global Resurgence," *The Virginian-Pilot*, 21 August 1989, 8.

18. Ruby Reeves Kennedy, "Single or Triple Melting Pot: Intermarriage in New Haven," *American Journal of Sociology* (1952): 55-66.

19. National Commission on Infant Mortality, *Death before Life* (Washington, 1988), 1.

20. Christianne Hale, "Infant Mortality in America," *Population Trends and Public Policy* 18 (August 1990).

21. Ibid.

9

Education in a
Heterogeneous Society

In tomorrow's knowledge-based and global economy, educated and skilled people will be the nation's most important asset. Trained and motivated people can develop the technologies and institutions needed to solve problems at home and to compete abroad. The recent economic development of countries such as Germany and Japan attest to the fact that people have become more important than natural resources to assure high incomes for residents and power and respect on the world stage.

The U.S. educational system has a mixed record: on the one hand, the U.S. population has relatively high levels of schooling compared to other industrial countries, but much of this schooling appears to be of poor quality as students elsewhere outscore U.S. students in standardized achievement tests in technology-oriented fields such as mathematics. Furthermore, U.S. education is not broadly distributed: the nation's best students are competitive with students anywhere, and their success contributes to our widely-admired system of higher education. However, almost one-third of all high school students fail to graduate, and many high school graduates lack the basic skills needed to fill even entry-level jobs.

An educational system which fails one-third of its students spells danger for the society. Furthermore, school success and failure has a racial and ethnic dimension. By 2020, over one-third of the school-aged U.S. children will be Latino or Black, the ethnic groups which are faring worst on average in today's educational system. If the educational achievement of all children is not improved, the United States faces the prospect of uneven educational progress which limits American economic competitiveness and increases inequality and social tensions at home.

POPULATION TRENDS AND THE EDUCATION SYSTEM

Numerous commissions have examined the American educational system, concluded that it is performing unevenly, and called for reform. Despite a wave of such reforms during the 1980s, the problems of the educational system were believed to be so severe that now-president Bush chose to campaign in 1988 with a pledge to become the "education president." In 1989, Bush convened only the third national summit of governors in this century to deal with the "crisis in American education," and early in 1990, the President and the Governors agreed on education goals for the year 2000 which include raising the high school graduation rate from 71 to 90 percent, making U.S. students once again number one in science and math achievement, and making all adults literate. Education is the major responsibility of state governments, and one governor has noted that "better schools is perhaps the major domestic issue today."[1]

The problems of the educational system are well-known. Not enough students stay in school, and while in school too many fail to learn. The call for educational reform is rooted in self-interest and democracy: President Bush called for reforms to "raise the level of learning in the classrooms of America" so as to keep the United States competitive economically.[2] The educational system must improve the quality and the distribution of schooling and training to promote a healthy democracy, which requires "equal opportunity for all our children and preservation of an informed population capable of self-government — a citizenry with a shared sense of democracy and a vision of our potential as a nation."[3]

Reforming the educational system will be made difficult in the years ahead because of the growth and diversity of the school-age population. Although the *proportion* of the population under age 25 will drop in future years as the nation ages, the *number* of children and young adults will actually increase. The population aged 3-24 is about 82 million today. If current trends continue, the 3-24 age groups would increase to 87 million by 2000, approach 100 million in 2020, and reach 110 million in 2050. About two out of every three Americans between the ages of 3 and 24 are enrolled in school, or about 56 million students. This number is projected to increase to 61 million by 2000, 66 million by 2020, and 73 million by 2050. About 85 percent of these students will be in either elementary or secondary schools.

Different proportions of various racial and ethnic groups are enrolled in school. School enrollment rates are highest among Asians (77 percent) and lowest among Latinos (66 percent). Among Anglo and Black children and youth, 69 percent of the 3-24 year-olds are in school.

Ethnic differences in enrollment are particularly marked at the youngest and oldest ages. For those aged 3 through 6, 65 percent of Asian children are enrolled in school, compared to 55 percent for Latino children. Anglo and

Black rates are between these extremes. A similar pattern emerges among persons aged 18 to 21 — presumably youth attending college. About 62 percent of Asians in this age group are enrolled in school, but only 39 percent of Latinos are enrolled, with the other two ethnic groups falling between these extremes. The well-known tendency for persons of Asian background to remain in school is reflected in these data. For example, among persons 22 to 25, 36 percent of Asians are in school, compared to only 17 percent for Anglos, 16 percent for Blacks, and 15 percent for Latinos.

The assumption that enrollment rates will remain constant in future years may be unduly pessimistic. Yet it is important to project the effects of current enrollment rates of an increasingly diverse student population. Ethnic shifts in school enrollment could be substantial in future years. Anglo enrollments are projected to remain constant during the 1990s, and then begin a long-term decline. By 2020, the number of Anglo students might decrease by 3 million from 1990, and their share of the growing total enrollment could fall from 71 percent today to 56 percent in 2020 and 47 percent by 2050. Black enrollments should increase in future years, but the Black student share of all students will remain at about 14 percent.

Between 1990 and 2020, Latino enrollments are expected to more than double — from 6 million to over 13 million, and their share of all students should almost double from 11 to 20 percent. By 2050, 27 percent of all American students would be of Latino origin. Similarly, Asian enrollments will more than double over the next three decades and could surpass 9.2 million by 2050.

Growth and diversity pose significant challenges for the nation's educational system. While the United States continues to produce some outstanding high school graduates, there are substantial differences in college entrance scores among the various ethnic groups. Anglos score considerably higher than other groups on the verbal section of the Scholastic Aptitude Test, while Asians do particularly well in mathematics. Black and Latino students score below average on both sections of the test.[4] As the ethnic proportions of potential college students change, these differences in test scores foreshadow a troubling picture in which educational tracking by ability could become educational tracking by ethnic group.

There is virtually unanimous agreement that the educational system should be improved. The National Academy of Sciences notes that "Business leaders want high school graduates who have a command of English, have reasoning and problem-solving skills, are able to read, write, and compute, and have an understanding of science and technology."[5] But the National Commission on Excellence in Education declares: "For the first time in the history of our country, the educational skills of one generation will not surpass, will not equal, will not even approach those of their parents."[6]

THE EDUCATION CHALLENGE

Tomorrow's jobs will require workers who have more skills and knowledge than today's workforce. The nation's schools must prepare the more diverse students of tomorrow to be productive workers. Schools face an enormous challenge, which becomes clearer when trends in academic achievement, student attrition, replenishment of teachers, and cultural diversity are examined. These are the four major issues that the nation's educational institutions must address.

There is widespread agreement that the schools are failing to graduate a significant proportion of students and failing to educate a significant proportion of graduates even for entry-level jobs. Whether measured by skills assessment tests or by employer complaints, many high school leavers cannot read or reason well enough to function effectively even in an entry-level job without additional training. Unprepared workers cost money. The Committee on Economic Development estimates that each year's high school dropouts cost the United States $240 billion in lost productivity and taxes during their lifetimes.[7]

Much of the impetus for educational reforms in the 1980s came from business leaders who complained that high school dropouts and graduates could not fill entry-level jobs. Examples of half or more of the job applicants for entry-level jobs being unable to read well enough to be mail clerks,[8] or unable to add and subtract well enough to be bank tellers,[9] made many business leaders advocates of educational reform. Business interest in the quality of education is not simply altruism. If the schools do not prepare students for jobs, then business must pay to train and retrain them. Some business leaders believe that the 1980s will be remembered for the structural and attitude changes among management and workers which improved product quality, and the 1990s will be remembered for the efforts made to improve the quality of the workforce.

The 1980s unleashed a variety of educational reforms to cope with the educational challenges of attrition, achievement, teachers, and culture. It is not yet clear whether these reforms are working to prepare more students for tomorrow's economy.

ATTRITION

The 1980s educational reforms have not yet reduced school dropout rates. Reliable attrition or dropout data are not available because school enrollment data cannot determine whether students who begin the ninth and tenth grade but do not graduate have moved to another state or left the United States, switched to a private school, or are no longer in school. What is known is that

20 to 40 percent of the students who begin ninth grade in a typical school do not graduate four years later, meaning that 3,800 U.S. teenagers drop out of high school every day, and that this dropout rate is highest for Blacks and Latinos.[10] The Black dropout rate fell during the 1970s from about one-fourth of all Blacks 16 to 24 to one-sixth of this group, but the dropout rate for Latinos has remained at about one-third during the 1970s and 1980s. In the largest cities, 40 to 50 percent of the high school students drop out before graduation.

The minority students who drop out of inner city schools can see the downtown skyscrapers which house big business employers, but they cannot hope to work there except as janitors or messengers. Unless dropout rates decrease during the 1990s the growing proportion of students most prone to drop out of high school ensures a lower proportion of high school graduates than today.

ACHIEVEMENT

Attrition is linked closely to the second educational challenge, achievement. High dropout rates for fast-growing minority groups, in conjunction with the below average academic achievements of many of those who do graduate from high school, mean that the average educational level of the entry-level workforce might be falling instead of rising as the United States approaches the twenty-first century. In other words, when achievement and dropout rates are combined with demographic trends, the result is a potentially explosive decrease in educational attainment, especially in cities with large numbers of Blacks and Latinos.

Trends in achievement test scores, and international comparisons of American and European or Asian students in knowledge of subjects such as mathematics or science, indicate that foreign youth often know more than American youth.[11] Some improvements in proficiency have been noted for the most disadvantaged students in the 1970s and 1980s, but these students began with too little knowledge for many jobs and they must learn more still to be employed without additional training.

Like drop-out rates, achievement varies by ethnic group. Anglos and Asians tend to score better on achievement tests than Blacks and Latinos. For example, in 1988 almost 90 percent of the 17-year-old whites performed at an "intermediate" level on reading proficiency tests, versus three-fourths of the Latinos and Blacks.[12] Asians score particularly high on standardized tests.

How can attrition be reduced and achievement raised in the 1990s? The issue of working high school students illustrates how hard it may be to enact meaningful educational reforms in an economy which has become accustomed to plenty of unskilled workers and is slow to adjust to demographic changes. In Japan, school is considered so important that high school students do not even consider working, but in the United States, an estimated half of the 11th graders and two-thirds of the 12th graders have part-time jobs.[13] There are no restrictions on the number of hours U.S. students who are 16 and 17 may work, and the United States has by far the highest proportion of working students among industrial countries. The demand for minimum wage workers in service industries such as fast food restaurants led the 1989 National Teacher of the Year to complain that too many high school students fit school into their work schedules instead of fitting work into their school schedules.[14]

Both older and younger teenagers are working more, and employers turning to 14- and 15-year-old workers have contributed to a doubling of child labor law violations discovered by the U.S. Department of Labor between 1985 and 1988. The drift toward working teenagers in the 1980s is due to lower unemployment, the need for additional income in poor families, and social trends which often favor consumption today instead of investment for tomorrow.

REPLENISHMENT OF TEACHERS

Changing the attitudes of students and employers is not the only challenge; there is also a teacher challenge. The United States has about 2.5 million teachers who earned an average $30,000 in 1988-1989. About two-thirds of these teachers are women, and almost 90 percent are white.[15] By some estimates, up to half of these teachers will retire or leave teaching for another occupation in the 1990s. This wave of exits from teaching should provide an opportunity for the ethnic make-up of the nation's teachers to become more similar to the ethnic composition of the students. Although "there is no conclusive evidence that minority teachers can teach minority students any more successfully than non-minority teachers,"[16] students in the multiracial U.S. society would benefit by early exposure to role models from a variety of racial and ethnic backgrounds.

Teachers may have to be given more autonomy to make decisions on how best to deal with more diverse students. An article about the Los Angeles school district was titled "Failing in 81 Languages" to emphasize the problems involved in hiring teachers for a school district in which the majority of students come from families in which a language other than English is spoken at home.[17] Teachers in such situations must often do more than teach English or history; they must also deal with very uneven educational and personal backgrounds. Some Asian students come from cultures which stress education, some Latino students are refugees from Central America who have never read books in any language and do not know how to use toilet facilities, forcing teachers to also become familiar with public health issues.[18]

The best way to teach increasingly diverse students has not been resolved, but there has been a demand for teachers from the same ethnic group as the students. Latino and Asian teachers are wanted both to be role models for students and to provide bilingual education. There are simply not enough teachers from each ethnic group certified to teach the diverse students who are making urban school districts modern-day Towers of Babel. This shortage of bilingual teachers has had an ironic side effect: the immigration which produced a more diverse student body is now encouraging school districts to seek Spanish and Farsi-speaking teachers abroad, so that attempts to serve immigrant children beget more immigration.

CULTURAL DIVERSITY

Minority teachers and bilingual education are closely linked to the fourth challenge: the cultural values that should be taught. In the past, schools played an assimilation role, transforming the children of immigrants from many lands into Americans within one or two generations. Today, Americans are less sure about what cultural values should be taught, and this confusion is reflected in debates over the role of the English language in American society and whether an emphasis on western civilization is ethnocentric. These cultural issues affect the schools, but cannot be resolved by them.

Schools have traditionally been the central institution behind the melting pot; diverse immigrant children entered, and Americans emerged. With the recent emphasis on cultural pluralism, the United States has become hesitant about the need for a single culture, and this uncertainty has contributed to confusion in the schools.

Public schools open without charge to all students have been a traditional hallmark of America's commitment to equal opportunity. During the 1980s, educational challenges which ranged from rising academic achievement to reducing dropout rates were identified, and widely-supported efforts to reform the schools were enacted in most states. Many of these reforms have not yet borne fruit; the educational challenge is to make these reforms effective before demographic trends compound them.

IMMIGRATION AND THE EDUCATION CHALLENGE

How will the educational challenges of achievement, attrition, teachers, and culture be affected by immigration policy? What benefits will the United States reap if it meets these challenges? What risks does it face if current immigration trends continue?

Educated, healthy, and motivated people are the nation's most important asset. Measuring the knowledge, health, and motivation of new workers is difficult because our measuring systems are inadequate. Knowledge, for example, is not the same as years of schooling; much learning takes place in the family, and without a supportive family, more years of education may not increase a young worker's knowledge.

The wealth of the United States depends on the number and the quality of its workers. In agricultural and industrial societies, increasing the quantity of labor often generates more economic output, since more people can farm new lands or staff the assembly line around the clock. However, in tomorrow's post-industrial society, workforce "quality" will surpass workforce quantity as the critical determinant of economic competitiveness.

The term "human capital" describes the skills that each individual brings to the work place. Human capital may be the ability to read blueprints, to repair equipment, or to operate a computer; in each instance, the skills of workers make people valuable to a business and the economy, much as physical capital such as a machine to make tires is valuable to a business and the economy. Of all the individual traits a person brings to the labor market, more years of education is the best predictor of more income, a higher status job, and more stable employment.[19]

Education is an investment in the sense that students normally do not hold full-time jobs while they go to school; in other words, students and society sacrifice some earnings and some work today in exchange for a future payoff of higher paid and more productive work.

During the Industrial Revolution, most societies promoted investment in physical capital or machines in order to foster economic growth. Today, society gets higher returns from investments in people than from investments in machinery, so that "investment in population quality and in knowledge in large part determine the future prospects of mankind."[20]

Unskilled immigrants, by definition, have little human capital. They enter the United States and fill jobs today which may be eliminated by technology or international competition tomorrow. But the effects of unskilled immigrants do not end with their own impacts on the labor market and economy; their children are an important part of tomorrow's workforce. In the past, the United States confidently predicted, albeit somewhat optimistically, that the school system could equalize differences in parental occupation and income, so that sons and daughters of both immigrant and native parents had equal chances for economic success. Schools no longer play this equalizing role with today's immigrant children.

The educational bridge between a childhood of learning and an adult work life has become the best single predictor of economic success and an indicator of the United States' potential for economic growth. Both immigrant and native-born parents realize that education is critical to their children's success.

However, complaints about the quality of the U.S. educational system are legion. A review of business programs promising jobs to high school graduates in New York City noted that many such programs failed because "not enough [job] applicants, high school graduates, passed the equivalent of an 8th grade math test."[21]

An educational system unable to cope with the problems of native-born children may be overwhelmed by the challenge of also educating the children of immigrants. If schools continue to produce frustration rather than skills for the many who drop out before finishing high school, the mismatch between workers and skills, noted in an earlier chapter, will worsen. If an influx of immigrant children slows education reforms, the inequalities that begin with poor parents may be magnified rather than narrowed in the schools. In this case, the United States may begin to import Third World characteristics along with Third World immigrants.

An examination of post-secondary schooling is also troubling. The good news is that the number of Americans 25 or older with at least a bachelor's degree has been rising. In 1910, only 2 percent of adult Americans had at least a college degree; in 1970, it was 11 percent, and by 1985, over 20 percent. But recent studies indicate that fewer Americans are completing college degrees within 4 or 5 years and that the "quality" of their degrees may have declined. A study of the high school class of 1972 is instructive.[22] First, only about 75 percent of the potential college class of 1976 actually graduated from high school, so the potential class of 100 was only 75, and only 50 attended a college or vocational school before their 30th birthday. Of the 50 who enrolled in post-secondary education, only 25 got a degree or certificate, so that only one-fourth of the high school class of 1972 earned formal recognition for post-secondary education by 1984.

Immigrants tend to be at the extremes of the education ladder. In 1980, for example, 24 percent of the immigrants but only 16 percent of native-born persons had four or more years of college. At the other end of the schooling distribution, foreign-born persons in the United States were more likely than native-born persons to have less than a high school education. Almost one-third of the foreign-born persons who entered the United States between 1975 and 1980 had less than eight years of schooling, almost twice the percentage of native-born persons with so little schooling. Furthermore, more than one-third of the foreign-born persons who entered the United States between 1980 and 1990 are likely to have less than eight years of schooling because (1) many of the Central American and Asian refugees and asylees who entered during the decade had little education and because (2) most of the 3 million aliens who applied for legal status under IRCA have very little education.

There are important differences in immigrant years of schooling by country of origin. Generally, the more recent the history of immigration to the United States, and the more difficulties the immigrants face in coming to the United

States, the higher their educational attainments. For example, the relatively few immigrants from Africa tend to have more education and economic success in the United States than the many immigrants from Latin America. There are other sharp differences: between 1970 and 1974, 44 percent of the immigrants from Asian countries completed college, versus 2 percent of the Mexican immigrants.[23]

Entry into the United States becomes easier after "pioneer" scientists and scholars send for their less educated relatives. The second and third waves of Asian immigrants, for example, demonstrate the polarized nature of immigrant schooling. The proportion of immigrants from Asian countries who have completed college has been falling, although it remains higher than the U.S. native-born proportion, and the percentage of Asian immigrants who have not completed high school has risen and now exceeds the U.S. native-born proportion of high school dropouts.

CONCLUSION

The new entrants to the workforce in the year 2000 entered the third grade during the fall of 1990. Can the educational system be reformed in the 1990s so that these students acquire the skills needed to sustain and improve tomorrow's economy? Optimists note that the children of Asian immigrants often do very well in the U.S. educational system, while pessimists point to the high drop-out rates of Latinos and Blacks. Both optimists and pessimists agree that the educational system will need to change to forestall a growing gap between the economy's need for skilled workers and the declining capacity of entry-level workers to fill entry-level jobs.

It is clear that today's students and tomorrow's workers will continue to be an ethnic mosaic, but it is not clear how the educational system should be changed in order to better train them. There are two visions of the educational system which often compete for the limited resources available for reform. The excellence ethic stresses the need to build upon the best, to devote additional resources to the best and the brightest students of whatever race so that the United States can maintain its technological edge. The hospital or catch-up ethic, on the other hand, stresses the need to bolster support for remedial programs that improve the chances of disadvantaged children to find jobs. In an ideal world, there would be support for both excellence and catch-up, but limited budgets often force trade-offs between them.

The educational system is the most expensive tax-funded program in most states; on average, states spend $4,200 to educate each public elementary and secondary school student. New York, for example, spends almost $7,000 to educate each of its 2.5 million public school students, and California spends $4,000 on each of its 4.5 million students. Both school systems have substantial minority enrollments: in California, 51 percent of the public school students are minorities; and in New York, 38 percent are minorities. Both states face major drop-out challenges: in New York City and Los Angeles, half or more of the students drop out before high-school graduation.

Like most other states, California and New York enacted educational reforms in the 1980s to cope with the mismatch of employers asking for more skilled workers and more students coming from poor families and speaking limited English. Additional monies for education were raised by arguing that the state's economy would suffer if the state's employers were unable to find qualified workers. But the results have been very uneven: indeed, the educational systems in states experiencing rapid population growth and a changing ethnic mix of students may be getting worse, not better.

Educational reforms cost money. California, which now spends $18 billion annually, would have to increase its funding for schools substantially to put in place all of the educational reforms which have been suggested. Support for public education remains strong in California, as evidenced by the 1988 passage of Proposition 98, which guarantees California schools about 40 percent of the state budget each year. However, it is hard to increase school funding in a state such as California because the state's constitution has been interpreted to require equal support for each school; local school districts do not have the option of taxing themselves to improve local schools. This means that California schools must compete with health care, transportation, and other state-funded programs for limited tax dollars in a system which requires a large infusion of funds to make a difference at a local level.

The problem of finding enough money to make a difference in local California schools is mirrored at the national level. The United States has a decentralized educational system: states and sometimes individual school districts decide how many courses are needed to graduate from high school and how rigorous these courses should be. Since there are 16,000 U.S. school districts and 100,000 schools, the resulting variance in school standards allegedly encourages some inequality-increasing migration, as affluent parents buy housing in good school districts, and discourages some economically-rational migration, as when unemployed parents in the midwest are reluctant to move south because of inferior schools.

Local choice means uneven schooling outcomes, and school-to-school differences have prompted calls for a national curriculum. Advocates of nationwide school standards want uniform core academic standards, such as 4 years of English and 3 of mathematics, and testing to assess what students have learned. Assessing how well schools perform against each other in a national curriculum is controversial because it reverses a history of local control over education, but advocates of national standards argue that standards are the only way to measure educational progress in a world of diverse students and teaching methods.

Regardless of how parents shuffle between school districts in order to get the best education for their children, there is an emerging consensus that the United States faces a public investment deficit because it has reduced funds for developing human resources. Scrimping on such necessary public investments helps to explain, according to most economists, the fall in the nation's productivity and the slowdown in economic growth.

Immigration and demographic trends may limit the resources available just to maintain, let alone improve, the educational system in the future. Strong support for public education has traditionally been taken for granted in American politics, but that automatic support is eroding. There are many reasons why voters in many states are less inclined to support higher taxes for education. However, demographic trends also threaten more erosion of support for educational funding. The demographic cause of the decline in support for educational funding is the divergence between students and voters. Anglo students will become a minority of all students after 2030, but Anglos will remain a majority of the voting population even as their share of the population shrinks. As these voters grow older, they may be more inclined to use limited tax dollars for public safety and health care programs rather than for education.

The American tradition of public schools open to all without charge may be threatened by the frustration of reforming an ever more complex and ethnically diverse educational system. Public schools were the central integrating institutions for the melting pot as well as the education factory which produced America's workforce. Both of these traditional schooling functions are threatened by demographic changes.

NOTES

1. Carnegie Forum on Education and the Economy, Task Force on Teaching as a Profession, *A Nation Prepared: Teachers for the 21st Century* (Carnegie Forum on Education and the Economy, 1986), 10.

2. As cited in William Endicott, "Bush Calls Education Summit," *Sacramento Bee*, 1 August 1989, 12.

3. Ibid., 14.

4. Leon F. Bouvier and Philip Martin, *Population Change and California's Education System* (Washington: Population Reference Bureau, 1984), 36.

5. National Academy of Sciences, *High Schools and the Changing Workplace*

(Washington: National Academy Press, 1984), 20.

6. Rockefeller Institute of Government, *New York State Project 2000: Report on Population* (Albany: State University of New York, 1986), 141.

7. Judy Mann, "Pushing for Payoffs," *Washington Post*, 29 March 1989, B3.

8. Motorola requires entry-level electronics workers to read at a 7th grade level and do 5th grade math. Of the 3,000 applicants for jobs at an Illinois facility, half failed these tests. Motorola estimates it will spend four times its $9 million plant investment to teach basic reading and math skills to employees. *Sacramento Bee*, 23 September 1989, 84.

9. The American Bankers Association reported in 1989 that ⅓ of all banks offer basic training in reading, writing, and arithmetic at a cost of $32 million annually because of poor worker skills. *Wall Street Journal*, 8 August 1989, 1.

10. Julie Lopez, "System Failure," *Wall Street Journal*, March 31 1989, R12.

11. Jeane Griffith, et al., "American Education: The Challenge of Change," *Population Bulletin* 44, no. 4 (1989): 20.

12. Ibid.

13. Jill Lawrence, "Work and School," *Sacramento Bee*, July 16 1989, A14.

14. Ibid.

15. Griffith, et al., "American Education," 16.

16. Julie Johnson, "Teachers Pay," *New York Times*, 22 July 1989, 16.

17. Sonia Nazavio, "Failing in 81 Languages," *Wall Street Journal*, 31 March 1989, R21.

18. Ibid., R22.

19. Dudley Poston (conversation with the author, May 1989) has shown with 1980 Census of Population data that the inter-related individual traits of years of education, having a professional occupation, and being proficient in English can pretty much rank immigrants from various countries by their average U.S. incomes. Foreign-born males who were 25 to 64 in 1980, for example, averaged $25,000 or more in 1980 if they had 14 or more years of schooling. Immigrants from most countries who had higher than average incomes usually had a professional occupation, and 99 percent were proficient in English.

20. Theodore Schultz, *Investing in People: The Economics of Population Change* (Berkeley: University of California Press, 1988), xi.

21. George Deukmejian, Letter to *Sacramento Bee*, 17 July 1989, B3.

22. Clifford Adelman, "The Class of '72," *New York Times*, 22 July 1989, 25.

23. Bouvier and Gardner, "Immigration to the U.S.," 22-23.

10
Pluralistic Assimilation and the Nation-State

The second great challenge facing the nation as it enters the twenty-first century is to assure that pluralistic assimilation succeeds as a mode of cultural adaptation. This challenge is critical given the escalating diversity of the population. If, under these circumstances, the nation is to maintain a sense of unified purpose, pluralistic assimilation is the correct path to follow. Cultural pluralism, on the other hand, can only lead to disunity and even an end to American identity.

CULTURAL PLURALISM

In its current radical form, cultural pluralism assumes a minority-majority relationship, not one where no single group is dominant. Some advocates of cultural pluralism argue that racial and ethnic minorities should maintain their identity, language, and culture — even remain separate — rather than assimilate into the mainstream society. Indeed, "many Americans today righteously reject the historic goal of 'a new race of man.'"[1] Interestingly, some of these advocates regard such separatism with unalloyed enthusiasm and encourage it.

> Whether out of vested interest in preserving an ethnic political base or philosophic opposition to cultural assimilation as a degrading process, such people promote a vision of the United States as a kind of loose federation of discrete ethnic blocs — a society whose rules and goals and procedures . . . will be established in time to come by a coalition of defiantly unassimilated groups.[2]

177

Consider that the United States will eventually be a nation without any majority group and that cultural pluralism, if successful, could degenerate into cultural separatism.

It is not too far-fetched to depict a scenario where the major groups — Anglo, Black, Latino, Asian — remain separate from one another; where new ethnic voting blocs predominate; where different languages are used within some enclaves; where cultures and values differ significantly among groups. Proponents of cultural pluralism point out that in certain immigrant enclaves, individuals can go through life without ever speaking English. In such enclaves, persons of different races, such as Anglos and Blacks in a Latino enclave or Hispanics in a Korean enclave, are often discriminated against and sometimes denied employment. In extreme cases, even the laws of the nation could be overlooked if they conflict with the norms and values of the enclave. Continued high levels of immigration and the failure of pluralistic assimilation could lead to such a scenario. Already, in places like Miami, the ability to speak Spanish is a pre-requisite for many jobs.

The new-found emphasis on group rather than individual rights is a natural partner to this type of cultural pluralism. Each group demands special privileges for its members. Can affirmative action programs, however justifiable and proper for women and Black and Native Americans, be extended to minority immigrants, without reinforcing this emphasis on group rights?

> These immigrants are eligible for affirmative action privileges upon their arrival, despite the fact that they have no conceivable claim upon America's conscience. It is hardly nativist or xenophobic to observe that such a situation is unjust. And the injustice has created bizarre distortions and conflicts. For example, the current system would allow a wealthy, Peruvian doctor to immigrate and claim affirmative action benefits at the expense of the son of a coal miner from Appalachia, based merely on his ethnicity.[3]

The current controversy over the suggested new curriculum for New York State schools provides yet another example of the growing move toward a divisive type of cultural pluralism. The "Curriculum of Inclusion" is intended to consider the needs of minority children.

> It raises the question of what vision of American society will inform what New York's school children will be taught. Should the schools emphasize that the multifarious cultural strands of American society coexist with and contribute to each other through citizenship in a polity that is open to all but is Western in its origins and major institutions? Or, as the tack force recommends, should the education system stress the separate — often non-Western — ethnic identities of New York's students, while treating the society's main institutions as instruments of 'European-American' domination?[4]

The tone of the report recommending the adoption of the new curriculum is loaded with extremist language. It is a call for the school system to inculcate in Black students, immigrants, and other minorities resentment and bitterness toward the chief institutions in American life.

In the name of tolerance, this kind of cultural pluralism sometimes rejects and sometimes condemns the unifying culture of America in favor of the separatist cultures of ethnic groups.[5]   With continued high levels of immigration, such movements will grow and intensify, leading the nation toward a divisive kind of cultural pluralism, a type not envisioned by its earlier proponents.

> Cultural pluralism is not the most attractive legacy we can leave our children. As a nation, we have barely survived the existence of two separate populations, black and white, and we have a long way to go in working out better relations between those two groups. What shall we do when the whole of America becomes a multiracial Alexandria?[6]

PLURALISTIC ASSIMILATION

Pluralistic assimilation could be the answer. It is particularly suitable for multiracial societies where no one group predominates. It differs from cultural pluralism in that allegiance is to the nation first and the group second; it differs from cultural assimilation in that the group maintains its identity.

The term, "assimilation" is used and not "integration." The difference between the two can be illustrated by an example from professional sports. In 1947, Jackie Robinson became a Brooklyn Dodger and big league baseball finally was integrated. But true assimilation of Black baseball players didn't take place for many more years. Only in 1977, when the Cleveland Indians fired Black manager Frank Robinson, could it be claimed that big league baseball was gradually becoming pluralistically assimilated. By then such a move was acceptable. With the hiring of Frank Robinson to manage the Baltimore Orioles in 1988 and his subsequent promotion to assistant general manager in 1991, and with the selection of Bill White, a Black American, as president of the National League in 1989, the pluralistic assimilation process is accelerating.   Integration is almost ceremonial; assimilation involves becoming a true member of the entire system, for good and for bad.

Pluralistic assimilation also serves to provide some heterogeneity within ever increasing societal homogeneity. As T.S. Eliot once wrote: "A people should be neither too united nor too divided if its culture is to flourish."[7]

Throughout the world, two opposing trends are emerging. On one hand, there is growing unification — witness the European Community. Yet there is a similar movement in the other direction — the demands for autonomy by the Welsh, Basques, Catalans and others. Going beyond governments, the trend is to an internationalization of ideas, cuisines, and even language — witness the ever growing reliance on English as a communication tool. These trends toward increasing homogeneity will inevitably succeed. Yet, within most societies and most groups, a certain reluctance can be noted. While embracing much of the new homogeneity, many groups express a desire to maintain some semblance of identity, some awareness of roots. "The more homogeneous our lifestyles become, the more steadfastly we shall cling to deeper values — religion, language, art, and literature. As our outer worlds grow more similar, we will increasingly treasure the traditions that spring from within."[8]

Earlier pressures for "Americanization" ignored this point. New immigrants were expected to shed their old culture and willingly embrace Anglo-conformity. It didn't work any better than did cultural pluralism which argued for the opposite position. However, pluralistic assimilation allows for diversity within a unified nation that itself is becoming multiracial and where there someday will be no majority.

An analogy may help further explain pluralistic assimilation. For many decades most European Americans lived under an Anglo-conformity umbrella. While minorities, such as Blacks, Hispanics and Asians were kept "out in the rain" so to speak, European-Americans tried to conform to Anglo norms. Gradually these Europeans gained acceptance and began sharing the umbrella. What had been an Anglo-conformity umbrella had become a European-American umbrella. In the meantime, the minority populations increased and demands for equal rights were vociferous. However there was no room under the umbrella. A tent became necessary. Here all groups could stay out of the rain and participate equally in the social system. Yet, the tent can only stand if the various poles are properly attached to the ground at each corner and in the middle. These ties are provided by the various ethnic groups: Asian, African, Hispanic, Native-American, and European that will comprise the United States of the twenty-first century.

Reducing levels of immigration is necessary but it is not sufficient if pluralistic assimilation is to succeed. Far more must be done.

First, American society must provide the means to make economic and social advancement possible for *all* Americans. This will involve easy and inexpensive access to higher education as well as technical training. It will necessitate a revamping of the nation's educational institutions to allow for the better preparation of *all* Americans for the occupations of the future — a "G.I. Bill" for the twenty-first century.

In other words, a new kind of structural mobility must be developed that is appropriate for the United States economy of the twenty-first century. Should these plans fail and Blacks and Latinos find themselves overwhelmingly in lower paying jobs while Asians and Anglos are predominant in the higher paying positions, conflict will be inevitable and pluralistic assimilation will fail.

Second, future immigrants must demonstrate their desire to join other Americans and become "one of us," changing the meaning of "us" in the process. Just as most early twentieth-century immigrants desperately wanted to become American, so too should those of the early twenty-first century. If the nation is to remain *E Pluribus Unum*, there can be no room for cultural separatism or for irredentist movements on the part of newcomers.

Naturalization is often seen as an indicator of total commitment by immigrants to their new homeland. Yet, far too often, people apply for citizenship for purely economic motives. Such a practice should be discouraged as much as possible. Perhaps citizenship should not be granted, almost automatically, to anyone who has been in the country at least five years and applies. Some evidence of total commitment should be sought. Perhaps citizenship should not be granted automatically to anyone born in the country. "The value of citizenship would be enhanced if the Constitution were amended to limit automatic citizenship to those persons who are born in the United States and also have at least one parent who is a citizen of the United States at the time of birth."[9]

Third, all forms of discrimination must end. This is an enormous challenge. The United States remains a racist society and that must change if pluralistic assimilation is to succeed. Recall that a major factor in the emergence of cultural pluralism is the fact that "immigrant groups . . . have been rebuffed in their attempts to seek entrance into the core society."[10] If pluralistic assimilation is truly desired as the ideal mode of adaptation for the future, Americans must cease thinking of the newest immigrants as "inferior" foreigners. The newcomers should be accepted wholeheartedly. These motivated individuals are not a "mob at the gates"; Americans should show them that the United States is a "benevolent community" eager to welcome these newcomers into their society.[11] Every effort must be made to assist the newest residents to participate fully and equally in this dynamic society.

This applies *a fortiori* to long-time American minorities. The Civil Rights legislation of the 1960s, as did the U.S. Constitution, promised a nation in which all persons would be treated equally. That remains distant on the horizon; one could argue that race relations are worsening rather than improving although some surveys indicate more understanding among groups than ever before. Even relations between minorities are fragile. With the newest immigrants' share of the population growing, it is vital to the survival of American society that a mechanism be found for all groups to know and understand one another.

Schools at all levels should develop programs to better understand the multilingual and multicultural background of all Americans. Too many majority Americans are beset with cultural superiority. "Belief in one's own culture does not mean disdain for other cultures."[12] If pluralistic assimilation is to succeed, Americans of all backgrounds must understand one another. Only then can all share and contribute to twenty-first-century America.

While the major ethnic groups will remain identifiable, all residents of the United States, irrespective of race or ethnicity, must learn to respect and appreciate one another simply as fellow Americans. Responsibilities must be balanced with rights. John F. Kennedy's inspired words from the 1961 Inaugural Address, "Ask not what your country can do for you, ask what you can do for your country," seem to have been totally forgotten in the selfish decade just concluded. For pluralistic assimilation to succeed, a stronger national community must emerge and the United States as a nation-state must do everything to ensure its continued unity through emphasis on language and patriotism.

THE NATION-STATE

A nation-state can be compared to other organizations, like clubs or universities. It has a certain number of members, or residents. Closure is thus an important characteristic of a nation-state. The nation accepts or rejects new applicants for "membership," like a club or university. This right to determine who shall be allowed in is another important characteristic of a nation-state. As long as there are nations, there will be members and strangers, and "admissions decisions have to be made, men and women taken in or refused."[13]

In the ideal nation-state, residents share certain values and beliefs — a national culture, so to speak. Yet, this condition is seldom realized. Many sub-Saharan nations, for example, are European-mandated geographical areas carved out at the 1885 Treaty of Berlin. These boundaries fail to take into account tribal or ethnic distributions.

At the other extreme lie countries like Japan. Much has been written about Japanese culture and how it contributes to that nation's remarkable economic success. With the minuscule exception of the aboriginal Ainus, the Japanese people are of one culture. There is general agreement over values and norms and overall social and individual behavior.

Between these extremes lie countries like Canada, Australia, and the United States. There, diversity is commonplace but only because the nation-state accepts certain newcomers who differ in some ways from the first settlers. Yet even in such countries limits to the acceptance of newcomers are considered appropriate. ". . . even a liberal nation has powerful propensities to exclude. The very idea of nationhood implies a coherence of shared tradition, experiences, and values — a national community."[14] Such a tendency toward closure and boundary-setting is inevitable in a world of nation-states.

For many nations, community remains an often elusive goal. Diversity is so great that the development of a national community is beyond reach. Yet without some sense of community, nations cannot long endure. Waltzer defines such communities as "historically stable, ongoing associations of men and women with special commitment to one another and some special sense of their common life."[15]

COMMUNITY AND CULTURE

Members of a national community possess a common culture. While cultures vary from society to society, it is culture that "provides the framework within which our lives become meaningful, based on standards of success, beauty, and goodness, and reverence for a god or gods, the forces of nature, or long-dead ancestors. Culture also shapes our personalities, what we commonly describe as human nature."[16]

Some nations encourage the development of more than one culture and, in the process, lose some sense of community. Canada is such a nation. There, both the English and the French cultures are deemed equal. Embattled Yugoslavia presents an extreme example. It has two alphabets, three major religions, four major languages, five major nationalities, and until recently, was divided into six major republics. One can legitimately inquire: "What is a Yugoslavian?" Canada, Yugoslavia, Belgium and sundry other countries differ enormously from countries like Japan and Sweden where cultural diversity is minimal and a sense of community is resent. Multilingual countries often exhibit a tendency toward disintegration. The current situation in the Soviet Union is perhaps the most extreme example of such a situation.

The United States, though multiethnic and multiracial, has consistently endeavored to assimilate its new residents into an ever changing American culture. That culture is not necessarily superior to others, but it has served the nation well and was particularly well-suited to the development of capitalism. However, it may be appropriate to ask whether American culture will be suitable for the resource-limited twenty-first century, when profits may no longer be the only worthwhile economic goal of society? Or will American culture adjust to more adequately meet the challenges of the future?

Equally successful (economically speaking) societies have generated quite different cultures. For example, although both Japanese and Americans praise achievement and hard work, Americans value self-assertion and competition; Japanese emphasize cooperation and self-denying obedience to the group.

> It is hard for a Japanese to understand that somebody would want to be one of them — a sheer contradiction in terms to them — as it is for an American

to imagine that every immigrant doesn't want eventually to become an
American. . . . Americans think everybody is going to be like them one day.
Whereas in Japan, foreigners are supposed to go back where they came
from.[17]

Irrespective of the type of culture, it is implicit in any national
consciousness to protect and maintain a society's culture. This is true of poor
and rich countries alike. Guamanians, though not an independent people, are
proud of their Chomorro culture. They want it maintained, despite the
incursions of modernization. Their desire to conserve their culture is
illustrated in their opposition to provisions of a proposed new Commonwealth
Act. Guamanians want the right to control foreign immigration into their
island. However "control of immigration is a sensitive issue because changes
would affect mainly Filipinos. They already are 20 percent of Guam's
population of 126,000."[18]

Perhaps Guamanians are aware of what has happened to the Hawaiians
over the past century. Immigration from China, Japan, Portugal, the
Philippines, the mainland and elsewhere have permanently altered the
character of the islands and Hawaiian culture is disappearing rapidly despite
courageous efforts to preserve it. In 1971 Garrett Hardin wrote that
constitutional principles may need to be challenged to reduce the rate of in-
migration to Hawaii. "The residents of a land of beauty have a responsibility
to be its trustees. If you broadly share your wealth, you will probably lose it
and if you are fair to everyone, you are fair to no one."[19] Societies, rich and
poor, developed and developing, jealously guard their cultures against too
much intrusion from outside.

IMMIGRATION AND CULTURE

Immigration is closely intertwined with problems of cultural maintenance.
This has been an issue throughout human history and has caused many,
sometimes bloody, conflicts. With the emergence of nation-states and their
clearer geographic boundaries, this issue becomes even more threatening.
Humans are territorial by nature. It is normal for residents of a nation-state
to expect newcomers who willingly migrate peacefully from another region to
become "more like us." If these newcomers are truly welcomed by the
residents, it is up to the latter to make them comfortable and allow them to
become "more like us." However the "us" itself is always evolving in part
because of the contributions of later immigrants.

Whenever the immigrant group refuses to adapt to the dominant culture,
conflicts can emerge. This is especially true when the number of such
immigrants is relatively large and comes from a single source. Whenever the

host group refuses to allow the newcomers to participate in the activities of the society, cultural conflicts can emerge. It is a two-way street; both sides must work diligently if a nation's culture is to survive albeit altered by input from the newest residents.

One can sympathize with the desires of immigrants to maintain their culture. Culture is ingrained in all. Nevertheless, if a person voluntarily decides to migrate permanently from one nation to another, some often painful adjustments in culture are necessary. Members of the host society should grasp these difficulties and tolerate cultural *faux-pas*.

These processes are universalistic, but they are particularly appropriate to the United States. As a nation of immigrants, the United States has witnessed "peaceful invasions" of newcomers gradually become Americans. As long as the newcomers desired to become American, and as long as the residents eventually allowed them to do so, the process proceeded quite adequately and the American culture remained dynamically intact. "It is America's peculiar good fortune that its immigrants have nearly always wanted to assimilate. The first generation might cling to 'foreign' ways, but the second generation has nearly always Americanized itself with a vengeance."[20]

Today's American newcomers from Latin America and Asia pose fresh challenges for the nation's culture. Do these new residents want to become "one of us"? Do the long-time residents want them to become "one of us"? The scanty evidence suggests that second-generation Asians, whether Korean, Filipino, or Vietnamese, are gradually accepting American values. There is a strong desire to learn English; there is a strong commitment to education and success. Furthermore, the sheer distance from the motherland almost dictates the necessity of becoming "one of us."

The situation among Latin American immigrants is different. For the first time in United States history, a majority of immigrants speak a single language. The motherland is nearby. There is no evidence of any decline in the level of immigration from Mexico, Central America, and elsewhere. Mexico, being by far the largest source of immigrants, poses a singularly important challenge.

Care must be taken to distinguish between Mexican-Americans and the newer immigrants from Mexico. Unfortunately, "United States society since 1848 . . . has lumped Mexican immigrants and Mexican-Americans, many of whom are third- and fourth-generation citizens, into one group and treated both as undesirable but needed foreigners."[21] If Mexican immigration had not increased in recent decades and if Americans had been more receptive, earlier Mexican immigrants might have soon embraced American culture as so many other groups did earlier in this century. Still,

> because the transition has been gradual, observers in the United States ironically conclude that, unlike other immigrants, Mexican-Americans are

unwilling to become part of United States society. It is, by contrast, more likely that Mexican-Americans have retained a 'Mexicanness' only because they were so long denied access to American institutions.[22]

Again cultural pluralism, and even separatism, resulted.

Many new immigrants from Mexico exhibit little desire to become "American" and the addition of such large numbers has reinforced and reinvigorated the Mexican culture among some Mexicans living in the United States. In a test of Mexican-American children in El Paso, sociologist James Lamare concluded: "Overall, Mexican-American children, regardless of generation, show only limited commitment to the American political community. . . . None of the five cohorts [studied] prefers the label 'American' over identification tags more reflective of their national origins."[23]   In a survey undertaken by the marketing research firm of Yankelovich, Skelly, and White, for the National Spanish Television Network, it was found that "In 1984, compared with 1981, more Latinos think of themselves as Latinos first, and Americans second."[24]

Some Mexicans come to the United States as "colonizers" rather than "settlers." Settlers include all the people who come to the United States with the expectation of starting a new life. A permanent and lasting break with the motherland is expected. Colonists, on the other hand, are not really departing from their homeland.

> [the Mexican immigrant] is transplanting a segment of his society to a new and expanded locale.   In some cases he is returning to an area which was dominated or under the control of his homeland at some time in the past. This is particularly the case for selected Chicanos who reside in Texas and the Southwest. Their land was won by the United States in battle and they look forward to its return to Mexican-type rule.   Such a Chicano does not see himself as breaking with the homeland but looks forward to close linkage with it, or even return.[25]

Increasingly, the inhabitants of much of the border area, in both the United States and Mexico, refer to their land as "Mex-America," a region that has an ethos of its own and where the international boundary shrinks into irrelevance.[26]

The historical refusal on the part of native-born Americans to accept immigrants from Mexico as full-fledged members of American society combined with the refusal on the part of many newer immigrants to show any desire to become members of American society is posing a major challenge to American culture. The challenge involves "the digesting into the United States mainstream of a vast segment of the population which sees itself as both linguistically and culturally different. This raises in turn the question:

Can it be done without disruptive collisions or confrontations?"[27] It can if both groups work at it and if immigration levels are limited.

LANGUAGE

For pluralistic assimilation to succeed, the nation must possess a dynamic culture that includes a common language through which all the residents can communicate. To say that a common language must be maintained is to say that English is necessary to keep the culture intact.

> Language is both a repository and a vehicle of culture. Not only does language convey ideas between people, but it has a fundamental role in shaping what those ideas are. In linguistically divided communities, it is not surprising that language constitutes both a cultural boundary and a marker of social stratification.[28]

This is not to deny the rights of various groups to encourage the use of their respective languages in the home. Nevertheless, English is the "glue" that helps keep American culture vibrant and dynamic.

Among earlier immigrants, learning English was of primary importance. Language was considered basic to assimilation. "The mastery of English was central for economic advancement and for sociopolitical commonality in a democratic polity based on citizenship."[29] The pressure for bilingualism particularly on the part of some Latinos has reversed these priorities. Spanish has remained the first language for many new immigrants and their families and English is the second language. A former president of the League of United Latin American Citizens (LULAC) says: "Spanish should be included in commercials shown throughout America. Every American child should be taught both English and Spanish."[30] The mayor of Miami argues that: "Citizenship is what makes us all Americans. Language is not necessary to the system. Nowhere does the Constitution say English is our language."[31]

In an era of increased global communication, all Americans should speak at least two languages, but the second need not be Spanish. Japanese, Russian, or German might be more advantageous to the American of the twenty-first century. What is of concern here is the attempt to minimize the importance of one agreed-upon language, English, for all those who share a nation.

Bilingual education should be utilized wherever needed. Its goal should be to speed up the process of acculturation into American society and not the permanent maintenance of a second language. If bilingual education alleviates communication problems then by all means let it be utilized. But its goal must be swift conversion into an English language education.

Unfortunately, the meaning of bilingual education has changed. Rather than being a process to ease the shift from the foreign to the English language, it has merged with cultural pluralism and thus the primacy of ethnic, racial, religious, and cultural subgroups supersedes all else.

> Bilingual education . . . would shape the pupil's education according to his ethnic or racial background in distinction to basing it on his needs as an individual or as a citizen of an English-speaking country. At best, it insists that the most salient facts by which the student's needs should be evaluated are his race and the country of his family's origin. At worst, students have been assigned to Spanish language classes because they had Hispanic surnames or because other members of their households spoke Spanish. Pluralism insists that the group, and the preservation and development of the group's identity, take precedence over both the unity of the nation and the identities of individuals.[32]

The debate over the role of English in U.S. society is intensifying outside the classroom as well. The demands of some Latino leaders for more and more bilingual training is creating a backlash among many majority residents. This is demonstrated in the overwhelming success of state-level propositions intended to make English the official language of the state. In 1986 almost 70 percent of California voters agreed that English should henceforward be the state's official language. Similar resolutions have been passed in numerous other states, such as Florida, Colorado, and Arizona. Interestingly, a majority of San Francisco Latinos agree that English should be the state's official language. In a March 1990 survey in that city, almost 70 percent of Latinos said that English should be the official language. As one respondent said: "It is better for Latino people to have this law, because we live in a country where most people do speak English."[33]

The bilingual issue must not be allowed to interfere with the adaptation of newcomers to American society. While the long-time residents should exhibit patience with the latest immigrants as they strive to learn a new language, in turn these newcomers should demonstrate a sincere desire to become proficient in the English language. English may not be the most beautiful language in the world, but it has become the international mode of communicating. It is to the advantage of newcomers and residents alike that all be able to communicate in the nation's basic tongue.

Too many countries have failed to attain true national consciousness because of bilingual and even multi-lingual controversies. In so many instances, the ethnic minority identifies first with its own subculture rather than the national culture. Canada is often cited as an example. It is, by law, a bilingual nation. Yet, Canada has experienced considerable difficulty in getting all of its citizens to be "Canadians." Many residents of French-speaking Quebec call themselves "Québecois" first, and "Canadiens" second.

The United States must choose its linguistic (and thereby cultural) path for the next century. Past successes with immigrants from Europe must be repeated with the newest immigrants from Asia and Latin America if the nation is to maintain its English-speaking culture for the foreseeable future.

PATRIOTISM

The eventual success of pluralistic assimilation is difficult without some aspect of a national community where there is an awareness of identity and a certain concern for other members of the group, even if that group's population is 250 or 350 million. Developing such a sense of community is difficult without a sense of national patriotism.

Patriotism is a much-maligned word today. Conservatives attempt to monopolize the concept, implying that liberals cannot be patriotic. This is sheer nonsense. All Americans, African, Asian, European, Latino, and Native, can and should exhibit patriotism, but it comes in many flavors. Samuel Johnson once wrote: "Patriotism is the last refuge of the scoundrel." However, Johnson did not say that only scoundrels can be patriotic. But perhaps only scoundrels can be chauvinistic.

There is room for a liberal patriotism where pride in the successes of American culture is displayed alongside an awareness of its many weaknesses and the need to improve; a patriotism not based on military chauvinism but one based, as Camus once wrote, on the ideal of what the country might be. For all its faults, and they are myriad, American culture is worth preserving and improving. The *ideal* of equal opportunity for all; the *total* commitment to a democratic order and to individual freedom; the Constitution whose 200th birthday was recently celebrated — these concepts must be preserved. The nation's avarice in consumption, corporate greed, and racism, in particular, must be confronted and eliminated. However, the nation must guard against diluting its culture while constantly striving to improve it.

This new patriotism must take into account global interdependence. Blind chauvinism, where one's country is considered superior to all others, who by definition are [considered] inferior, is no longer appropriate, if it ever was. Indeed, George Washington was uncomfortable with fervent national chauvinism, even in behalf of the new United States. "While favoring a temperate patriotism, Washington and other revolutionary statesmen stressed that the true aspirations of Americans should not be to perfect their republic alone, but to realize the 'great republic of humanity' at large."[34] Given the extensive interdependence of the world community, such a view is more appropriate today than ever and is required to contribute both to national goals and to a more orderly world.

This new patriotism is not blind, mechanical nationalism, but an attachment to the state compatible with the reality of the contemporary interdependent world community. "Nationalism of this kind requires that the bulk of the population display feelings of patriotism — not aggressive patriotism but patriotism reconstructed into responsible civic consciousness."[35]

CONCLUSION

"Patriotism," "Community," "Nation-state," are terms closely related to one another. It is no exaggeration to state that the United States is shifting away from the goals these concepts imply, making the goal of pluralistic assimilation that much more difficult to reach. The 1980s have witnessed a growing "meism" in all generations and a "groupism" among minorities. At the same time, ethnic groups have grown further apart and ugly racist incidents have cropped up in numerous places.

By limiting immigration, the nation will at least have a better chance at achieving the goals of a true national community inhabited by individuals proud to be American, but equally aware of its shortcomings and its role in the global economy of which we are all members. This can only take place if these selected immigrants, and other minorities, are accepted by the majority as full members of the community and themselves express a sincere desire to join this community. Ideally, the nation "is a 'terminal community,' the largest community that, when the chips are down, effectively commands men's loyalties, overriding the claim of both, the lesser communities within it, and those that cut across it within a still greater society."[36]

These ideals may not be attained if immigration levels are allowed to remain at current, or higher, levels. Such demographic patterns could only lead to large ethnic ghettos where the English language is practically unknown, where patriotism is oriented toward the motherland, and where the concept of community is limited to the specific area itself.

> These developments portend a new turn in American life. Instead of a transformative nation with a new and distinctive identity, America increasingly sees itself as preservative of old identities. We used to say *e pluribus unum*. Now we glorify *pluribus* and belittle *unum*. The melting pot yields to the Tower of Babel.[37]

The forces leaning towards extreme cultural pluralism are directing the nation on a path toward a conceivably radically different future.

Chauvinism is not called for, but in light of the potential hazards to the nature of our society by uncontrolled immigration and a weakened concept of citizenship, policy-makers cannot afford to neglect the larger question of the national interest while attempting to placate competing interest groups.[38] A determined effort to assure the success of pluralistic assimilation is the most appropriate route to follow if the nation is to remain *E pluribus unum*.

NOTES

1. Arthur Schlesinger, Jr., "When ethnic studies are un-American," *Wall Street Journal*, 23 April 1990, 6.

2. Christopher, *Crashing the Gates*, 278.

3. Mark Krikorian, "Affirmative Action and Immigration," *Christian Science Monitor*, 11 September 1989, 2.

4. Scott McConnell and Eric Breindel, "Head to Come," *New Republic*, 8 and 15 January 1990, 19-20.

5. Gary Imhoff, "The Position of U.S. English on Bilingual Education," *Annals of the American Academy of Political and Social Science* (March 1990): 9.

6. Thomas Fleming, "The Real American Dilemma," *Chronicles* (March 1989): 9.

7. T.S. Eliot, *Notes Toward the Definition of Culture* (New York: Harcourt, Brace, and Co., 1949), 49.

8. Naisbitt and Aburdene, *Megatrends 2000*, 120.

9. Bikales, *A More Perfect Union*, 127.

10. Portes and Bach, *Latin Journey*, 25.

11. Robert Reich, *Tales of a New America* (New York: Times Books, 1987).

12. Arthur Schlesinger, Jr., "When ethnic studies are un-American," 4.

13. Michael Waltzer, "The Distribution of Membership," in Peter G. Brown and Henry Shue, *Boundaries: National Autonomy and its Limits* (Totowa, N.J: Rowman and Littlefield, 1981), 10.

14. Peter Schuck, "Immigration Law and the Problem of Community," in Nathan Glazer, ed., *Clamor at the Gates: The New American Immigration* (San Francisco: Institute for Contemporary Studies, 1985), 289.

15. Waltzer, "The Distribution of Membership," 32.

16. John Macionis, *Sociology* (Englewood Cliffs: Prentice-Hall, 1989), 62.

17. George Fields, "Racism is Accepted Practice in Japan," *Wall Street Journal*, 10 November 1986, 2.

18. "Guam's Future," *Honolulu Advertiser*, 20 November 1987, 13.

19. As cited in Eleanor Nordyke, *The Peopling of Hawaii* (Honolulu: University of Hawaii Press, 1987), 110.

20. William Pfaff, "Rethinking the Multicultural Ideal," *Los Angeles Times*, 4 March 1989, 21.

21. Rodolfo O. De la Garza, "Mexican-Americans, Mexican Immigrants, and Immigration Reform," in Nathan Glazer, ed., *Clamor at the Gates: The New American Immigration* (San Francisco: Institute for Contemporary Studies, 1985), 99.

22. Ibid.

23. James W. Lamare, "The Political Integration of Mexican-American Children: A Generational Analysis," *International Migration Review* 16, no. 4 (1981): 173.

24. Yankelovich, Skelly, and White, *Spanish USA, 1984*, 1984.

25. Morris Janowitz, *The Reconstruction of Patriotism* (Chicago: University of Chicago Press, 1983), 130.

26. Arturo Islas, *Mex-America: A State of Mind* (New York: William Morrow, 1989).

27. David M. Reimers, *Still the Golden Door: The Third World Comes to America* (New York: Columbia University Press, 1985), 151.

28. William Beer and James Jacobs, eds., *Language Policy and National Unity* (New York: Rowman and Allenheld, 1985), 2.

29. Janowitz, *The Reconstruction of Patriotism*, 136.

30. As cited in Richard Lamm, testimony before the Joint Economic Committee of the U.S. Congress, 29 May 1986, 12.

31. Ibid.

32. Imhoff, "The Position of U.S. English," 10.

33. Frank Viviano, "Poll Shows Ethnic Groups Torn by Bias, Cultural Ties," *San Francisco Chronicle*, 27 March 1990, A6.

34. Peter Schuck and Rogers M. Smith, *Citizenship without Consent: Illegal Aliens in the American Polity* (New Haven: Yale University Press, 1985), 142.

35. Janowitz, *The Reconstruction of Patriotism*, 152.

36. Rupert Emerson, *From Empire to Nation* (Cambridge: Harvard University Press, 1960), 95-96.

37. Arthur Schlesinger, Jr., "When ethnic studies are un-American," 2.

38. Kevin McCarthy and David F. Ronfeldt, *U.S. Immigration Policy and Global Interdependence* (Santa Monica: Rand Corp, 1982), 16.

11
The Politics of Immigration
Policy

One thing is certain: the author of this book will be vilified in some quarters for advocating less immigration. Charges of racism, lack of concern for the poor of the world, insensitivity to the economic needs of the United States, and perhaps other accusations will be levelled. Despite the "liberal" arguments offered throughout this book, advocating limiting immigration into a nation of immigrants is simply not considered "the thing to do" by certain people, especially in this era when group rights are emphasized at the expense of individual rights and national well-being.

POLITICAL PRESSURE

For almost a century — from 1882 to 1965 — the nation tried to reduce the high levels of immigration. At first, these concerns were also racist, beginning with the Chinese Exclusion Act of 1882 and culminating with the Quota Laws of the 1920s and their reaffirmation in 1952. The 1965 revisions tried to eliminate the racial and ethnic barriers of previous legislation, though not entirely successfully. Anxiety over the number of immigrants was expressed, particularly in the first decade of the twentieth century. Furthermore, the authors of the 1965 revisions did not anticipate any increases in the number entering the country; they simply wanted to change the qualifications needed to gain entry. For example, Attorney-General Robert F. Kennedy told the Senate that 5,000 Asian immigrants might come the first year "after which immigration from that source would virtually disappear."[1] Thus, for over a century no attempt was made to *raise* immigration levels; many attempts, some successful, were made to *lower* immigration levels.

In the 1980s, political attitudes shifted. Even the 1986 legislation (IRCA) aimed at reducing illegal immigration went through compromise after compromise before being passed by Congress. Its eventual form was a watered-down version of the originally proposed legislation. In 1990, as we have seen, legislation that will substantially raise immigration in future years was passed into law.

Legislators generally follow the opinions of the people who vote for them quite closely. The liberalization of positions on abortion by previously "pro-life" legislators when they realized that a majority of the population were "pro-choice" typifies such behavior. This is not the case with immigration. Survey after survey has shown that the vast majority of Americans favor limiting, and even reducing, immigration levels.

Even Julian Simon, an ardent advocate of increased immigration, after reviewing polls taken between 1930 and 1980, concedes that: "At all times, the responses seemed to indicate that Americans were not in favor of more immigration."[2]

In a 1985 Associated Press and Media General Poll, 55 percent of respondents felt that "U.S. immigration laws should be changed to make immigration more difficult." Only 9 percent felt it should be made "less difficult."

A February 1986 Roper Poll found that 77 percent of respondents agreed that the "U.S. should reduce the quotas of the number of legal immigrants who can enter the U.S. each year." Only 17 percent disagreed.

A May 1989 Tarrance and Associates poll of California respondents found that 59 percent felt that the U.S. admits "too many" immigrants each year; 9 percent felt that the U.S. admits "too few."

Another Tarrance and Associates Poll of Texas respondents in late 1989 asked the following question: "As you may know, the United States accepts a number of legal immigrants from foreign countries each year. In your opinion, does the United States presently accept too few legal immigrants, too many legal immigrants, or about the right number of legal immigrants, each year?" Only 5 percent replied "too few" while 59 percent said "too many." Another 27 percent said "about the right number" and 9 percent were unsure. Among Texas Latinos, 61 percent replied "too many," while only 5 percent said "too few."

In a 1990 nation-wide poll conducted by the Roper Organization, 74 percent of Latinos, 78 percent of Blacks, and 77 percent of the general public believe immigration should not be increased; 45 percent believe immigration should be reduced and only 9 percent favor increasing immigration. Furthermore, 87 percent of Americans believe the nation has population problems and 35 percent consider those problems "major." Finally, only 31 percent think there is a labor shortage in the United States and of those who think a shortage exists, only 27 percent support importing foreign labor while 75 percent support giving tax breaks to employers for training underqualified Americans.[3]

To the best of this author's knowledge, no American poll has ever found a majority favoring increased levels of immigration. Why then does the Congress go against the wishes of a significant majority of the American people?

First, ethnic pressure groups have lobbied long and hard against any attempts to limit immigration. Groups like the Mexican-American Legal Defense Fund (MALDEF) and La Raza even campaigned against the 1986 IRCA legislation that was aimed solely at reducing illegal movements into the country. Legislators assume that these organizations speak for their entire constituencies. As the polls indicate, this is far from true.

Second, certain economic determinists and business leaders have convinced many legislators that a labor shortage is imminent and that, even without a labor shortage, increasing the labor supply is economically advantageous for the country. The *Wall Street Journal* has been at the forefront of this movement. In a recent *Journal* article, the author concluded:

> We cannot wait 20 years to see what will happen when the baby-boomers retire and ask what happened to their Social Security trust fund, The U.S. needs to admit more immigrants now to get us out of the demographic bind we put ourselves in by restricting immigration in the first place.[4]

The fact that such increases would also result in lower wages is omitted. Julian Simon goes even further: "My recommendation would that we simply jump immigration visas to 1 million a year. And in three years, if we find no big problem develops, jump it again. And again . . ."[5]

Third, from the other extreme of the political spectrum, some liberals are convinced that the nation has a duty to continue taking in the poor surplus populations of depressed areas of the world. Some would expand the meaning of "refugee" to include anyone belonging to certain ethnic or religious groups, irrespective of whether individuals were persecuted or not. Such positions may prove valuable at re-election time in some areas, but they fail to consider the overall impact on the nation of these potentially massive movements of people.

From these three different positions has emerged a strange political coalition — liberals, conservatives, ethnic lobbyists -all committed to raising immigration levels. On the other hand, the majority of the people opposed to such moves are, on the whole, unorganized. Furthermore, these people are generally less committed to their positions than the lobbyists, conservative economists, and pro-immigration liberals. With some regional exceptions, many people who favor immigration reductions do not rank this among the top problems of the nation. As a result, politicians do not fear retribution at the polling booth, as they do on issues such as abortion and taxes.

Ironically, continued high levels of immigration and possible upswings in unemployment could lead to increased concern on the part of the citizenry. This could raise the "immigration issue" to the top of the list — alongside abortion and taxes. Then, and only then, would politicians take heed of the concerns of their constituents. But by then, it could be too late. The momentum for population growth would be in place.

In the meantime, anyone who dares to suggest that immigration levels should be reduced is immediately castigated by one or more of the three groups. The advocate of reduced immigration would be labelled a racist (by certain liberals), naive and anti-business (by certain conservative economists and their followers), or anti-Hispanic or anti-Asian (by ethnic lobbyists).

POLICY DEVELOPMENT

One might argue that the United States has an immigration policy — the current legislation. But such policy cannot be determined in a vacuum. As discussed earlier, rather than settle for a policy on immigration, the United States should have, and needs, a population policy. All three demographic variables must be considered: fertility, mortality, and immigration.

An optimal population size should first be determined. How many people can the nation support and at what levels of consumption? Flexibility should be the basic guideline. Optimal population size could vary based on many variables: rapid environmental depletion or new means to cope with degradation; unanticipated economic demands or an improvement in robotics; ease or difficulty in cultural adaptation, and so on. A committee of prominent scholars in ecology, sociology, economics, demography, political science, linguistics, and other relevant disciplines should advise the federal government on the changing situation. Limits could be re-adjusted from time to time. The point is that some optimal numerical goal should be set, albeit temporarily, to allow for the development of a coherent population policy.

Once a goal were set, demographic adjustments would follow. Every effort should be made to increase life expectancy. If successful, that would necessitate some reductions in fertility or immigration (or both) if a numerical goal was not to be surpassed. Fertility cannot be managed in a democratic society, nor should it. However, lower fertility could be encouraged by improved sex education and making contraceptives, such as the newly-approved Norplant System, more readily available particularly for adolescents. Abortion restrictions could be eliminated. Both fertility and mortality rates should be closely monitored so as to better gauge the extent of immigration needed to meet numerical limits. Fertility and mortality rates cannot be determined by government regulations, but immigration levels can and should be determined in such a manner.

As with total numbers, immigration limits could be adjusted, perhaps every five years, depending on changes in fertility and mortality. For example, the fertility rate is apparently climbing, for the first time since 1972. With a population size goal in place, this could mean more stringent limits on immigration.

Whether in determining overall population totals or in determining the extent of immigration, flexibility would be of prime importance. The optimal goal would reflect changes in the environment, the economy, the culture; immigration levels would reflect changes in fertility and mortality. The result would be a reasonable population policy that would contribute to an ecological balance between Americans and the environment — whether physical, economic, or social.

RECOMMENDED LEVEL OF IMMIGRATION

New limits on immigration are needed if the nation is to maintain its cultural unity and its place in the world of the twenty-first century. The guide to determining such numbers should be the one stated in the title of the report of the Hesburg Commission in 1981: *U.S. Immigration Policy and the National Interest.*

> We may as a nation wish to take into account the individual desires of foreigners, seconded by their American relatives, to live here rather than where they were born, but such desires should not serve as the principal guide to policy. Consciously defined national interests should determine immigration numbers and the principles of selection among the many applicants.[6]

Immigration should be limited to approximately 450,000 annually resulting in net immigration of 350,000. This number is not carved in stone and immigration policy is not limited to sheer numbers. Adjustments will be necessary from time to time. Furthermore, the characteristics of persons and their match of skills to the needs of the economy should be as important as how many are admitted.

Ethnic, racial, or religious background should not determine who is granted entry into the United States. In addition, given the world-wide interest in immigrating to this country, immigration from as wide a range of sources as possible should be encouraged. Such a policy would also serve another important function. To the extent that new immigrant groups represent a diversity of countries, it would be less likely that any single group would gain the political power necessary to accomplish a shift in foreign policy, to create a political dichotomy on domestic economic or social issues, or even worse, to create separatist sentiments in a geographically concentrated foreign enclave.[7]

Refugees should qualify under the UN definition of that term. That is to say, they must be *political* refugees with documented proof that their lives would be in danger if they returned to their homeland. So-called economic refugees are not refugees under any accepted international definition. A limit of 50,000 refugees annually is recommended within the 450,000 total. However, under certain extreme conditions, more could be accepted.

Immigrants allowed to enter the country on a permanent basis should be divided about equally between relatives of United States citizens and individuals (and their immediate families) who qualify under a set of economic preferences. Thus, total annual immigration of 450,000 would be divided approximately as follows: 200,000 immediate relatives of citizens; 200,000 qualifying under specified economic preferences (a marked increase over current levels); 50,000 as refugees.

Family reunification means immediate relatives of United States citizens: parents and children. Visas would be granted on a first come, first served basis, with no more than a specified percent of all family reunification immigrants coming from any one country.

Occupational preference would be given to individuals who qualify on the basis of some kind of a point system similar to that used in Canada and Australia. Points could be given for competence in English, education and special training, age, and capacity to invest in the United States. The system could be adjusted from time to time depending on the needs of the United States. Persons admitted under this occupational preference system could bring their immediate families with them, but they would be counted against the maximum for each sending country.

Illegal immigration must be terminated as soon as possible. The nation can ill afford to perpetuate within its midst a poverty ridden subgroup without any rights in law here, solely to minimize the labor costs of farmers and sweatshop operators. While sympathizing with illegal immigrants, these individuals cannot be allowed to flout the laws of the nation. Employers should be closely monitored to assure compliance with federal labor laws. Those found hiring illegal residents should be fined. The nation's borders and international airports should be more closely guarded with additional Border Patrol personnel if necessary. If it is found that illegal immigration still persists, further stringent measures should be introduced, such as a new tamper-proof identification card for all employees.

WHY 450,000?

This level of immigration is selected because it is consistent with an end to population growth within the next fifty years, providing overall fertility is soon reduced to 1.8.   It also approximates the recommendations of the Hesburg Commission in 1981.[8]

The United States could perhaps temporarily support millions more people if that were necessary, but quality of life, however defined, would deteriorate rapidly. Therefore, rather than ask why limit population growth, the question should be: "Why not?"

Unfortunately, for now that limit cannot be the nation's current size — 254 million. A momentum for growth is present in the nation's age composition; furthermore, immigration should not come to a complete end but should be reduced. Together, immigration of 450,000 annually (or net immigration of 350,000) and continued fertility at recent levels would yield a population of 316 million by 2050 — a gain of over 60 million in 60 years. By then, growth would have come to an end.

As for population decrease — the fear of some Americans — there is no evidence of any such drop under this low scenario over the next 75 years. It would then take many more years before the population reached its current level of 254 million. Rather, the signs point to more Americans than ever, over 300 million by 2020. There are no grounds for Americans troubling themselves with the perceived demographic complications their counterparts will face a century from now. Few, if any, Americans of 1890 were concerned with the issues of 1990.

For those still worried about possible decreases in population, the Bureau of the Census projections cited earlier in this book offer an interesting solution. Under their highly publicized medium scenario (that is, fertility of 1.8 and net immigration of 500,000), the United States population would peak at 302 million in 2038 and then begin to fall slightly to 292 million in 2080. However, when using the same assumptions for fertility and immigration but gradually increasing life expectancy to 88 years by 2080, the population would peak at 318 million in 2050 and remain at about that level until 2080. No population decline would occur. Perhaps, rather than fret about not enough babies and not enough immigration, the neo-doomsayers should join others in advocating measures to increase the life expectancy of all Americans.

For those Americans who feel that the population is already too large, this scenario is not very optimistic. Yet, it may be the most realistically possible at this time, given the mood of Congress. In the long run, under this scenario the population does begin to fall and thus, patience is highly recommended!

Some would argue that with such low levels of immigration, labor shortages would be chronic. Yet, even under this low scenario, the labor force of 2050 would be about 25 million larger than it is today. Assuming continuation of the present pace of technical innovation, wide categories of jobs would no longer exist. A tighter labor market in the coming decades would stimulate the U.S. economy to rationalize its use of labor to better compete with Japan and Germany whose economies have boomed with slow labor force growth and, in the case of Japan, almost zero immigration.

Beyond the economy, quality of life looms large. Even California's freeways might become less congested places with slower population growth. Perhaps there would be fewer over-burdened landfills, prospective energy shortages, and reduced depletion of our natural resources. The reduction and eventual end to population growth might be just the inducement needed to finally improve our entire infrastructure.

THE IMMIGRATION ISSUES

Four arguments have been presented for lower levels of immigration. In addition, the challenges of ethnic diversity and pluralistic assimilation were discussed.

LABOR FORCE

The underclass is growing larger every year. At the same time, the jobs of the future demand higher levels of education. This is creating a mismatch between the education and training of individuals and the economic needs of the twenty-first century. The low fertility of recent decades should have contributed to reducing the size of the underclass as the sheer number of young adults declined. That has not been the case partly because of the high levels of immigration which in some cities have kept the numbers in the underclass high. Reduced immigration could alleviate the problems of the underclass and could elevate some of its members into the mainstream of American society.

ECONOMIC

The nation is moving toward a two-tiered economy. As long as large numbers of people are available for the low level jobs, there will be no incentive to modernize industries and farms to compete internationally on the basis of better American technology in the twenty-first century. High immigration has worked to retard the modernization of American industry. This has encouraged American business to rely on cheap workers rather than technological improvements. Reductions in immigration would contribute to the maintenance of American competitiveness in the twenty-first century.

CULTURE AND PLURALISTIC ASSIMILATION

The continued high level of immigration poses serious questions for American culture. Some form of cultural adaptation must be found that will allow for a smooth transition by immigrants to the United States. All previous immigration waves almost ended thereby making it possible for new residents to assimilate into American society. This is no longer the case. If pluralistic assimilation is to be the adaptation mode of the future, rather than cultural pluralism or cultural separatism, immigration levels must be reduced.

ENVIRONMENTAL

The United States is the fastest growing industrial nation in the world. Such rapid population growth reduces the quality of life of all its residents and poses severe challenges for the environment. Limits should be placed on such growth. Higher fertility would lead the nation toward the half billion mark in population. The challenge is to find the ideal balance between low fertility and moderate levels of immigration that will allow for the ultimate population to be not much greater than the present population. Limiting immigration would go a long way towards solving the nation's environmental and population problems.

RACIAL SHIFTS

Shifts in the composition of the United States population are inevitable as long as fertility remains low. The shift is not a problem as long as the newcomers can adapt to American society and providing the residents give them the opportunity to become "one of us." A lower level of immigration will reduce the intensity of the racial shift. That is to say, it will occur at a slower pace than with higher immigration. This too should aid the process of pluralistic assimilation.

CONCLUSION

This book is strongly pro-immigrant. Just as a company must be concerned with the success of its new employees and a ship's captain with the state of the crew, so too, a country must be concerned with the success of its new residents. If they succeed, the country will succeed; if they fail, the country suffers a shattering blow.

Large-scale immigration may have served a useful purpose in the past, but past success is not sufficient to argue that similar levels of immigration will be good for the United States in the future. It was historian Arnold Toynbee who warned that the same elements that build up an institution eventually lead to its downfall.

Millions of people would move to the United States if they were permitted to do so. Sympathy can be extended to individuals who desperately want to improve their lot in life. This nation is justifiably proud of the fact that it remains the preferred place of residence for so many of the world's people. Yet accepting more immigrants is not in the best interests of the United States. As one of the more favored places in the world, the United States should join with other fortunate nations to assist developing countries so that the quality of life of all people on the planet may improve in the next century.

Technological, economic, cultural, as well as demographic changes are occurring at a rapid pace. Whether it be the miniaturization of computer chips or the increased reliance on robots, there is little doubt that the nation is experiencing a dramatic growth in technological innovations.[9] Interrelated with such changes are shifts in the labor force and the economy. Minorities are comprising an ever greater share of the work-force. At the same time, the economy is generating increasingly sophisticated jobs. The economy itself is being redefined as it escapes the deficit spending of the 1980s and finds itself competing on an increasingly international level.

The nation's life is also undergoing considerable adjustment. There is a growing realization that all is not well. Pretentious affluence at levels heretofore undreamed of is present alongside unacceptable levels of hunger and poverty. A growing concern is noted, particularly in some cities and states, that the composition of the population is changing rapidly. Together these startling shifts in technology, economy, culture, and demography will have a tremendous impact on every segment of society.

Should current immigration levels be maintained or increased, the future of the United States, as a twenty-first-century national community, is dim. In place of a national community, the nation could consist of several ethnic communities, speaking different languages and adhering to different cultures. Some people may prefer this type of future American society. The recommendations above reflect the opposing view that pluralistic assimilation is the proper goal for the nation for the twenty-first century — a nation that is united but yet is diversified enough to allow for cultural variation among its citizens.

The nation's identity is at a crossroads. It is time for representatives of all groups — ethnic, political, educational, religious, business and labor — to meet together and ask: What kind of a United States do we want in the twenty-first century? "Who are we? What do we wish to become? And most fundamentally, which individuals constitute the 'we' who shall decide these questions?"[10] In the process of answering these questions, the American society of the twenty-first century will be defined.

NOTES

1. As cited in Scott McConnell, "The New Battle over Immigration," *Fortune*, 9 May 1988, 94.

2. Simon, *Economic Consequences*, 349.

3. FAIR, "Immigration Reports," June 1990, 1.

4. Peter Francese, "Aging America Needs Foreign Blood," *Wall Street Journal*, 27 March 1990, 4.

5. Julian Simon, "Economic Pluses Usually Arrive with Immigrants, Professor Says," *Washington Times*, 30 March 1990, 10.

6. As cited in Otis L. Graham, Jr., "Re-thinking the Purposes of Immigration Policy," unpublished manuscript, 1990, 23.

7. Pastora San Juan Cafferty, et al., *The Dilemma of American Immigration: Beyond the Golden Door* (New Brunswick, N.J.: Transaction Press, 1983), 29.

8. Marshall, as cited in *Final Report of the Select Commission on Immigration and Refugee Policy*, Appendix B.

9. See, for example, Alvin Toffler, *Powershift: Knowledge, Wealth, and Violence At the Edge of the 21st Century* (New York: Bantam Books, 1990).

10. Schuck, "Immigration Law," 285-86.

Bibliography

Thomas. 1985. "A Case Study of Immigrants in the Restaurant Industry." *strial Relations* 24 (Spring): 205-221.

E. Digby. 1964. *The Protestant Establishment: Aristocracy and Caste in rica*. New York: Vintage Books.

, William S. 1950. *American Immigration Policy*. New York: Harper and ⅃.

/illiam, and James Jacobs, eds. 1985. *Language Policy and National Unity.* ✓ York: Rowman and Allenheld.

Richard. 1990. "The Price of Freedom." *Time*, 14 May, 71.

, Gerda. 1982. *A More Perfect Union*. Washington: Federation for American migration Reform.

George. 1988. *International Differences in the Labor Market Performance of nigrants*. Kalamazoo: Upjohn Inst.

1990. *Friends or Strangers*. New York: Basic Books.

ⅇ, Randolph S. 1916. "Trans-National America." *Atlantic Monthly* 118 (July):

ⅇr, Leon F. 1988. *Immigration: Diversity in the U.S.* New York: Walker and ᴐ.

1991. "Shifting Shares of the Population and U.S. Fertility." *Population and vironment* (forthcoming).

, and Vernon Briggs. 1988. *The Population and Labor Force of New York.* 'ashington: Population Reference Bureau.

, and Robert Gardner. 1986. "Immigration to the U.S.: The Unfinished Story." ᴐpulation Bulletin 41, no. 4: 13-14, 22-23.

, and Philip Martin. 1984. *Population Change and California's Education ystem*. Washington: Population Reference Bureau.

, and David Simcox. 1989. "Population Change in Meso-America: The Tip of he Iceberg." *Population and Environment* (Spring).

ⅇs, Vernon M., Jr. 1990. "The Declining Competitiveness of Immigrants — Review: George J. Borjas' *Friends or Strangers: The Impact of Immigrants on the U.S. Economy*." *Scope* (Summer): 7.

Bibliography

Abbey, Edward. 1988. "Immigration and Liberal Taboos."
New York: Henry Holt.

Adams, Willi Paul. 1983. "A Dubious Host." *The Wilson*
110.

Adelman, Clifford. 1989. "The Class of '72." *New York 1*

Ahlburg, Dennis A., and J.W. Vaupel. 1990. "Alternativ
Population." *Demography* 27, no. 4: 645-648.

Alba, Richard D. 1985. *Italian-Americans: Into the Twiligh*
Cliffs: Prentice-Hall.

_____, ed. 1985. *Ethnicity and Race in the USA: Toward t*
Routledge and Kegan Paul.

_____. 1989. Paper presented at conference on "People
Policies for 1990 and Beyond." Albany: Rockefeller In

"America the Vital." *Wall Street Journal*, 16 March, A-12.

Archdeacon, Thomas J. 1983. *Becoming American: An Eth*
The Free Press.

_____. 1990. "Melting Pot or Cultural Pluralism? Changi
Ethnicity." *Revue Européenne des Migrations Internationc*

Arriaga, Alfonso Sandocal. 1990. "Perspectivas y retos para e
4.

Broder, David. 1989. "On the Roads Again: Governors in the Lead." *Washington Post*, 8 August, 12.

Buchanan, Patrick J. 1989. "Islam's Global Resurgence." *The Virginian-Pilot*, 21 August, 8.

Business Week. 15 July 1985, 56.

Cafferty, Pastora San Juan, et al. 1983. *The Dilemma of American Immigration: Beyond the Golden Door*. New Brunswick, N.J.: Transaction Press.

Carnegie Forum on Education and the Economy, Task Force on Teaching as a Profession. 1986. *A Nation Prepared: Teachers for the 21st Century*. Carnegie Forum on Education and the Economy.

Carr, A. Barry, and David W. Culver. 1972. "Agriculture, Population and the Environment." In *Population, Resources and the Environment*, edited by R. Ridker. Commission on American Growth and the American Future. Washington: Government Printing Office.

"Census reports it missed up to 6.3 million people." *The Virginian-Pilot*, 19 April 1991, 3.

Choldin, Harvey M. 1986. "Statistics and Politics: The 'Hispanic' Issue in the 1990 Census." *Demography* 23, no. 3: 403-418.

Christopher, Robert C. 1989. *Crashing the Gates: The De-Wasping of America's Power Elite*. New York: Simon and Schuster.

Chua-Eoan, Howard G. 1990. "Strangers in Paradise." *Time*, 9 April, 35.

Coale, Ansley. 1974. "The History of the Human Population." *Scientific American* 231 (1974): 51.

Cole, Kenneth. 1987. "Clean Water: National Issue, Regional Concern." In *States' Summit '87: Issues and Choices for the 1990s*. Council of State Governments Annual Meeting, Boston, December.

Commission on Population Growth and the American Future. 1972. *Population and the American Future*. Washington, DC: Government Printing Office.

Davis, Kingsley. 1948. *Human Society*. New York: Macmillan and Co.

De la Garza, Rodolfo O. 1985. "Mexican-Americans, Mexican Immigrants, and Immigration Reform." In *Clamor at the Gates: The New American Immigration*, edited by Nathan Glazer. San Francisco: Institute for Contemporary Studies.

Deukmejian, George. 1989. Letter to *Sacramento Bee*, July 17, B3.

Dimarzio, Msgr. Nicholas. 1988. Testimony presented before the Sub-committee on Census and Population of the Committee on Post Office and Civil Service, U.S. House of Representatives, 12 April.

Dubois, W.E.B. 1961. *The Souls of Black Folks*. Greenwich, Conn.: Greenwood Press.

"Duke Shows His True Colors." *Newsweek*, 25 December 1989, 12.

Eliot, T.S. 1949. *Notes Toward the Definition of Culture*. New York: Harcourt, Brace, and Co.

Emerson, Rupert. 1960. *From Empire to Nation*. Cambridge: Harvard University Press.

Endicott, William. 1989. "Bush Calls Education Summit." *Sacramento Bee*, 1 August, 12, 14.

Espenshade, Thomas J. 1987. "Population Replacement and Immigrant Adaptation: New Issues Facing the West." *Family Planning Perspectives* 19, no. 3.

FAIR. 1990. "Immigration Reports." (June).

Fields, George. 1986. "Racism is Accepted Practice in Japan." *Wall Street Journal*, 10 November.

Fields, Howard. 1989. "New Study Claims Census Figures Low." *AARP News Bulletin* 30, no. 1: 2, 3.

"Five Year Estimates of Immigration under Current Legislative Options, 1990-1995." *Scope* (December 1989). Washington: Center for Immigration Studies.

Fleming, Thomas. 1989. "The Real American Dilemma." *Chronicles* (March): 9.

Francese, Peter. 1990. "Aging America Needs Foreign Blood." *Wall Street Journal*, 27 March, 4.

Frisbie, W. Parker. 1986. *Trends in Ethnic Relations: Hispanics and Anglos*. Austin: Texas Research Center Papers, Series 8.

Gans, Herbert J. 1979. "Symbolic Ethnicity: The Future of Ethnic Group Culture in America." In *On the Making of America: Essays in Honor of David Reisman*, edited by H.J. Gans, et al. Philadelphia: University of Pennsylvania Press.

Gardner, Robert W., et al. 1985. "Asian-Americans: Growth, Change, and Diversity." *Population Bulletin* 40, no. 4: 11.

Geyer, Georgie Anne. 1990. "Bush was right about the Chinese students." *The Virginian-Pilot*, 1 February, A-15.

Gibson, Campbell. 1975. "The Contributions of Immigrants to the U.S. Population Growth: 1790-1970." *International Migration Review* 9 (Summer): 157-176.

Glazer, Nathan. 1983. *Ethnic Dilemma*. New York: Hawthorne Press.

Gordon, Milton. 1964. *Assimilation in American Life*, chapter 3. New York: Oxford.

Graham, Otis L., Jr. 1986. Testimony before the Joint Economic Committee of the U.S. Congress, June.

_____. 1990. "Re-thinking the Purposes of Immigration Policy." Unpublished manuscript.

Grant, Lindsay. 1988. "Too Many Old People or Too Many Americans?" *The NPG Forum* (July): 1.

Griffith, Jeane, et al. 1989. "American Education: The Challenge of Change." *Population Bulletin* 44, no. 4: 16, 20.

"Guam's Future." *Honolulu Advertiser*, 20 November 1987, 13.

Haddad, Yvonne Y. 1986. "A Century of Islam in America." In *The Muslim World Today*. Washington: American Institute of Islamic Affairs (Occasional Paper No. 4).

Hale, Christianne. 1990. "Infant Mortality in America." *Population Trends and Public Policy* 18 (August).

Haub, Carl. 1987. "Understanding Population Projections." *Population Bulletin* 42, no. 4.

Hawkins, Augustus. 1988. Statement in Hearing before the Subcommittee of Investment, Jobs, and Prices of the Joint Economic Committee, Senate Hearing 100-78, April.

Henry, William A., III. 1990. "Beyond the Melting Pot." *Time*, 9 April, 28-31.

Higham, John. 1975. *Send These To Me*. New York: Atheneaum.

"How to make anti-poverty policies popular." *The Economist*, 27 April 1991, 23.

Howe, Irving. 1977. "The Limits of Ethnicity." *New Republic*, 25 June, 19.

Hudson Institute. 1987. *Workforce 2000*. New York: Hudson Institute.

Illegal Aliens: Influence of Illegal Workers on Wages and Working Conditions of Legal Workers. 1988. Washington: GAO, PEMD-88-13BR.

Imhoff, Gary. 1990. "The Position of U.S. English on Bilingual Education." *Annals of the American Academy of Political and Social Science* (March): 9, 10.

International Labor Office. 1986. *Economically Active Population — 1950-2025*. Geneva.

Islas, Arturo. 1989. *Mex-America: A State of Mind*. New York: William Morrow.

Janowitz, Morris. 1983. *The Reconstruction of Patriotism*. Chicago: University of Chicago Press.

Johnson, Julie. 1989. "Teachers Pay." *New York Times*, 22 July, 16.

Kallen, Horace M. 1924. *Culture and Democracy in the United States*. New York: Boni and Liveright.

Kennedy, Paul. 1987. *The Rise and Fall of Great Powers*. New York: Random House.

Kennedy, Ruby Reeves. 1952. "Single or Triple Melting Pot: Intermarriage in New Haven." *American Journal of Sociology*: 55-66.

Kirschten, Dick. 1990. "Legislating by One Senator's Rules." *National Journal*, 27 October, 2603.

Krikorian, Mark. 1989. "Affirmative Action and Immigration." *Christian Science Monitor*, 11 September, 2.

Lamare, James W. 1981. "The Political Integration of Mexican-American Children: A Generational Analysis." *International Migration Review* 16, no. 4: 173.

Lamm, Richard. 1986. Testimony before the Joint Economic Committee of the U.S. Congress, 29 May.

Lawrence, Jill. 1989. "Work and School." *Sacramento Bee*, 16 July, A14.

Lieberson, Stanley. 1985. "Unhyphenated Whites in the United States." In *Ethnicity and Race in the USA: Toward the 21st Century*, edited by Richard Alba. London: Routledge and Kegan Paul.

_____, and Mary C. Waters. 1988. *From Many Strands: Ethnic and Racial Groups in Contemporary America*. New York: Russell Sage Foundation.

Long, John F., and D.B. McMillen. 1987. "A Survey of Census Bureau Publication Projection Methods." In *Forecasting in the Social and Natural Sciences*, edited by K.C. Land and S.H. Schneider, pp. 141-178. Dordrecht, Netherlands: Reidel.

Lopez, Julie. 1989. "System Failure." *Wall Street Journal*, 31 March, R12.

Macionis, John. 1989. *Sociology*. Englewood Cliffs: Prentice-Hall.

Mann, Judy. 1989. "Pushing for Payoffs." *Washington Post*, 29 March, B3.

Marshall, F. Ray. 1981. As cited in *Final Report of the Select Commission on Immigration and Refugee Policy*, Appendix B. Washington: Government Printing Office.

Massey, Douglas S., and Felipe Garcia Espana. 1987. "The Social Process of International Migration." *Science* 237 (August): 737.

Maurice, Charles, and Charles Smithson. 1984. *The Doomsday Myth*. Palo Alto: Hoover Institution.

McCarthy, Kevin, and David F. Ronfeldt. 1982. *U.S. Immigration Policy and Global Interdependence*. Santa Monica: Rand Corp.

McConnell, Scott. 1988. "The New Battle over Immigration." *Fortune*, 9 May, 94.

_____, and Eric Breindel. 1990. "Head to Come." *New Republic*, 8 January and 15 January, 19-20.

"Mexico beckons, protectionists quiver." *The Economist*, 20 April 1991, 24 and 157-176.

Michener, James. 1985. *Texas*. New York: Random House.

Miller, G. Tyler. 1990. *Resource Conservation and Management*. Belmont: Wadsworth Publishing Co.

Miller, Marjorie. 1989. "Despite New Laws, U.S. Still a Lure in Mexico." *Los Angeles Times*, 21 August, 1.

Mincy, Ronald. 1989. *Wall Street Journal*, 9 May, B1.

Mines, R. and P. Martin. 1984. "Illegal Immigration and the California Citrus Industry." *Industrial Relations* 23: 139-149.

Moore, Dawn Glesser. 1988. Testimony before the Subcommittee on Census and Population of the Committee on Post Office and Civil Service, U.S. House of Representatives, 12 April.

Morrison, Peter. 1977. *Forecasting Population of Small Areas: An Overview*. Santa Monica: Rand Corporation.

Moynihan, Daniel P. 1977. "Defenders and Invaders." *Washington Post*, 13 June.

Muller, Thomas and Thomas Espenshade. 1985. *The Fourth Wave: California's Newest Immigrants*. Washington: Urban Inst.

Murray, Alan. 1990. "Bush Sees Labor Shortage, Looks Abroad." *Wall Street Journal*, 7 February, 2.

Murray, Charles. 1984. *Losing Ground: American Social Policy, 1950-1980*. New York: Basic Books.

_____. 1985. *Wall Street Journal*, 15 May, 34.

Myers, Norman. 1990. "People and Environment: The Watershed Decade." *People* (London) 17, no. 1: 17, 19.

Myrdal, Gunnar. 1944. *An American Dilemma: The Negro Problem and Modern Democracy*. New York: Harper and Row.

Naisbitt, John, and Patricia Aburdene. 1990. *Megatrends 2000: Ten New Directions for the 1990s*. New York: William Morrow.

National Academy of Sciences. 1984. *High Schools and the Changing Workplace*. Washington: National Academy Press.

National Commission on Infant Mortality. 1988. *Death before Life*. Washington.

Nazavio, Sonia. 1989. "Failing in 81 Languages." *Wall Street Journal*, 31 March, R21, R22.

Nordyke, Eleanor. 1977. *The Peopling of Hawaii*. Honolulu: University of Hawaii Press.

Novak, Michael. 1971. *The Rise of the Unmeltable Ethnics*. New York: MacMillan.

Papademitrious, Demetrious, and Thomas Muller. 1987. *Recent Immigration to New York: Labor Market and Social Policy Issues*. Washington: National Commission for Employment Policy.

Pearson, Robert. 1989. "Economy, Culture, Public Policy, and the Urban Underclass." *SSRC Items* (June): 23, 25.

Peirce, Neal. 1989. "Breakthrough for Wetlands: EPA's Reilly Lobbies a Maryland Law." *The Virginian-Pilot*, 22 May, A-7.

Pfaff, William. 1989. "Rethinking the Multicultural Ideal." *Los Angeles Times*, 4 March, 21.

Pimentel, David. 1980. Testimony before the Select Commission on Immigration and Refugee Policy.

_____, and Marcia Pimentel. 1990. "Land, Energy and Water: The Constraints Governing Ideal U.S. Population Size." *The NPG Forum*, 5.

Piore, Michael. 1976. "Illegal Immigration to the U.S.: Some Observations and Policy Suggestions." In *Illegal Aliens: An Assessment of the Issues*. Washington: National Council for Employment Policy.

Portes, Alejandro, and Robert Bach. 1985. *Latin Journey: Cuban and Mexican Immigrants in the United States*. Berkeley: University of California Press.

Reich, Robert. 1987. *Tales of a New America*. New York: Times Books.

Reimers, David M. 1985. *Still the Golden Door: The Third World Comes to America*. New York: Columbia University Press.

Reiss, Bob. 1977. "The Melting Pot." *Potomac Magazine, Washington Post*, 17 July, 27.

Ridker, Ronald. 1972. *Resource and Environmental Consequences of Population Growth in the United States: A Summary*. Commission on American Growth and the American Future. Washington: GPO.

Rockefeller Institute of Government. 1986. *New York State Project 2000: Report on Population*. Albany: State University of New York.

Santiestevan, Henry, and Stina Santiestevan, eds. 1984. *The Hispanic Almanac*. Washington: Hispanic Policy Development Project.

Schlesinger, Arthur, Jr. 1990. "When Ethnic Studies are Un-American." *Wall Street Journal*, 23 April, 2, 4, 6.

Schuck, Peter. 1985. "Immigration Law and the Problem of Community." In *Clamor at the Gates: The New American Immigration*, edited by Nathan Glazer. San Francisco: Institute for Contemporary Studies.

_____, and Rogers M. Smith. 1985. *Citizenship without Consent: Illegal Aliens in the American Polity*. New Haven: Yale University Press.

Schultz, Theodore. 1988. *Investing in People: The Economics of Population Change*. Berkeley: University of California Press.

Sheets, Kenneth R. 1983. "War Over Water: Crisis of the Eighties." *U.S. News and World Report*, 31 October, 7.

Sidgwick, Henry. 1881. *Elements of Politics*. London: MacMillan.

Simon, Julian. 1988. "Getting the Immigrants we Need." *Washington Post*, 3 August, 8.

_____. 1989. *The Economic Consequences of Immigration*. Cambridge: Basil Blackwell.

_____. 1990 "Economic Pluses Usually Arrive with Immigrants, Professor Says." *Washington Times*, 30 March, 10.

Skerry, Peter. 1985. "The Ambiguity of Mexican-American Politics." In *Clamor at the Gates: The New American Immigration*, edited by Nathan Glazer. San Francisco: Institute for Contemporary Studies Press.

_____. 1989. "Borders and Quotas: Immigrants and the Affirmative Action State." *The Public Interest* 96 (Summer): 94-97.

Smith, Lamar. 1990. "Immigration hurts native-born." Readers' Forum. *Washington Times*, 20 April.

Solomon, Jolie. 1989. "Managers Focus on Low-Wage Workers." *Wall Street Journal*, 9 May, B1.

Steinberg, Stephen. 1981. *The Ethnic Myth: Race, Ethnicity, and Class in America*. Boston: Beacon Press.

Swicegood, Gray, F.D. Bean, E.H. Stephen, and W. Opitz. 1986. "Language Usage and Fertility in the Mexican-Origin Population of the U.S." *Demography* 25, no. 1: 17-34.

Thernborn, Goran. 1987. "Migration and Western Europe: The Old World Turning New." *Science* 237 (September): 1185.

Thernstrom, Stephan. 1985. "Comment." *Journal of American Ethnic History* 5: 77-78.

Thomlinson, Ralph. 1965. *Population Dynamics*. New York: Random House.

Toffler, Alvin. 1990. *Powershift: Knowledge, Wealth, and Violence At the Edge of the 21st Century*. New York: Bantam Books.

"Total Jobs Keep Rising Despite Many Layoffs and Talk of Recession." *Wall Street Journal*, 24 March.

Turner, Frederick Jackson. 1920. *The Frontier in American History*. New York: Henry Holt.

U.S. Bureau of the Census. 1989. *Projections of the Population of the United States, by Age, Sex, and Race: 1988 to 2080*, by Gregory Spencer. Current Population Reports, Series P-25, No. 1018. Washington: Government Printing Office.

U.S. Department of Labor. 1989. *The Effects of Immigration on the U.S. Economy and Labor Market*. Washington: U.S. Dept. of Labor.

_____. Bureau of Labor Statistics. 1988. *Projections 2000*.

United Nations. 1982. *International Migration Policies and Programs: A World Survey*. New York: United Nations.

Valdivieso, Rafael, and Cary Davis. 1988. "U.S. Hispanics: Challenging Issues for the 1990s." *Population Trends and Public Policy* (December): 12, 13.

Viviano, Frank. 1990. "Poll Shows Ethnic Groups Torn by Bias, Cultural Ties." *San Francisco Chronicle*, 27 March, A6.

Vonnegut, Kurt. 1987. *Bluebeard*. New York: Delacorte Press.

Waltzer, Michael. 1981. "The Distribution of Membership." In *Boundaries: National Autonomy and its Limits*, edited by Peter G. Brown and Henry Shue. Totowa, N.J: Rowman and Littlefield.

Waltzer, Philip. 1990. "Blacks told to prepare to be majority." *The Virginian-Pilot*, 9 February, D3.

Waterfield, Larry. 1989. "Shrinking Working Pool Threatens Food Industry." *The Packer*, 27 May, 1A, 6A.

Wattenberg, Ben J. 1989. *The Birth Dearth*, 2nd edition. New York: Pharos Books.

Wattenberg, Ben J. 1989. "The Case for More Immigrants." *U.S. News and World Report*, 27 March, 29, 182-186.

_____, and Karl Zinsmeister. 1989. *The Comparative Advantage of the First Universal Nation*. Washington: The American Enterprise Institute.

Weeks, John R. 1988. "Demography of Islamic Nations." *Population Bulletin* 23, no. 4: 4.

Weintraub, Sidney. 1989. "Implications of Mexican Demographic Developments for the United States." In *Mexican and Central American Population and U.S. Immigration Policy*, edited by Frank D. Bean, et al. Austin: Center for Mexican American Studies.

"What Japan Thinks of Us." *Newsweek*, 2 April, 24.

White, Theodore. 1982. *America in Search of Itself: The Making of the President — 1956-1980*. New York: Harper and Row.

Will, George. 1990. "Congealed in Traffic." *Washington Post*, 11 March, B7.

Yankelovich, Skelly, and White. 1984. *Spanish USA, 1984*.

Yinger, J. Milton. 1981. "Toward a Theory of Assimilation and Dissimilation." *Ethnic and Racial Studies* 4 (July): 261.

Zangwill, Israel. 1914. *The Melting Pot: Drama in Four Acts*. New York: Macmillan.

Zevi, Tullia. 1989. As quoted in Alexander Stille, "A Disturbing Echo." *Atlantic Monthly* (February): 20.

Index

219

About the Author

Leon F. Bouvier retired in 1986 from the Population Reference Bureau, where he served as vice-president. He is currently Adjunct Professor of Demography at Tulane University School of Public Health. He received his Ph.D. in Sociology from Brown University in 1971 and has held research and teaching positions at the University of Rhode Island, Georgetown University, the East-West Population Institute and Old Dominion University. In 1978, Bouvier served as a demographic advisor to the Select Committee on Population of the U.S. House of Representatives; in 1980 he served in a similar capacity for the Select Commission on Immigration and Refugee Policy. Among his publications are *Population: Demography and Policy* (with R. Weller); *Socio-Religious Factors in Fertility Decline* (with S.L.N. Rao), and *Immigration and Social Diversity*. Bouvier is married to Theresa Fallon and is the father of four children and has eight grandchildren.

About the Center for
Immigration Studies

The Center for Immigration Studies is a non-profit research and policy analysis group founded in 1985 and devoted to publication, education and dialogue on immigration into the United States and its effects on broad national, social, environmental and demographic interests. The Center now concentrates on four broad areas of interest: (1) Overseas population and social trends driving immigration to the United States; (2) The effects of current U.S. immigration policies and practices on domestic population and fertility; (3) The implications of current immigration for labor market conditions and public assistance costs; (4) The options for enforcing immigration laws effectively and humanely in ways consistent with democratic values. The Center is governed by an eleven-member policy board and is supported by grants from foundations, private individual donors and other tax-exempt charitable and educational organizations.